Praise for *The Freedom Formula*

"When you're deeply passionate about your work, it's easy to let it consume your life. But doing so only hurts you, as *The Freedom Formula* so expertly reminds us. David Finkel's approach to restructuring your priorities will help you make the most of your time—whether you're at your desk or on vacation."

—Gino Wickman, bestselling author of
Traction and creator of EOS

"Growing CoBank into a sustainable $130 billion financially strong and dependable advocate for rural America was an audacious goal that directors, leadership, and employees put their heart and soul into for over a decade. Save yourself some of the blood, sweat, and tears and follow David's lead from the start. Brilliant book!"

—Robert B. Engel, former CEO of CoBank and current
CEO and Managing Director BLT Advisory Services LLC

"If you're stuck in a cycle of overworking, struggling with time-management, or just can't find time to unwind, you need to break free. *The Freedom Formula* will help you do just that—while maximizing the value created during your working hours. You can't afford not to read it."

—Dr. Greg Reid, author of the *Think and Grow Rich*
series through the Napoleon Hill Foundation

"David Finkel's *The Freedom Formula* dispels the myth that leaders have to sacrifice what is good in life for professional success. You can have both and this book shows you how."

—Dr. Geoff Smart, chairman and founder of ghSMART
and *New York Times* bestselling author of *Who*

"*The Freedom Formula* begins as if it were a thriller novel. David Finkel's newest offering bursts through the clutter of business books and reveals powerful information in a fashion that is intensely interesting to read. Better yet, the information in *The Freedom Formula* has proven to create measurable results!"

—Andy Andrews, *New York Times* bestselling author of *The Traveler's Gift* and founder of WisdomHarbour.com

"If you're looking for concrete ideas to succeed at work and in your business without sacrificing your life, this book has something of value on every page. Destined to become a classic whose messages will withstand the test of time."

—Jason Jennings, *New York Times* bestselling author of *The Reinventors*

"No hype, no BS, no fluff. Just solid gold ideas to create more value at work with less time and effort."

—Stephen Pressfield, *New York Times* bestselling author of *The War of Art* and *The Legend of Bagger Vance*

"If you're overworked, stressed out, and unsure how to step off the treadmill, David gives you a way to think and act. This book is filled with powerful tools and an upgraded model to get better results and more enjoyment from your life."

—Stephanie Harkness, entrepreneur and former chairman of the National Association of Manufacturers

"David delivers more value per page than any other author I know. Buy and read this book!"

—Patty DeDominic, past president of the National Association of Women Business Owners and former chair of The Foundation for SCORE

The
FREEDOM
Formula

The
FREEDOM
Formula

How to Succeed in Business
Without Sacrificing Your Family,
Health, or Life

DAVID FINKEL

BenBella Books, Inc.
Dallas, TX

BenBella Books, Inc.
10440 N. Central Expressway, Suite 800
Dallas, TX 75231
www.benbellabooks.com
Send feedback to feedback@benbellabooks.com

Printed in the United States of America
10 9 8 7 6 5 4 3 2 1

Library of Congress Cataloging-in-Publication Data has been requested.
ISBN 9781948836401
eISBN 9781948836654

Editing by Leah Wilson and Laurel Leigh
Copyediting by James Fraleigh
Proofreading by Chris Gage and Amy Zarkos
Text design by Publishers' Design and Production Services, Inc.
Text composition by PerfecType, Nashville, TN
Cover design by Sarah Avinger
Cover photo © iStock / Gearstd
Printed by Lake Book Manufacturing

Distributed to the trade by Two Rivers Distribution, an Ingram brand
www.tworiversdistribution.com

Special discounts for bulk sales are available. Please contact
bulkorders@benbellabooks.com.

*To Adam, Matthew, and Joshua. You fill my life
with joy, and I love you with all my heart.*

Contents

Why Working Longer and Harder Doesn't Work (and What Actually Does)

It was one of those overcast San Diego nights when it feels like you are sitting in a cloud. I was alone, immersed in the large hot tub on my patio. Soaking in the 104°F water, it occurred to me this was the first time I'd used the hot tub since I'd purchased the house almost a year prior, even though it was one of the primary reasons I had bought this executive home carved into the hillside of Mt. Helix, along with its stunning views overlooking Mexico to the south and the Pacific Ocean to the west. The house was twice as large as the one I grew up in. I was twenty-eight years old, still single, and running a successful business coaching company. I was earning more money than I ever expected to earn. I should have felt happy, as if I'd arrived. But I didn't.

Instead, I was bone tired, burnt out, and anxious. My life consisted of being on the road two weeks out of every month, teaching workshops and keynoting at industry conferences. Then it was back to the office, catching up on all the management challenges of my rapidly scaling company, which I had a tendency to micromanage. I had no life because, when I wasn't working, I was exhausted.

As I slipped into the hot, steamy water at the end of another eighty-hour week of meetings, conference calls, troubleshooting, coaching, and writing a syndicated column, I thought the stress might melt away. Instead, I felt anxious and alone—a sense of isolation that was reinforced by muffling fog and the remote geography of the house, not a neighbor in sight. I became short of breath and my heart started pounding.

Is this it? I wondered, feeling suddenly nauseated in the middle of all that bubbling, swirling liquid. *Is this all my life is going to be? An endless stream of business fires to put out, and all these people counting on me for their livelihoods, and all these clients I don't want to disappoint?*

It felt like I was on this treadmill and someone—me—had turned up the speed higher and higher. If I didn't keep running to stay on, I'd go flying off the back. *Is this all there is?*

Sure, the money was great, more money than I'd ever seen my parents earn or imagined I would, but this wasn't what I'd signed up for. I wanted to do work that mattered and that paid handsomely, which I felt would allow me to live my life on my terms, to be the one in charge. But in the end, I wanted one thing more than anything else. This one thing was the single deep desire that had sparked me to open up shop. It's what drove me to keep going when tough times hit.

I wanted *freedom.*

Freedom from people telling me what to do and how to do it. Freedom to do things my way. Freedom from having my future depend on the whims or decisions of others. And—gulp—*time* freedom. Instead of constantly working to feed my business and feeling trapped, I wanted my business to work for me. While it was wonderful to have what outwardly looked like success, I realized I wanted more than just professional success. I also wanted to be married and have a family—kids I could be present for—but if I kept going the way I was, I'd either still be single or divorced twice over by my early forties.

That Harry Chapin song rang in my head. You know, the one that says,

> *But there were planes to catch, and bills to pay*
> *He learned to walk while I was away . . .*

I thought of my father, who as part of a small medical practice was gone taking calls three nights a week and every third weekend. I thought about the soccer games he "watched" from the parking lot as he spent much of the game hunched over, talking into one of those early, shoebox-sized mobile phones while dealing with emergencies.

Then and there, I made a decision. I wanted out of the pressure cooker, to escape the long hours and demands. Was it too much to ask to have business success *and* a personal life, too? I wanted to work. I loved what I did. It was engrossing and fulfilling. I liked the impact I had on clients and their companies. I enjoyed the financial rewards. But I didn't want my work to dominate my life like an alien blob that kept eating more and more of my time.

That decision launched a twenty-year journey to find, experiment with, and synthesize better ways to grow companies and achieve professionally. The net result of those years of work is the book you're holding. *The Freedom Formula* is a two-decade synthesis of everything I've learned about creating and sustaining breakthrough business success without sacrificing family, well-being, and all the other things that offer personal fulfillment beyond the bottom line. The formula is based on my direct experiences working with tens of thousands of business leaders, professionals, entrepreneurs, and executives who, like you, craved a simple, comprehensive, structured approach to consistently get the most by having their team regularly focus its best time and attention on the things that create the most economic value for their company.

Let me take a guess to see if I know a little bit about you and your daily life. You check email the moment you lift your head off the pillow in the morning and just before you go to bed at night. You bring work with you on vacation, sneak a glance at your phone during family dinners, and take business calls at your kids' sports games or anytime you should be present for the loved ones in your life. You work late and through the weekend, often bringing work home as you miss precious time with your spouse, significant other, children, family, and friends, unable to attend events because of a business deadline or crisis that requires your immediate attention. The real-time accessibility of today's technology has completely blurred the boundaries between your office and your personal life, chaining you to the demands of your business, employer, or professional practice and requiring you to be "on" for colleagues, employees, and clients 24/7/365.

If it feels like I'm describing you, you're not alone, and you already know that the forty-hour work week has become virtually obsolete. Slowly and steadily, we've given over huge chunks of our personal time to work.

A recent article in the *Harvard Business Review* reported on an international study by the Center for Creative Leadership showing that professionals, executives, and business owners in the United States and thirty-six other countries now work a whopping seventy-two-hour week. According to the Wells Fargo/Gallup Index, 57 percent of business owners in the United States now work six days a week, and more than 20 percent of them work *seven* days a week. Don't even get me started on vacation time! On average, US employees who get paid time off took only 54 percent of their vacation days, leaving 46 percent unused. And if you do slip away for a few weeks of vacation, odds are high that you work while away. According to a TripAdvisor poll, 77 percent of Americans and 40 percent of people in developed nations like Australia, Brazil, and Germany work while on vacation despite complaints from their family members.

It's almost as if you've been forced to make a choice between your company and your life, sacrificing time with your family, your health, or yourself for the sake of business and career success. Work has taken over, eroding your personal life and keeping you on that treadmill that never shuts off. On the one hand, you want to succeed at your job or in your business, so you work long hours. As you've grown incredibly competent at what you do, sometimes it feels like the pressure has only increased, because now your company relies more than ever on your daily presence and production to succeed. It feels like each day you start with even higher expectations about what you can get done, which in the past you managed by working more "efficiently." But at a certain point, you maxed out what efficiency was able to do for you, so you turned to the temporary fix of longer hours and working from home or over the weekend. But soon that temporary expediency—never intended to be permanent—became a fixture in your life.

It doesn't matter whether you run your own business or professional practice or play a key leadership role at a large corporation— the pressure and frustrations are universal. My clients initially tell me things like,

"I'm overwhelmed and don't know where to start. So much of my day is spent putting out fires and reacting to customer demands. The only way I can get my key projects done is to come into the office earlier and stay later, and work on the weekends when at least I have fewer interruptions."

"All I do is work. Even when I'm with my family, I'm still responding to emails and texts for work. The saddest part is that my family has just gotten used to it. When I do actually put down my smartphone, they act surprised, as if I'm just a temporary visitor."

"Sometimes I think life would be better if I just let go of the business and worked for somebody else or moved down in the organization. At least then I wouldn't have to bring all the stress and pressure home with me at night."

"I'm scared. If something were to happen to me or one of my key people, my department might fail. At a minimum, I'd be sucked back into dealing with a massive workload and would never see my family until we recruited a replacement person and got him or her up to speed. But that would take months! That causes me so much anxiety. I feel like I'm walking on eggshells."

We live in a very different world than past generations. High-speed internet access and almost universal connectivity, combined with powerful mobile tools, have given us a degree of geo-flexibility that not so long ago wasn't possible. You can access your files, peers, and virtual workspace from anywhere. I'm sure you've experienced the dark side of this, too. Blurred boundaries, a feeling like you've always got to be "on"—a persistent low-level anxiety over missing something important or falling behind pushes us to work more and enjoy less. It's one of the reasons my wife and I take our family camping so often; it's as if going deep into the woods were the only way to disconnect.

We all know the world isn't going to go backwards to the halcyon days of old, which had their own challenges. In today's world, high-achieving professionals face a central challenge, one you are confronted with daily: How can you have an engaging, satisfying, and successful career without sacrificing your family, health, or personal life in the process? It feels like a binary "either/or" choice. But it doesn't have to be this way. You can have both.

There is a simple, concrete, step-by-step formula that can help you create more value in less time. You can be "on" for an intense forty-hour work week—or less—and still be present for the other important areas of your life. You can climb the corporate ladder, create wealth, and scale your company in ways you never thought possible, and *The Freedom Formula* will show you exactly how.

This book will offer you a realistic and doable way out—a road map—that will help you take your life back without compromising those things that matter most to you. This proven four-step formula will help you and your team consistently focus your best time, talent, and attention on those Fewer, Better activities, projects, and strategies that create the most value and highest return for your company.

And because a core part of the formula offers a doable structure for reclaiming hundreds of your best hours every year, you and your staff will be able to create breakthrough results and enjoy wild professional success while still having rich personal lives. To be clear, the formula will require a rethinking of your priorities, use of time, and team focus. It will push you to reimagine what work looks like day to day as well as to master the mechanics of a better way to leverage your time and team for maximum impact.

I won't be sharing theory here. I developed the formula empirically, through two decades of experimentation and refinement, working directly with tens of thousands of business leaders who reached the same ceiling of success that you're likely dealing with, a point where working longer and harder wasn't a smart, sustainable strategy to get what they *really* wanted.

In these pages, you'll meet business leaders from across the world who have dealt with the same challenges and struggles you're facing.

You'll meet Michelle, the COO of a successful medical company, and learn the inside story of how she found a way to work best with her brilliant but at times overly ambitious CEO so that their company could focus on a smaller number of highest-value, greatest-return strategies and initiatives. This not only led to years of high growth but, more importantly, helped Michelle regain her equilibrium in the process.

You'll meet Anne, an entrepreneur in California who was injured in a cycling accident, requiring months of recovery time. I'll share with you the step-by-step work she did in the prior five months to build strategic depth into her company that not only saved her business from disaster when she was unable to work for so long, but in fact allowed her team to generate the largest growth surge in her company's fifteen-year history.

There's Marvin, a highly successful senior partner at a small Atlanta law firm who was able to use the formula to cut his work weeks by ten hours while increasing his firm's profitability by $800,000 per year.

And Bob, the former CEO of a large financial institution, who shares the simple insight that helped him transform a struggling bank into one of the world's most profitable financial institutions, with per-employee profits *ten times* the industry average.

Each of these business leaders faced many of the same challenges you do, and they applied the straightforward solutions you'll discover in this book to find their way to even greater business success while restoring sanity to their personal workload. Once they made the decision—as you will—that things couldn't go on this way, and invested the energy to make a change, they were amazed by the simplicity and effectiveness of the solution. Day by day, quarter by quarter, they have been implementing these small but highly specific changes to reap life-changing results.

I didn't start out with a refined design for the Freedom Formula. Initially, it was just me groping in the dark, reading over a hundred business books a year, experimenting with my time, team, and company, struggling to find a better way to scale the firm without sacrificing everything else. As I started to enjoy small successes, I shared the ideas with other business leaders who participated in our coaching programs. Early on, these were almost exclusively small-cap companies with sales less than $25 million a year. This laboratory sped up the testing and refinement process. As my company grew and our reputation in the market expanded, we began working with mid-cap companies and both autonomous divisions and key leaders within multibillion-dollar enterprises. We worked with business owners, company executives, and even departmental managers as our clients asked for help finding ways to keep growing without burning out their best people. This work gave us reach into companies with an aggregate market value of more than $500 billion. It was in this laboratory that the formula I'll share with you was refined.

The formula starts with the simple premise that you don't get paid for time served but rather for value created. To create value you do need time, but you need a very different kind of time than merely raw, undifferentiated hours. Not all hours are created equally. You know this intuitively. You recognize that two hours of your best time, consolidated into one, interruption-free block, focused on your highest-value work, is worth a magnitude more in value to your company than ten or even twenty hours of you plowing through email or bouncing between projects, meetings, and low-level tasks.

We have helped our clients break the direct, one-to-one relationship between hours worked and value created. They grew to appreciate that, done right, they should expect one hour of their best time to generate the value of hundreds or even thousands of hours of generic work output. They learned that by focusing their team's best talent and attention on their highest-value activities in genuinely productive ways, they could enjoy massive growth that was largely independent of the actual hours they worked. This includes the VP of sales who helps her team create a lead-scoring system that ensures they focus their best sales energy on their highest-value prospects. Or the product lead who brings his top engineers into a room to brainstorm and create the best approach to solving a tough engineering challenge on a new piece of software they are developing. Two well-spent hours in that conference room may control hundreds of hours of individual programming. My point is that while hours are an essential ingredient of creating value, they are much less important than (1) selecting how to invest those limited hours and (2) aggregating those best hours into solid blocks big enough to do your highest-value work.

Structure and environment will win over willpower and discipline. Or rather, discipline may win a sprint, but environment and structure almost always will determine the outcome of a marathon. Make no mistake about it, your success at work is a marathon, not a sprint. To win out over the long haul, you must create more and more value for your company, and structure and environment are two essential components to set yourself and your team up to succeed.

This is why I won't just tell you what you need to do to create more value for your company, but instead I'll walk you through the mechanics—step by step—of how you actually can do this. I'll give you a concrete structure to design your week so that you have consistent blocks of interruption-free best time during which to do your highest-value work. This is what you're really on the payroll to do, not grind out hours. I'll share with you ways in which you can design your workflow, systems, and teams so that you get more done with less time and effort. Most importantly of all, I'll show you how to sustain these gains over time by building on the solid foundation of systems, team, and culture. To be clear, the formula is not a patch or a quick fix. It's a proven, superior map to get your entire team aligned investing their best time doing those things that matter most for your company. In this book, I'll cut through the theory and take you directly to the strategies and steps that have been proven to work in the only laboratory that matters—the marketplace.

The Freedom Formula is presented in two parts. **Part I: The Four Steps to Freedom** shares the core four-step formula for consistently directing your team's best time and attention into your highest-value activities. This proven, bottom-up approach to deploying your team's talent for maximum impact gives you a structure that works even under the relentless pressure of the tight deadlines, endless emails, and constant alerts and interruptions of the unremitting, always-on world in which we live.

You'll quickly see how you can determine exactly what you do that creates the most value and, more importantly, how to design your week to let structure and environment help you reclaim five or more hours of your best time each week to reinvest in these highest-value activities. You'll learn how Tom Santilli did exactly this, scaling his e-commerce company 400 percent in seven years while reducing his eighty-hour work weeks to under twenty hours. (Tom's story is told in chapter one, "Step One: Embrace the Value Economy.") You'll engage in techniques for determining your company's, division's, or team's best Focus Areas and reducing these strategic decisions to a rolling series of one-page Action Plans every ninety days. (See chapter three, "Invest in Your

Fewer, Better.") This proactive pattern helped Nate Anglin double his aerospace company's net income in just eighteen months. Chapter four, "Develop Strategic Depth," covers precisely how to sustain these gains as you battle the reactionary forces of entropy and the status quo to enjoy the compounded effect of these best practices over time. You'll learn how to protect your team against the loss of a key person and why one of the most important things you can do to build strategic depth into your company may be just taking a real vacation.

Part II: The Five Freedom Accelerators builds on the four-step formula by sharing five powerful accelerators to get you results *faster*. These accelerators help you engage your team in this journey with you, allowing you to travel faster and more sustainably. Topics include how to grow your key team's abilities and groom your leaders to build depth and harness greater autonomy. You'll examine the important role that intentionally crafting your company culture plays in helping your team absorb your best practices and most important filters so that they automatically make better decisions. And you'll discover how to leverage better design to sustain this work and combat the inevitable forces of entropy that threaten to distract or even destroy the results you've built by following the formula.

I remember one business owner we worked with several years ago named Terrance. He owned a seasonal hospitality business in southern Utah. Every year from May through October, he steeled himself for another six-month season. The rest of the year, he "only" had to put in a light fifty- to sixty-hour work week, but come May this jumped to twelve to fourteen hours a day, seven days a week. This was hard enough on Terrance physically, but emotionally it was killing him:

> "Every day, I'd have to be up and out of the house before my kids even woke up," Terrance shared. "By the time I got home at 9 or 10 PM, they'd be asleep. This was my life every season for six months out of the year. I felt like I was missing my kids' childhood."

When we first began coaching Terrance four years ago and he told me his story, it broke my heart. I'm a dad with three young sons myself. I've experienced how fast their childhood seems to disappear. There are personal milestones in your kids' lives that you never can rewind. I remember how it used to feel when my older two sons would reach for and hold my hand anywhere we walked together—into a store, on a trail, or even down the stairs to breakfast. It was one of the sweetest parts of being a dad for me, the feeling of their tiny hands in mine. Then the day arrived when they were about eight years old, and they stopped reaching for my hand. Just thinking about this makes me want to cry. Of course, it's normal and healthy—they're growing up. But I miss it.

So when Terrance told me about how for years he sacrificed baseball games, family meals, and bedtime stories with his four kids to take care of his business responsibilities, I felt for him. There is good news at the end of his story, though. After just eighteen months of applying the formula you're going to learn about in part one of this book, Terrance had reclaimed a big part of his life. I remember having a private conversation with him at one of our quarterly business workshops, and he shared how applying the formula impacted him and his family:

> "I finally started questioning many of the hours I was putting in. My coach challenged me to be much clearer on what I did that actually created the highest value for my company, and to find ways to systematically and effectively hand off many of the other responsibilities to my staff. It was scary at first, but we did it in baby steps. When I saw that the work was getting done, and that my staff actually valued the trust I placed in them, it emboldened me to keep going with the formula."

It was at this point, when Terrance started doing his quarterly one-page Action Plans for his company as well as increasing his team's strategic depth—both of which you'll find out exactly how to do in part one of this book—that he made the biggest breakthroughs:

"After eighteen months of this, I finally was able to cut my summer hours by twenty hours a week, and my family and I took our first-ever vacation during the season—which is when my kids have their summer break from school. It was amazing. I feel like I've got my life back again."

Like Terrance, you fundamentally can change the way you structure your day, week, quarter, and business environment so that you achieve incredible professional success and enjoy even richer personal and whole-life success, too. One word of caution: change sparks resistance, internally and externally. Old ways and patterns of behaviors dig in and launch a rearguard action to hold any change—good or bad—at bay. So, if you notice yourself arguing or struggling with what I'm sharing, that's normal and to be expected. In fact, it's a sign of growth. It means that you are pushing past old ways that you've outgrown. My best coaching advice is to try out the formula in your personal workday before you apply the concrete steps across your entire company, department, or team. Let the ideas prove their value to *you*. Yes, the formula worked for Terrance. Yes, it has worked for me and my companies. Yes, it's worked for thousands of other business leaders around the world, many of whom you'll meet in this book. But start with yourself—prove it to yourself. When you apply the Freedom Formula to reclaim your time and your life, you'll wonder how you ever could have done it any other way.

David Finkel

CEO
Maui Mastermind®

PART I

The Four Steps to Freedom

CHAPTER 1

Step One:
Embrace the Value Economy

I want to invite you over to an evening at the Finkels'. As you walk into our calm and peaceful home, I greet you at the door and lead you to our clean and immaculately set kitchen table. My kids are sitting quietly, napkins on laps, patiently waiting for their turn to share about their day. Each of them respectfully listens to their brothers share and then asks insightful, probing questions, making it evident how much they care about one another—not! That's fantasy land.

You walk in, and the first thing you notice is the noise. My god, the noise. How can three boys be so loud? You see my wife telling me about a Cub Scout activity we need to attend that weekend, while my youngest son, Joshua, is playfully trying to get my attention by throwing Cheerios at my head. My son Adam is yelling, "Listen!" while his twin brother, Matthew, is poking me and thrusting his iPad in my face, hoping that in the chaos and confusion I'll reflexively put the PIN code in so he can get extra screen time to play Minecraft.

Ah, home sweet home. A riot of noise, chaos, movement, and interruptions. If you've ever had a houseful of young kids, then you know exactly what I'm talking about. I wouldn't trade my mess of a family for anything in the world, but sometimes it sure can be hard to find a moment to catch my breath and actually *think*.

You've guessed my point. The strategy of waiting for my family to spontaneously show self-restraint, patience, and calm listening skills is doomed to fail. Just like in your company, the strategy of passively waiting for this wave of demands, fires, and tasks to pass so that you magically will be left with some time, space, and quiet to get to those important projects you've been meaning to work on for weeks . . . well, that too is a fantasy. In the ocean, one wave is followed by another, and another, and another; likewise, in your company, this wave of immediate needs will be followed by another, and another, and another. Tomorrow will be just as overfull and stressful as today unless you embrace what I call the Value Economy and make different choices. If you want to create a space to work on your most important projects, you've got to *actively* make this happen.

In my family life, I've learned that I need a few hours to myself every weekend to go for a hike, or to read a book, or to just quietly listen to music and think. In your company, you also need to structurally create a block of time free from distraction and interruption. Value needs a moment to collect its thoughts and gather its forces. **Entropy is only ever tamed by the counteracting investment of active energy to bring some order and structure to your week.**

But you say, "They're waiting for me to set the meeting," "respond to their question," or "get them that report." If you can't regularly reclaim two, four, or six hours of your week in one- to three-hour blocks to do the high-value work you're really on the payroll to do, then all the movement and frenzied activity of responding to requests and processing your inbox is just a sham. Or, as Shakespeare put it, "Full of sound and fury, [but] signifying nothing." This was the experience of Tom Santilli, CEO of a successful technology wholesaling company in Florida.

TOM HAD BUILT HIS COMPANY, xByte Technologies, from the ground up, but years into the venture, his eighty-hour work weeks—filled with fires, emails, and constant interruptions—were getting to be too much. He had two young kids at home whom he wasn't seeing enough, and he felt torn between the demands of the business and being present with the important people in his life.

If Tom was tired, so was his wife, Lee. She was tired of Tom missing out on family dinners, not being more involved in family activities, and of watching Tom's long hours impact his health. She watched as Tom said one thing—"My family is the most important thing in my life"—but behaved differently: long hours, missed meals, and the stress of work brought home.

None of this was lost on Tom. In his heart, he knew he needed to find a way to get away from the crushing pressures of running the business day to day, but he didn't know *how*. He felt caught between the business's need for long hours to maintain the momentum and success and his personal needs of caring for his family and himself. Tom was like a lot of business leaders I've met over the years who are trapped by their business responsibilities, prisoners of their prior success. They've become like the mythological Atlas, holding the weight of a small world on their shoulders. They carry the hopes and promise of their company forward, and in many ways feel like they're leaving their family and selves behind. What they are doing seems to work in the domain of business—after all, it has generated impressive results so far, even if late at night they recognize it was only part of their ambitions for their lives. But they are afraid to stop working so hard because they don't know any other way to ensure that the whole thing doesn't come crashing down. They dream of a way to enjoy professional success without sacrificing the other aspects of their lives. For Tom, as for a lot of people, it just wasn't obvious *how* to do this.

In Tom's case, it was his wife who pushed him onto the path to find a way out. Lee had gone online to research potential solutions when she found my business coaching company. Her husband was smart, he was committed, but he also was more than a little bit obsessive about how he and his staff operated the business. Lee knew that there must be a better way. So, in 2007, she enrolled Tom in one of our programs. Today, Tom says,

> "She knows how cheap I am, so when I learned that she already had paid for the program and that it was nonrefundable, I

felt like I had to participate. I'm so glad I did, because that was the start of a major change in how I ran the company. I know I wasn't the fastest student at first, but over time what I learned about how to run the business better made a huge difference for me. Looking back, I can't believe how I used to run the company. I was doing so much that I just shouldn't have been the one doing. It was nobody's fault but my own. I just didn't know any better."

One of the things Tom learned was that many of the hours he worked each week not only created little value, but also were a key factor in slowing the business's development. He realized that he did three things for his company that created the most value—nothing else he did even came close. First, he made sure his purchasing team was buying right—the right products that would sell quickly with expectations of strong margins. Second, he kept a close eye on big-picture pricing decisions that his online and phone sales teams made so they didn't inadvertently give away the margins that his purchasing team had worked so hard to establish. And third, he made high-level strategic decisions, such as key hires and capital investments. Sure, he did a lot more for the company than that. He scrutinized his operations team, to make sure shipments were going out on time; and his quality team, who did the sample testing of the pre-owned computer servers and component parts they sold. And he paid careful attention to his company financials. But when he looked at his own role in the clear light of day, he realized the three places where he made his highest-value contributions were making sure they bought right, priced profitably, and made sound high-level strategic decisions. Everything else was just bread and dessert. What he quickly came to learn in our work together was that he was spending most of his time—*over 50 hours a week*—essentially eating empty calories:

"As part of the coaching process, it quickly became clear that most of the hours I was working did very little for the company. I just felt like I had to do those things or personally oversee that they were done. Looking back, I can see it was more about my compulsion to be in control than it was about what made the most rational return on my time." ♦

Maybe you are a lot like Tom was back then. You're capable, committed, and, by the yardstick of professional success, incredibly accomplished. But you've reached a point in your career when you recognize there has to be a better way than to jump on the endless treadmill of growth by daily grinding out more hours. You want to be successful leading your company, division, department, or team, but you are no longer willing to sacrifice everything outside of work to do it. You've already given up too much at the altar of career success, things that you'll never get back, like time with your family or relationships that ended because you were too busy working, working, working.

Here's the thing—the idea that you need to work long hours to succeed in business is a fallacy. In fact, many of those hours you're working now actually hurt the long-term success of your company by making it less stable and scalable and more heavily reliant on you. Hours worked does not necessarily lead to a better, stronger business. What you really need, now that you've developed a core set of high-value competencies, is to work much more strategically.

What if the root cause of all you sacrificed in the name of career success was an outdated model you held about how the world of business works? A model you never consciously questioned but rather were passively fed by cultural myths and conditioning? **What if there was a shadow economy operating in parallel with what we thought was the one we have been living inside? And what if this shadow economy was the real force behind the throne of business success?**

The Two Economies

You've been taught that the path to success comes from working hard. You've been indoctrinated with cultural memes like:

- "Work hard."
- "Success comes from outworking your competition."
- "You can have anything you want if you just work hard enough for it."
- "The early bird catches the worm."
- "Sweat equity."
- "If you want something done right, do it yourself."
- "If you're committed to succeed, then you have to put the hours in."

I call this model of the world the Time and Effort Economy. In this model, you get results by working harder. Want to accelerate your success? Put in more hours. Still not enough? Spend nights and weekends taking business calls or answering work texts and emails. Vacations? Sure, just make sure you bring your phone, tablet, or laptop with you so you can stay in touch with the office.

In the Time and Effort Economy, people get paid for hours, effort, and attitude. It's the nose-to-the-grindstone world of blood, sweat, and sacrifice. If the Time and Effort Economy were a Hollywood movie, the poster child would be Rocky Balboa, bloodied but still slugging away, absolutely committed to being the last person standing at the end of the fifteenth round.

"Rocky," you say. "I can live with that." After all, he became the heavyweight champion of the world. First, let's remember that was Hollywood in the 1970s, not the real world. And even if it were true, for every Rocky who makes it to the top through grit, gore, and guts, there are literally tens of thousands of others who get knocked out after a promising start. Plus, can't we see there must be a better way to succeed in business than just absorbing the punishing hours, month after month, year after year?

This chapter takes its title from a better, more potent model for business success: the Value Economy. In the Value Economy, you succeed by creating value for your company. You need time to create value, but a very *different* kind of time. You need blocks of your best, uninterrupted time to strategically focus on those things that you do for your company that create the most value. Low-value email and third-party requests? You'll get to them, but only after you've invested the best hours of your week into your highest-value creation activities. **The low-value stuff gets your *remnant* time, not your best time.**

A quick word: Neither model is true or false. They simply are implicit constructs we've created about how the world of business works. Questions like, "Is this model true?" are less useful than asking, "How effective is this model in getting me the results I want?"

Your model becomes the filter through which you let in, or keep out, inputs from the world. Your model is one of the biggest forces that shapes how you interpret, structure, and make meaning out of the world. Your model, true or untrue, literally becomes the moderating filter that intermediates all that you encounter in the world. Your model, which is a gossamer creation of your mind, literally can change everything about what you believe possible and how you act in an area of your life.

Here's an example. I started playing field hockey at age thirteen. After a couple of years, I was spotted by development scouts as a player with potential. They selected me to play on the US Under-18 and Under-21 National Teams. It was an incredible opportunity for me. There I was at age fifteen, training four days a week with the Senior National Training Squad at Moorpark College in Simi Valley, California. I had just had my first burst of teenage growth, shooting up from five foot four to five foot ten inches in less than eighteen months. Gangly and awkward, I weighed in at 146 pounds, more like a puppy who hadn't yet grown into his own body than an elite athlete.

Three days a week, at the end of two hours of practice, we headed over to the track to do interval workouts including 400-meter sprints to push our subaerobic threshold ever higher. I was shunted to the back of the pack by the grizzled group of veteran players I trained with. These were full-grown men in their early to mid-twenties who were in peak physical shape. The rest of the squad came past the finish line well under the required seventy-second limit, but not me. "Seventy-eight . . . seventy-nine . . . eighty . . . eighty-one . . . and bloody Finkel, " my coach would say, his voice dripping with disgust, as I straggled across the finish line. After our allotted three minutes and thirty seconds of recovery time, we'd line up for another sprint, and again I'd come in ten to fifteen seconds—an eternity—after everybody else. After a couple of years of this, is it any wonder that I absorbed a view of myself as slower than my training mates?

I can still remember the day all of that changed. It was four-thirty in the afternoon on a sunny, hot day. We had just finished a typical two-hour practice. We walked over to the stadium track to do our conditioning workout. I was seventeen years old and by this point had been training with the Senior National Team for two full years. This day for some reason my coach, Ric, screamed for me to get in the front of the pack at the starting line instead of the back where I just naturally positioned myself to be out of the way of all the other, faster men running with me.

The whistle blew and I took off, this time in front of the pack. I still remember the feel and pattern of my breath as I sprinted around the first turn on the track, pumping my arms as fast as I could, hands and neck relaxed, and in the lead. On the straightaway, I lengthened my stride and again I felt my breathing find a rhythm. Almost like a dream, I came off the final turn and into the home stretch toward my coach, who stood with his stopwatch calling out times. "Sixty-three . . . sixty-four . . . sixty-five . . . sixty-six!" I had come in with the first and fastest group, third out of twenty athletes with a time of sixty-six seconds. I was equally dazed and elated. This just couldn't be possible.

We jogged and then walked for our allotted recovery time, and then lined up for our second interval sprint. Sixty-seven seconds. Then our third 400-meter sprint—sixty-six seconds. Our fourth—again, sixty-six seconds.

My world changed that day as, somehow, I cracked open the limiting view I had previously held. Any track expert will tell you that it's impossible for an athlete to go from 400-meter interval times of eighty-one and eighty-two seconds to times of sixty-six and sixty-seven seconds in one day. You can't shave a full fifteen seconds off in one day. But of course, that is exactly what happened. Looking back, I can see that what it really meant was that for many months I had those faster times inside me, but my model of myself and what I was capable of held me back. I finally had grown into my body—by this point, I was six feet tall, 170 pounds—but until that day, I held myself back because of my past picture of who I was.

What really had changed that day? Nothing more than my belief of what I was capable of—my model of my own capabilities.

Likewise, I experienced a powerful breakthrough in the world of business when I realized that eighty-hour work weeks weren't the secret to success, and that by consistently focusing my best time and attention on my highest-value activities, I could generate results that previously seemed impossible. After several years of doing this as an individual, I learned the power of running my company under this same premise, focusing my team's best time, talent, and attention on our company's most valuable projects and opportunities. As had been the case with running sprints, I saw an "impossible" leap forward.

I began teaching an early version of the formula to my business coaching clients, and their results supported the universal applicability and impact of focusing an individual and a team's best time and attention on a few highest-value opportunities and initiatives. I watched as my clients' companies grew faster and enjoyed large profit increases, while their key leaders were able to rein in their hours and take actual vacations—for many of them, something they had forgone for years prior to doing this work.

What most impacted my experimentation with the formula was becoming a dad. When my sons Adam and Matthew were born in 2009, I had been experimenting with this formula for over a decade. If push came to shove and my company needed me to get on a plane to keynote another large conference or to work nights and weekends for an intense quarter to finish up a new book, I did. But when I held my newborn sons in my arms for the first time and felt that overwhelming mixture of emotions, working those same hours simply wasn't an option. Their arrival introduced a brand-new constraint to use of my time. Like an astronaut carefully calculating the optimal use of their consumables of oxygen, fuel, and water, I began reformulating ways to make maximal use of my limited work hours, best attention, and travel days.

This book is my best attempt to lay out in one unified place the patterned program I came to embrace. The pathway for you to keep growing isn't rooted in brute force. It doesn't require long hours or nights and weekends. In fact, it insists on just the opposite. I know this is heretical to the Time and Effort Economy, but I've seen the impact firsthand—in my own life and in the lives of my clients who apply this formula.

Today I run two wildly successful companies and put a hard stop on my work week of forty hours. I'm home for dinner by 5:30 PM— I'd better be, since I'm the one who cooks in my household. I exercise six days a week and take a minimum of ten weeks of real vacation time every year. The start to all of this was my decision to leave the Time and Effort Economy and fully live in the Value Economy. It's a decision you get to make that holds the promise of changing *everything*.

THE TIME AND EFFORT ECONOMY SAYS: My boss will be upset if she sees I'm not busy.

THE VALUE ECONOMY SAYS: My boss will be upset if she sees that I'm not producing results.

TIME AND EFFORT ECONOMY: If I don't keep checking my inbox and apps, I may miss something important.

VALUE ECONOMY: If I keep interrupting my best work by checking my inbox and apps, I won't be able to contribute my best value to our company.

TIME AND EFFORT ECONOMY: To be a good, committed team player, I've got to respond to work requests at night and on weekends, even if that means interrupting family time to take that call or answer that email.

VALUE ECONOMY: To be a good, committed team member, I've got to be brave enough to stand up for a company culture that is committed to results, not just a flurry of activity. When my home life is rich and fulfilling, I do my best work and stay with my team longer.

TIME AND EFFORT ECONOMY: I've set my email and apps to give me push notifications. After all, this model says, be responsive and accessible.

VALUE ECONOMY: I intelligently use filters and better design to consistently reclaim blocks of interruption-free best time. After all, this model says, to be effective, you must spend your best time on your highest-value work for the company.

TIME AND EFFORT ECONOMY: Work hard and become indispensable. If no one else can do what you do, you'll always have a job.

VALUE ECONOMY: When you work smart, create huge value, and especially when you build the systems, team, and culture that will carry that value forward and protect those gains even if you weren't there doing the work, you'll have true economic protection. You'll have become so valuable that your company, or a competitor, will pay handsomely for your ability to provide these enhanced, sustainable results.

You can see the very different ways the two economies perceive the world and push you to play day in, day out. Most of the gains of simply working harder are incremental gains. You put in one hour extra of work, you get one extra hour of economic value out. In most cases, this is a linear relationship: x units extra in, x units extra out. Also, these gains are capped: there are only so many hours in the day and week. In fact, grinders living in the Time and Effort Economy often reach a point where extra hours bring diminishing returns. After this threshold of fatigue or burnout, there is a degrading relationship where they now only get a fractional unit of value out for each extra hour in, with this rate of decay often increasing as they try to brute-force even more gains through still more hours.

Rather than just working more hours answering emails, responding to texts, or taking care of the low-value, third-party requests that clutter your days, investing your best hours at the points of maximal impact means that each hour worked generates a magnified return: 10× . . . 100× . . . 1,000× or more.

STEPHANIE WAS THE CEO of a contract medical manufacturing company in Santa Cruz, California. In the early days, before she took over the company, they were an undifferentiated, commodity player struggling in the late 1980s to stay afloat against a horde of competition, especially from overseas firms with cheaper labor costs and almost no environmental regulations.

Stephanie realized that to survive, she needed to find niches where her company could create more value for their customers. She led their first big strategic move into plastic parts for consumer electronics, producing components for early Apple products like the iPod. To compete in this arena, she knew they needed an overseas production facility to provide the speed and quality of their US-based manufacturing at a cost that appealed to their price-sensitive customers. This move led to years of growth for her company. She invested her best time in wooing large customers, making key strategic decisions, and building a leadership team that could run the day-to-day operations smoothly and autonomously.

In the mid-1990s, she shifted the company from commodity plastic parts to partnering with electronic suppliers who needed engineering-intensive solutions. This decision led to higher margins. But as the company readied itself for an eventual sale, Stephanie carved out her best time to think carefully about how she could position the company for the biggest, most successful exit:

> "I realized that in order for us to harvest the biggest sale price, we needed to position our company at the crossroads of two things: the key trends in the marketplace and the highest multiple-generating manufacturing niches we could effectively compete in given our strengths."

Stephanie's solution for her company—nestled in the Santa Cruz foothills, close to the innovation hotbed of Silicon Valley—was to move into medical device manufacturing. She took the manufacturing strengths of precision and operational excellence they had developed domestically making parts for highly demanding customers like Apple and Intel and combined that with their geographic advantages and rich network of contacts at innovative start-up companies, venture capital firms, and teaching institutions focused on medical research. One challenge: They had never made medical devices. So Stephanie's company invested in the doctors, engineers, designers, and assemblers. They purchased new capital equipment and brought in the expert regulatory consultants they needed to succeed in this world.

It took them five years to redesign their factory, hire the talent, and build a cohesive team. But the investment paid off with record growth and profitability. In the end, they became one of the industry's hottest players:

> "We began making surgical kits and tools in clean room conditions. We'd hermetically seal the packaging and sterilize it,

and the next time it was opened was by a surgical team in an operating room somewhere in the world. It was exciting and heady stuff to realize that our products were cutting-edge and enhancing and saving lives. We built a reputation as the go-to place if you were a medical device start-up company [that] had a difficult-to-manufacture plastic device. Jack, our head of manufacturing, and his team loved the engineering puzzle of working with these vibrant companies. It just worked for our talent set and other strengths."

And work it did. The company grew and become a tempting acquisition target, with billion-dollar firms jockeying to buy the company. In the end, Stephanie's focus on value, not hours and effort, helped her guide the company to a sale ten times greater than what the typical plastics injection-molding company ever would have commanded. ◆

What if you don't run a large company or division? What if you're a self-employed professional or someone leading a small professional services firm? If you are wondering how the formula applies to you, let's take the case of Marvin, managing partner of a three-lawyer firm in Atlanta, Georgia.

THIRTY YEARS INTO HIS CAREER, Marvin was a gifted attorney. His clients willingly paid his $600 hourly billing rate, knowing that he was one of the best business attorneys in his community. When I first began working with him and his firm three years ago, he fought me tooth and nail over this "Value Economy thing." He said, "David, I just need to find a way to keep the work coming in the door. I don't have the time to do coaching sessions every two weeks. Every coaching session costs me twice—once for the session itself and a second time for the hour of lost billing I had to give up."

You might wonder why Marvin even joined the program with an attitude like that, but at the same time he said these things, part of him realized that he was just working too much. He regularly billed seventy hours a week, which put his average work week at eighty hours or more. He worked all of Saturday and most of Sunday. He was intrigued by the idea that he could work less, still make the same income, and find even more enjoyment in owning the firm. That was why he made the leap to join the program, but now he was second-guessing that decision.

I convinced him to stick with the program for just twelve months and we'd see where things stood. One of the first areas we looked at when we began working together was his firm's pricing, billing, and collections practices, always a high-leverage, easy place to start to make an immediate impact on a professional services firm.

Over the first two months of coaching, I walked Marvin through several key decisions, and we had his top administrative leader in on most of those sessions to implement the decisions we made during them. It turns out that while Marvin was very profitable when he did client work for $600 per hour, that wasn't his most profitable use of time. He actually made quite a bit more when he positioned himself as a rainmaker and legal-matter magnet that brought the firm new work, which could then be staffed down to associates, paralegals, and legal secretaries billing at $195 to $350 an hour. This was better for his clients, as it saved them money, and it was better for the firm since the margin on this staffed-out work was quite high. And, by building better systems to control for quality and improve efficiencies, staffing down the work allowed his firm to take on 30 percent more work without increasing headcount. From the outside looking in, this work was a home run.

I still remember the day, ten months in, when Marvin came to me and said he was quitting the program. He couldn't justify the two hours of one-to-one coaching time it took each month; he needed that time to do billable work. Struggling to keep a straight face, I said to him, "Before you make that final decision, let's just have your accountant pull the numbers so we can get a clear before-and-after picture of your return on time invested so you can make the best decision." He agreed.

When the analysis came back, it turned out that Marvin's firm had increased its bottom-line profit—not gross revenue, *profit*—by $850,000. What's more, Marvin's billing records showed that at the same time the firm was making close to a million dollars more profit, he had reduced his work by ten hours a week. How was this possible? Simple: I've learned that for most professionals, rarely is your highest-value work doing "billable" activities. Billable activities, even at Marvin's hourly rate, are valuable, but not the highest value. It took some convincing, but for Marvin, a few hours a month spent making the bigger strategic decisions—such as how to strategically staff down work but control for quality, push billing rates upward, and set collections guidelines—were literally worth a hundred times more per hour of his time than if he had used those same few hours a month for more billable work. Needless to say, he's still a client to this day. ♦

Here's the thing: We all live in the Value Economy . . . eventually. At some point, all companies will judge the impact and value of team members based on contribution, rewarding the very best of the best both financially and nonfinancially. If they don't, some other company will. The marketplace may be many things, but dumb is not one of them.

This is why the first step of the Freedom Formula calls on you to embrace the Value Economy. We have to start here, because just like when I was starting my 400-meter sprints at the back of the pack to stay out of the way of all those faster, muscle-bound athletes, the first thing holding you back from sprinting ahead faster and getting your life back is your mental model.

ONE OF THE BUSINESS OWNERS I coach is Kes Andersen, who runs Pathfinder Signs, a successful multimillion-dollar outdoor advertising company, responsible for more than ten thousand outdoor signs. When I first introduced him to this formula, he was getting up at 4 AM every day to take calls from his field teams to make sure that if they had any problems with the large signs they were going to install that day, he could solve them. While the field teams needed to get out and do their installations that early to avoid traffic, why was Kes doing the same?

> "My wife used to ask me why I didn't just let my team handle that stuff," Kes admits. "What I didn't want to tell her—heck, I didn't even want to admit to myself—was that I liked the feeling of being in control that those 4 AM calls gave me. Or to be more accurate, I hated the feeling of being out of control that having someone else oversee those field teams would have meant for me." ◆

Break the Five Time and Effort Chains

In chapter four, "Develop Strategic Depth," I'll share how Kes worked himself out of those 4 AM calls and increased his production capacity by 25 percent without hiring more staff. But now I want to ask you a few blunt questions: Does your compulsion for control cause you to micromanage your team and stop you from growing their capacity to "own" more functional areas of your business? If you're being honest with yourself, wouldn't you have to admit that at least a small part of why you struggle letting go to members of your team is that you hate that feeling of being out of control and that you get something out of being needed? Have you built a fragile team that is overly reliant on the talent, expertise, and relationships of one or two key players?

In my experience, there are five chains that can trap you in the Time and Effort Economy. When you look beneath the surface of circumstance and culture, these chains are the real root causes that ensnare millions of bright, talented business leaders around the world. These are capable business professionals who unnecessarily work too many hours and sacrifice too much of their personal lives relative to the value they create and the success they enjoy. Once you break free of these chains, you'll immediately rise to new levels of professional success. Best of all, you'll do it while enjoying a rich and fulfilling personal life.

Chain #1: Faulty Model

Somehow we have fooled ourselves into thinking that if we only work harder, longer, faster, that we can work our way out of the hole. But that's the faulty model of the Time and Effort Economy. It's like someone stuck at the bottom of a deep pit shoveling away. When you ask them how they plan on getting out, they shout up, "I'll just dig faster!"

There have been many times in my business career where, if you had observed my *behaviors*, you'd have to conclude that my strategy was one of "digging faster." I've felt, as you've probably felt, that I was dying a death of a thousand cuts, overwhelmed and exhausted. It's one thing to know this cognitively, but quite another to consistently behave this way.

Chain #2: Chasing After Control

| *Controlitis*—the inflammation of your control gland

At various times I've found myself saying, "If you want something done right, you've got to do it yourself." Business leaders tend to be control freaks, and I'm no different. I hate the anxiety of wondering if someone else will do the job right. I regularly feel pulled back into assuming control and more closely directing my team. I like the feeling of coming up with the idea or solving the problem. I feel important. Needed. In control.

But recognize the high price you and your company are paying for your urge to control every detail of your business and team. I'm not suggesting that you just abdicate responsibility; rather, I urge you to build on a stable base of sound business systems, a talented and well-trained team, and a culture that helps ensure that your team properly handles any ambiguous situation that arises.

Part of what keeps you locked down by the chain of control is the curse of your own competency. I'll be frank here and acknowledge that you likely are exceedingly good at what you do. Over the course of your career, you've become one of those competent people who just gets stuff done. When you watch a member of your staff struggle to get a result, you know you could do better, and it's excruciating to hold yourself back. Your control gland becomes inflamed, and you feel compelled to jump back in and take more on. But the more you directly try to control, the more trapped you become in the Time and Effort Economy, as your hours and attention get eaten up by the insatiable hunger of your staff when they learn that the best way to please you is simply to let you decide the next steps.

This is really what woke Kes up every morning at 4 AM to check in with his production teams. This is really what pushes so many of us to hold another meeting or send another round of emails to get updates on the details of how project X or situation Y is progressing.

Recognize that when you feel out of control, it pushes you to personally oversee and handle more, in the false belief that only you can do it. This just more permanently traps you in the endless rounds and increased pressure of doing more and more. If you're not careful, this is one of the thickest chains holding you back from the good life you truly desire.

Chain #3: Lack of Clarity

Without clear priorities and objectives that every member on your staff understands, efforts get scattered and poor decisions get made. This leads to underperformance, which pushes you to chase after more control to set things back on the right path, which further robs the business of depth because you're not prioritizing time to develop your team so that they can take on more responsibilities. It's a negative reinforcement loop.

Lack of clarity is evident in the overwhelmingness you feel when you're drowning in the hundred messages a day you have to process in your inbox and app feeds. It's tempting to escape into the micro-pleasure of checking off easy, low-value tasks. Being responsive to the unending daily interruptions feels more comfortable than facing your anxieties about starting in on one of your larger, more important projects.

This also impacts your team. The lack of strategic structure for how priorities get established, goals set, and plans made causes your team to flounder and struggle. Of course, you're always there to pick up the pieces and take back more control, but by this point you understand where that leads. That's why one of the core steps of the formula is for you to clearly identify—in writing—what you and your team need to focus on this quarter and this week.*

Chain #4: Lack of Depth

When you have a team that lacks the experience or talent to accomplish the goals you've set, you often find yourself pulled back into more closely doing and managing the functions of your department, division, or business. It becomes a chicken-and-egg scenario: if you had the right people on the team, you could let go of more. But because you have to handle so much of the work volume, you don't have the time and attention to hire or develop the right people who could take off much of the load currently on your shoulders. Round and round you go.

Chain #5: Outdated Time Habits

The world today is fundamentally different than the world we evolved to thrive in. In the developed world today, an abundance of calories

---

* In chapter three, "Invest in Your Fewer, Better," I'll give you a proven process to develop your rolling *one-page* ninety-day Action Plan. You'll also meet a powerful tool called the Big Rock Report to focus your team's best attention on the weekly execution of your Action Plan.

has caused an epidemic of obesity and lifestyle diseases like heart disease, stroke, diabetes, and cancer. We evolved for a world in which food was scarce, where sugar meant fruits with their precious nutrients, and fat meant the calories we needed to survive a long winter.

Similarly, our time sense evolved in a business world where time and effort were once the things we were paid for. But that has shifted over time, and with the transformation of modern communication and technology, brute strength and raw hours mean a lot less than they did centuries ago. Work no longer has to take place in an office or factory; you literally can work from anywhere. Yet the geographical freedom we experience—and which our ancestors couldn't have imagined—has a dark side. More and more of us feel compelled to always be on, checking our devices, responding to messages. The changing, 24/7, interconnected world has completely altered the way we live and work, but many of us simply haven't updated our time habits to design the structure and systems we need to effectively and sustainably produce today.

AT A FORTUNE 50 CONSUMER ELECTRONICS COMPANY, I coached Paul, one of two senior VPs in charge of their most profitable division. My job was to help him find ways to get their highly educated workforce to work better together to develop new products faster in their hypercompetitive, multibillion-dollar niche.

Paul wanted to get the company to leverage technology to speed up development projects and better allocate their high-priced staff across a portfolio of projects. This high-tech company was still managing development projects by spreadsheet, with data being entered and controlled top-down—crude and inefficient. Not only did this make it difficult to best deploy their engineers; it throttled development speed, as team managers got status updates via an endless series of progress meetings. These managers literally would go down the list of deliverables one person at a time, getting status updates sequentially, wasting hours and hours of some of the world's top engineers, who had to sit through these poorly run meetings and wait for their turn to give updates. Some of the managers tried to be more efficient by asking for email updates, not realizing that the interruptions to their talent's day slowed down progress and risked the multibillion-dollar prize if this company didn't get their products to market faster.

Of course, you realize that there is a much better way to leverage technology to manage larger-scale, decentralized projects like these. A cloud-based project management system, where individual engineers could spend an average of ten minutes a day updating their pieces of the bigger puzzle, would have given this company a valuable, real-time picture of project status and how to best shift its engineers around to reach the finish line faster. Still, even with this obvious improvement available, it took Paul a year to get his boss and his boss's boss to let him move forward with it. Why? Because entrenched team members enjoyed a personal advantage in the old system, which kept information tightly controlled at the VP and senior VP levels, even though it hurt the company as a whole. ♦

To sustain the changes you want and break this final chain, you must rethink any of your outdated time habits and confront cultural elements that may be deeply rooted in your company.

At the beginning of this chapter, I introduced you to Tom and how his wife Lee "forced" him into our program by pre-paying for it. How did things turn out for Tom? Over the course of our first seven years working together, Tom grew his company 400 percent. His shareholders were thrilled. At the same time, he reduced his work week to less than forty hours. Lee and their children were thrilled. And two years ago, Tom stepped out of the CEO role and became chairman of the board, effectively halving his hours. With a large equity stake in his own company and a role that he loves, Tom was thrilled.

You already know that understanding this concept in your head isn't enough; you've got to *behave* it in your workday. While many business leaders give lip service, perhaps even champion the Value

Economy concept, their behaviors tell a different story. They personally work a mass of long, undifferentiated hours. Their best time gets sucked into solving other people's problems or responding to lower-value requests, and as a consequence, they cram their best work into slivers of time here and there.

They *say* they embrace the Value Economy, and yet they still assess their team in large part on the hours and effort they put in. They don't always do this overtly, but subtly, they push their team to play in the Time and Effort Economy. "Mary is always so responsive. She's really a team player." Or, "Armando, I sent you that email two hours ago and haven't heard back from you yet!" What message are you sending to your team? What if Armando intentionally turned off his email and phone for three hours to create the updated project plan to thrill your number one customer? Or to bring three of his best engineers into a conference room to brainstorm the best way to solve the major design challenge that was blocking progress on your next major product release? How will your pushing him to be "responsive" to email shape which economy he lives in going forward?

Don't say, "I already know this." Instead, ask yourself, "Am I doing this?" If I were there shadowing you for a week, what would your behaviors reveal about which economy you really are working in? Would I see you throw hours and effort at problems or to meet deadlines? Would I observe you judging and rewarding your team—with attention, actions, and incentives—for their attitudes and apparent effort? Or for their concrete results and actual value created?

Merely saying you believe in the Value Economy isn't enough. You must embrace it by shifting your behaviors to align with it. **It's your behavior that reveals which economy you currently operate from. What does your behavior say?**

Embracing the Value Economy means breaking the one-to-one relationship between hours worked and value created. The rest of the book will give you the precise mechanics to do just that, but what's critical to understand at this point is that you don't get paid for time served, but rather for value created. And to create value, you must push past the chains that, in the past, trapped you in the Time and Effort Economy. In chapter two, we'll look at a proven time structure that will help you reclaim five or more hours of your best time every week, which you can reinvest in your highest-value activities. This is the first application step to move fully into the Value Economy.

Free Gift for Readers: The Freedom Tool Kit ($1,275 Value)

Because I know that not everyone learns the same way, my coaching team and I have created a complete tool kit to help you apply the ideas you'll learn and share them with your staff. This *free* value add for readers like you includes downloadable PDF versions of all the tools you'll be introduced to in the book, along with dozens of valuable video training sessions and other tools to help you enjoy greater professional success and a rich personal life, too. It even includes a powerful ninety-day quick-start program to help you and your team immediately apply the formula to grow your business. To get immediate access to the Freedom Tool Kit, go to **www.FreedomToolKit.com**.

CHAPTER 2

Step Two:
Reclaim Your Best Time

AS A MOTHER AND BUSINESS OWNER, Sylvia felt torn in two. Her formal work week was close to one hundred hours, not counting the extra informal hours she put in doing the billing, bookkeeping, purchasing, hiring, and "all the rest" after school closed. The business of running two large Montessori schools in Southern California—looking after 427 other people's children—caused her to miss key moments in her own two daughters' lives. With steady enrollment, a strong teaching staff, and $4.3 million in revenues each year, the schools were successful. But as much as Sylvia's family depended on her to provide a comfortable home and financial security, it killed her not to be present for the piano recitals, the soccer games, and all the other daily joys and trials of being a mom.

Her husband, Sean, a military veteran, did his best to pitch in and help, but he knew Sylvia was going to do things her way regardless of what he said. The pair had met while serving in the US Marine Corps. They retired from military service together, and, soon thereafter, Sylvia decided to start a school of her own, thinking it would make a difference for her students and give her family a greater quality of life. Sean moved into the support role, taking the lead at home and struggling to fill the hole Sylvia had left behind there from her overwhelming hours running the business.

The guilt was constant. Sylvia remembers the day her then twelve-year-old daughter, Karla, called her at work in tears because she'd been cyberbullied by a group of girls at school.

"I need you here, Mom," Karla sobbed. "I need you now!"

Sylvia just happened to be in the middle of a major crisis at the time. One of her students, a six-year-old with a severe peanut allergy, had been exposed when one of the other kids shared some mini Reese's cups. She was in the ER with the little boy, waiting for his parents to show up while the doctors treated his anaphylactic shock.

"Honey, I'm so sorry, but this can't wait; I'll be there as soon as I can," Sylvia explained.

Then Karla, true to the style of an angry tween, hurled a zinger: "You're more of a mother to those kids than you are to me!" ◆

Sylvia was struggling with the age-old question we all face as we continue to build our careers and provide for ourselves and our families: How can I be successful at work and still have a life? How can I give everything to everyone and still make a living? But, short of cloning herself, she didn't see any other way than to keep putting in brutal hours, even though she saw the toll it was taking on those she loved most—her children. Maybe one day she could earn enough to retire herself and her family in comfort. But by then her two girls would have grown up and moved out of the house. She'd have missed out on their childhood altogether.

Something had to change. She knew this but didn't know how to make that change. As you doubtless have observed, she'd been living in the Time and Effort Economy, working beyond what is humanly sustainable, for diminishing returns, and at great personal cost.

Hard Stops

You know that time is one of the most powerful variables you control in the success equation. Now it's time to put a hard stop on your day and live and work better for that clear line in the sand. You already know what some of your biggest time wasters are, both in and out of the office, but seeing them in stark black and white may drive the point home. Here's a quick pop quiz to help you decide exactly where a large chunk of your time is being wasted:

Top 10 Low-Value Time Thieves

How many hours on average do you spend per week doing the following activities?

Hours	Event
	Sitting in nonproductive or wasteful meetings.
	Dealing with low-level interruptions that easily could have been handled by someone else.
	Handling low-value emails.
	Handling low-value requests from coworkers.
	Writing reports that have no impact on the bottom line and that no one bothers to read.
	Streaming YouTube cat videos, checking social media, or indulging in other forms of escapism for a "mental health break."
	Doing low-level business activities that the company easily could outsource at a much lesser cost to the business than your time.
	Putting out fires that easily could have been prevented.
	Doing office work you could pay someone $25/hour or less to do (filing, faxing, copying, typing, shipping, cleaning, etc.).
	Doing personal errands you could pay someone $25/hour or less to do (laundry, cleaning, yard work, simple repair work, picking up dry cleaning, etc.).
	Total: hours per week

Now multiply your total by fifty weeks per year. That's how many hours you are personally wasting on low-value work at present. When I did this exercise at a recent business conference I was keynoting, members of the audience averaged eighteen hours per week of wasted time! That's over nine hundred hours each year, or a full twenty-two working weeks a year that were wasted.

The cost doesn't stop there; it continues with your key staff. Assuming that they use their time as well as you do, multiply these wasted hours per year by the number of key staff on your team. This is the direct cost to your company of operating in the Time and Effort Economy. And what about the follow-on indirect cost of burnout, employee turnover, and disengagement? When you factor in all the direct and indirect costs of "business as usual," the real cost is staggering.

Imagine if you and your company reinvested these wasted hours into your highest-value activities. What kind of impact would that have?

My Buffet Strategy to Time Management

Ask yourself how often you operate reactively, squandering your best attention on low-value email, staff interruptions, and other seemingly urgent but low-value tasks that your team could have handled on its own. You fit in the high-value activities when you can—often when everyone has gone home, the office is quiet, and the phone has stopped ringing—but by then you're too exhausted to think. It's almost like you are filling your plate at a buffet, where other people's urgencies and high-calorie, low-nutrition tasks dominate your plate, leaving little room for your most valuable, enterprise-nutritious activities.

Together, we're going to flip this model on its head. From now on, you are going to fill your time plate first with the highest-value activities, in structured blocks of your best time, so that no matter what you fill the other space with, you'll get more of your highest-value work done in the best manner possible. One of my biggest challenges as a coach is getting the business leaders I work with to break the connection between one hour worked and one hour of value created. A successful consultant who gets paid $500 an hour for each billable hour worked, for example, may think that's the highest use of her time. But, in fact, the more valuable expenditure is the time she puts into securing a new client who will bring in hundreds of billable hours over the relationship, or deciding which niches to focus on, or which to ignore, or growing her consulting team to be able to systematically get more valuable work out the door faster and at a higher quality.

Instead of living by the old linear equation of one hour of time being equal to one unit of value, what if you could squeeze fifty to one hundred units of value out of that hour? How about one thousand units of value? How would that change your business? How would it transform your life?

Remember, you don't get paid for hours worked; rather, you get paid for value created. Timecards and grueling days don't help you create value. Investing blocks of your best work time on those Fewer, Better activities that create the most value for your organization is your first functional step toward breaking the hours-worked fallacy. The most successful business leaders galvanize and focus their entire organizations to invest their collective best time into those Fewer, Better activities that make the biggest difference. One of the most powerful ways to break the direct link between one hour worked and one unit of value created is by harnessing, leveraging, and unleashing the value of your team's hours worked for best and highest effect. This is how the Jeff Bezoses and Richard Bransons of the world can create billions of dollars of market value annually independent of the hours they personally put in.

Reflect on the example of Paul Robinson, owner and CEO of a rapidly growing IT services company in San Diego, California, called Ensunet.

PAUL GREW UP IN A HOUSEHOLD that valued excellence and personal effort. His dad, Arnie Robinson, won a gold medal for the long jump at the 1976 Olympic Games in Montreal. For ten years, Paul applied his dad's determined, focused work ethic to grow his fledgling company. And it worked, to a point. He grew the company to a six-figure income. But long hours and hard work by themselves stalled, as they always do. For several years, Paul remained stuck at this level, essentially being a six-figure, self-employed IT professional.

When he started to apply the Freedom Formula, especially the time model that you're about to explore, he grew his company by 1,000 percent over the next 36 months. Recently, I had a chance to talk with Paul at a workshop I was teaching for 120 business leaders. I asked him directly if his business breakthrough had occurred because he was putting in more hours. He looked at me, smiled, and said, "David, I didn't have any more hours to put in, I already was working eighty-hour weeks."

What initially made the biggest impact was focusing his best time on his highest-value activities, which gave his business its first round of growth. These activities included securing bigger contracts and finding the key staff to directly help his company fulfill on them.

> "That gave me the courage and cash flow to focus on growing our systems and team, which gave us our second round of growth," Paul told me. "There's no way hard work alone would have done this for us." ♦

I understood. Once upon a time, I was living at the Olympic Training Center in Colorado Springs, training for the Olympics myself. It struck me that when I moved in as a resident athlete, I didn't train longer hours, but the quality of every hour that I trained was measurably greater. The same holds true for the most successful business leaders. They don't work more hours; that's a myth. Rather, the hours they work are qualitatively more valuable than those of average business executives because they focus on the right things, at the right time, in the right way.

Breaking the Link Between Hours Worked and Value Created

Hour Worked	Unit Value of Output	Who Creates This Way
1 hour worked	1 unit of value created	Average employee
1 hour worked	10 units of value created	Capable manager
1 hour worked	100–1,000 units of value created	Talented business leader
1 hour worked	1 million units of value created	Rock star leader

All it takes is a few small changes. Think of it as choosing more wisely at a buffet. You can load up on junk food: desserts, fried food, or whatever is on offer at the pasta bar. Or you can first eat a plateful of nutritious food like vegetables and proteins—and then go back and load up on any crap you want. Not only will you have gotten your nutrition already, but your first plate of healthy food will have partially filled your stomach, so you end up eating less of the junk food later.

It starts with identifying the most nutritious activities and distinguishing them from the junk food in your daily business diet. I call this tool your Time Value Matrix™.

The Time Value Matrix

To upgrade your use of time, you first have to identify what you do that truly creates value for your enterprise. The first step to creating more value per unit of time is to concretely define what your real value-creation activities are.

If you've read anything on time management, you've come across Pareto's Principle, inspired by the work of nineteenth-century economist Vilfredo Pareto. Commonly called the "80-20 Rule," Pareto's

Principle states that 20 percent of your actions generate 80 percent of your results (high value) and 80 percent of your actions generate the other 20 percent of your results (low value). I've used this valuable distinction as the foundation for a refined time-value model.

If you take the 20 percent of your actions that generate 80 percent of your results and apply the 80-20 rule to it a second time, then 20 percent of that 20 percent produces 80 percent of 80 percent of your results. That means 4 percent of your effort (the 20 percent of 20 percent) generates 64 percent of your results (80 percent of 80 percent).

Hang in here with me for one more math moment and apply the 80-20 rule one final time. That means that just 1 percent of your effort (20 percent of 20 percent of 20 percent) generates 50 percent of your results! That's right—a tiny fraction of your highest-value work produces half of all your results.

No, this is not an exact science. Nor does this just work automatically. But Pareto's Principle illustrates a valuable point: all time is not valued equally. Four hours of your best time on Tuesday may have produced a far greater return than thirty hours of low-value tasks you "checked off" on Monday, Wednesday, and Thursday.

The goal of step two of the Freedom Formula is to reclaim blocks of your best time, structured in a way that enables you to focus on your highest-value activities. The starting point is to create your own personal Time Value Matrix (*fig. 1*), sorting your activities into four types of time:

- **D time** is the 80 percent of unleveraged, wasteful time that only produces 20 percent of your total return. I call this the 80 Percent Mass and give it a relative value of 1.
- **C time** is the leveraged 20 percent of your time that produces 80 percent of your results. I call this Leveraged Time. It has a relative value of 16 (¼ less input generating 4 times more output). That means every hour of C activities creates 16 times the economic value of one hour of D time.

- **B time** is the highly focused 4 percent that generates 64 percent of your results. I call this 4 percent your Sweet Spot. It has a relative value of 64: one hour of B time produces 64 *times* the value of the same time spent on a D activity.
- **A time** is the top of the pyramid—the Magic 1 Percent. Fully 50 percent of your results come from these activities. (A time has a relative value of 200 times that of D time.)

Your low-value, D-time task might include screening out phone solicitations, filling out your expense reimbursement spreadsheet, or creating a low-stakes, time-consuming report that no one really looks at or uses anyway. If you didn't have to do these tasks, or if you only fit them into your least productive remnant time, you'd have more of your best time for your higher-value work.

Your C-time activities could include delegating to a staff member, working one-to-one with a client, or sending a progress update to your team. These things matter, but they don't matter the most. You

TIME VALUE MATRIX™			
	Input	**Output**	**Relative Value**
A time *Magic 1%*	1%	50%	200 × D
B time *4% Sweet Spot*	4%	64%	64 × D
C time *Leveraged 20%*	20%	80%	16 × D
D time *80% Mass*	80%	20%	1 × D

Copyright © Maui Mastermind®

Figure 1

need C-level activities; they make up much of how you push projects ahead and take care of your day-to-day responsibilities. The key is to recognize and remember that there is a higher order of activities, your A- and B-level activities, that are a magnitude more valuable.

Your B-level activities might include working one-to-one to coach and develop a key team member, planning out your high-value activities for the week, or participating in a key brainstorming session.

Your A-level activities might include creating your one-page quarterly Action Plan for your company or department, making a key hire, or working with one of your top alliance partners to launch a new joint campaign.

At this point, it's normal if the line between A- and B-level activities is blurred. Over time, as you start to pay attention, it will become easier to discern the finer distinction between your particular A-level activities and your B-level ones. What matters now is that you see that A- and B-level activities are a magnitude more valuable than the mundane C- and D-level tasks that clog your to-do list.

Right now, invest ten minutes in listing your own A-B-C-D activities. Start with your A- and B-level activities. Ask yourself, "What are the most important results that I'm really on the payroll to create?"

If you're the CEO, you might answer, *being the strategic visionary who helps my company decide at the highest level which strategies or initiatives get the most and best company resources.*

If you're the head of marketing, your answer might include *to make sure we build a brand that resonates with our core market and differentiates us from our competitors so that we can continue to sell to and service our customers.*

If you're a self-employed professional, you might include *creating a reliable platform that brings a steady stream of new clients into your firm.*

If you're head of HR, you might include *recruiting and retaining top talent—company-wide—for your organization.*

YOUR TURN: What are the three most important results that you *really* are on the payroll to create? For each of your key results, list three of your most important behaviors or activities that generate each of these key results. On the next page, you'll see an example *(fig. 2)* that I filled out for myself with my business coaching company, Maui Mastermind. I encourage you to visit **www.FreedomToolkit. com** to download a blank version of the Time Value Matrix tool so you can do this same exercise yourself.

Again, don't worry if you haven't quite decided on the distinction between your A- and B-level activities just yet. What matters at this point is that you get in your gut the qualitative difference between A and B activities and the C- or D-level tasks that fill your day.

Now list your C- and D-level tasks. These likely are the things that currently fill the mass of your day. Look at your to-do list and calendar to jog your memory about all the tasks you regularly spend your day getting done. The first step of upgrading your use of time is to get clear—in writing—what you do that creates the most and the least value.

Understand that these lists are not static. What you currently consider A- or B-level activity will inevitably change as your business grows or your role evolves within an organization. For example, if meeting one-to-one with a prospective client currently is an A-level activity for you, make sure that in six to twelve months, you've increased the value you create for your company so this activity is pushed down to a B- or C-level activity. Ideally, working with a joint-venture partner who can generate dozens of leads for you every month will become an A-level activity, or training your sales team to meet with prospective clients one-to-one, or creating a sales video that generates passive sales. By that point, meeting one-to-one with a prospective client is no longer as important for you to do personally. This is good. This is growth.

Understanding the distinctions between A-, B-, C-, and D-level activities will help you shift your focus from putting in hours to upgrading the type of work you do. Over time, this will create huge business breakthroughs. If you are an entrepreneur, you can grow your business by 25 to 50 percent or more if you

Top 3 Results I'm on the Payroll to Generate	3 Activities or Behaviors I Do That Generate This Result
Spokesperson for company to bring large numbers of prospective clients into the door of our business	• Write and promote bestselling new books. • Lock down large-scale promotional opportunities for our company, like regular columns with leading business websites and publications. • Give large-scale keynote talks to groups in our target audience.
Strategic visionary and decision maker	• Make high-level strategic decisions about what to invest our staff time and attention into and where to invest company resources (and what tempting distractions to say no to). • Regularly ask and prod my company to think about what comes next, and make sure that a portion of our best resources is focused on testing, exploring, and preparing for future growth engines for the company. • Communicate, both in words and actions, our values and culture throughout the company.
Coach, develop, and lead our leadership team	• Invest one-to-one time with our key leaders to help them grow and effectively lead their respective areas of the company. • Make sure that each of our key leaders has a clear understanding of our company strategy and how their part of the company needs to contribute to the overall plan so that we accomplish our most important goals. • Hold our leadership team accountable for their pillar plans and key results.

Figure 2   Sample list of David's key results and highest-value activities

just create an extra day or two each week to focus on taking those action steps that would grow and expand your business. If you are an executive, you can meet corporate targets faster and demonstrably increase the growth and success of your division, without working every weekend. If you practice law or some other profession, you can increase your firm's profit without simply cranking out more billable hours or personally performing more procedures. Whatever your field, the result of upgrading your existing hours to better and higher uses is magical—greater value created in less total time worked.

Interestingly, your A- and B-level activities may not always be what you think. Take Dr. Gurpreet Padda, a physician who runs a thriving pain management practice in St. Louis, Missouri.

AT THE TIME DR. PADDA FIRST LEARNED these time-value strategies, he owned a dozen different businesses, from a surgical practice to a medical billing company to several commercial real estate projects and even a few restaurants. He was stretched to his maximum capacity and had no idea how to scale.

When I first started working with Dr. Padda a decade ago, he thought the highest use of his time was the hours he spent in surgery, performing the pain-intervention spinal procedures at which he was a world-class expert. But the more he took these time-mastery concepts to heart, the clearer it became that, while lucrative, these surgery hours were not his best and highest use of time for his companies because, barring cloning himself, they weren't scalable. They actually were C time for him. He realized that his true A- and B-level activities were things like making key strategic decisions such as which business lines to expand into or avoid altogether, key hires, and high-dollar negotiations with seven- or eight-figure stakes. By restructuring his time, following the strategies discussed later in this chapter, Dr. Padda realized an additional $1 million a year in personal income.

"I knew time was my most precious resource, but the insight that I had a higher order of time beyond my hours in surgery was a fresh one."

Dr. Padda is an outlier example of just how effective these time mastery strategies can be when combined with the business growth principles and tactics I'll discuss later in this book. Today, Dr. Padda owns thirty-two different businesses with more than five hundred employees. He runs several medical clinics, multiple restaurants, a microbrewery, and two organic farms.

"And I still find these time value strategies just as valuable and relevant today as when I first learned them from you a decade ago." ♦

Focus Days and Push Days

Remember the buffet analogy? Now that you know what your healthiest, highest-value activities are, let's structure your week so that you intentionally fill up your first plate of food with your highest-value activities. This is where a time distinction I call Focus Days and Push Days comes into play.

A Focus Day is a specific day of the week you set aside to work primarily on a few key A- or B-level projects. On your Focus Day, you'll block out three to four hours of your best time to invest in your highest-value A- and B-level activities. Push Days are all the other days of your work week that you use to just "push" your normal projects another step forward. Focus Days help you create long-term impact on your business; Push Days help you keep your day-to-day operations rolling forward. I suggest that you start by designating one day each week as your Focus Day, and within that Focus Day, you permanently schedule one three- to four-hour "focus block" that you reserve for your highest-value activities.

Enroll your team in supporting your Focus Day. Encourage your key staff to set aside their own Focus Days, too. What do you do with the other four to five hours of the day that aren't in your focus block? Whatever you normally would do. Your focus block is so nutritious and valuable for your organization that it is okay to let the rest of the day go to your C- and even a few D-level activities. On the next page is a sample weekly schedule showing how your week might work when you use this simple yet potent concept *(fig. 3)*.

On your Focus Day, get outside of your old business routine and instead work on the highest-leverage, highest-value, highest-return part of your business. This could mean building out a baseline operational process to use with new clients, investing time in coaching your key team members, refining your hiring system, or visiting your two most important customers or prospects to deepen the relationship or close the sale.

I've developed my team to the point where I now take three Focus Days a week: Tuesday, Thursday, and Friday *(fig. 4)*. I use Monday and Wednesday as my Push Days. These are the days that I push my normal responsibilities and projects forward step by step. That's when I'm accessible by phone and email, and I hold many of my phone meetings. It's when I get the "job" of my business done.* I set aside my Push Days for the usual operational tasks of a business leader along with the organization and execution of any big ideas, deals, or plans that were mapped out, signed, or conceived on my Focus Days. But even on my Push Days, I also set aside a one-hour focus block to work on A- or B-level activities.

Think of your focus block as an appointment with yourself, when you are at your best, in the morning or the afternoon, whenever you feel sharpest, to do those highest-value A- and B-time items only you

---

* As you know, in many office settings, it's generally not a good idea to make Monday a Focus Day because that's when most people catch up from being away from the office, while Fridays usually are reserved for wrapping things up before the weekend. Adjust the model to suit the days of the week you and your team work.

	Mon. (Date)	Tues. (Date)	Wed. (Date)	Thurs. (Date)	Fri. (Date)
8:00					
9:00	Focus Block		Focus Block		Focus Block
		Focus Day			
10:00					
11:00					
12:00					
1:00					
2:00					
3:00				Focus Block	
4:00					
5:00					

WEEKLY SCHEDULE

Figure 3   Sample weekly schedule

can do for your company. Put it in your calendar to guarantee your-self a focus block of at least one hour of uninterrupted time even on your Push Days. Even if you do this in small, incremental steps with two Push Days a week, you'll start to notice a significant impact on your productivity level.

On Focus Days, I am all in. This is when I turn off the phones and email from 8:00 to 11:30 AM and again in the afternoon from 1:00 to 2:30 PM, so that I can concentrate on my highest-value activities.

For me, Focus Days often involve writing: books, like the one you are reading now; training tools for our business coaching system; or business plans for my teams to implement. That time also may involve holding high-value meetings or being in the studio recording a new business-growth training course. (In case you're wondering, I do check in for 30 to 45 minutes around noon and again at the end of the day to answer important phone messages or emails.)

Often on my Focus Days, I'll leave the office and work remotely. Sometimes I go into my conference room and work there. Getting out of my normal environment removes the temptation to do the C- and D-level work that lives in every corner of my office. I also put an away message on my email and empower my assistant to screen my calls and handle or delay any of my emails. This frees me up to fully focus on my most valuable activities.

This simple methodology allows you to reclaim those critical blocks of your best time. **Remember, the world won't volunteer to turn off; it takes a structured, well-designed approach to make these blocks of time to invest in your highest-value activities.** If you're passive about this, your time will be fractured into small pieces. Ten minutes here, five minutes there. High-value focus doesn't just happen on tap, anymore than I can say to one of my sons, "Okay, junior, let's have some quality time!" You have to give yourself the time and breathing room to let it happen organically.

This is about using all this extra time wisely, because it's actually *not* time that's the scarcest resource—attention is. Your best attention, the time when you are at your best in terms of productivity and focus, is the most powerful weapon in your arsenal.

For many of us, that first hour of the day, when we are sufficiently rested and fresh, is the most valuable. Lesser organizational leaders and managers crave control and immediate emotional rewards, so the first thing they do when entering the office is check their email. In fact, they likely already checked it twice before reaching the office. What a wasted opportunity! Most email just helps you tread water. Instead, when you get to your office, invest your golden hour in something that truly makes a difference. I've gotten into the habit of neatly laying out the one project I want to work on during my focus blocks the night before, so that when I walk into my office it's the

DAVID'S TYPICAL WEEK
with Focus Days and Reserved Focus Blocks

	Mon. (Date)	Tues. (Date)	Wed. (Date)	Thurs. (Date)	Fri. (Date)
8:00	Focus Block		Focus Block		
9:00		Focus Day		Focus Day	Focus Day
10:00					
11:00					
12:00					
1:00		Focus Day		Focus Day	
2:00					
3:00					
4:00		**15.5 HOURS/WEEK**			
5:00					

Figure 4

first thing I see on my desk in the morning or on my computer when I unlock my screen. Making progress on this high-value item makes the rest of my day gravy.

Imagine the power of a four-hour Focus Day block and four days of one-hour focus blocks, giving you eight uninterrupted hours each week to invest in your top priorities. Now multiply that by the forty-eight weeks a year you work (you *are* taking off a minimum of four weeks' vacation a year, right? If not, why not?). That's the equivalent of forty-eight full eight-hour days of your very best time—nine working weeks of you at your best doing upgraded activities. You can see how this is a key early step in breaking the link between one hour of time worked and one hour of value created.

The more you create these uninterrupted blocks of time, the more you can upgrade your use of that time and inject value into your daily activities. Instead of going from one thing to the next to the next, you'll be amazed by how much you get done when you are more intentional, keeping this principle of quality blocks of time in mind. Many business leaders allow their time to be "sliced" to death. They have five minutes to focus on a project before an email interrupts them. Then they move to a meeting, only to have fifteen minutes to prep for the next meeting that starts soon after the first. Then they get hit with two staff requests as they leave that meeting on their way back to their office. And so goes their day. You already know it's extraordinarily difficult to create your best value in small slivers of time. You need those blocks of uninterrupted best time in which to think, plan, create, and execute on key items.

RECAP: Set aside one Focus Day every week. Block out a three- to four-hour block of focus time during which you'll work exclusively on the highest-leverage, highest-value, highest-return activities (A and B) that add real value. Then, schedule in a focus block of at least one hour every Push Day.

The Four D's

After you've identified what you do that truly creates value (your A and B activities), look closely at your D activities as the place to mine the raw ore of more time. By applying the four D's of Deleting, Delegating, Deferring, and Designing Out, you'll free up five or more hours each week to reinvest in A and B activities. When you upgrade your time, you'll have more space and time within which to create more value.

The first three of the D's are obvious: you can delete it, delegate it, or defer it until a later time. Let's take a closer look at the fourth

D—design it out. I remember one professional complaining to me about how his day kept getting interrupted by unsolicited phone calls. I pointed out to him that on his company's phone tree, which all callers reached when they dialed his company, his extension was listed first! Essentially, he was saying, "Press one and interrupt my day with random calls." He laughed when I pointed this out and said, "I get it. I need to make myself the last option." I smiled and told him maybe. Or, I suggested, he could take himself completely off that phone tree and just make sure the people he wanted to get calls from had his direct, but unlisted, extension.

I'll have a lot more to say about leveraging better design to accomplish more with less in chapter nine, but right now I want you to take a simple action step. Pick one of your regularly occurring D-level activities. How could you design out this task so it never comes up to begin with?*

The Scourge of Email

As you drill down into the daily operations of your organization, you'll hunt and kill a multitude of time thieves, but one D that stands out above the rest is low-value email. Many of us are drowning in email, never realizing that the very way we habitually use it has made it much harder to get it back under control. Over a two-year period, I asked thousands of business leaders that my company coaches, "What's the single greatest interruption that kills your productivity?" The overwhelming answer, by a three-to-one ratio, was email.

It may be promotional junk mail disguised as something more important or perhaps you are being cc'd on something that requires

---

* Leverage the downloadable Time Value Matrix Tool to give you a structure to do this across multiple D-level tasks. You can download this tool at **www.FreedomToolKit.com**.

Apply the four D's to your D-level activities and regain more hours every week.

Delete It
Some D activities just plain shouldn't be done by anyone. Look at the action item and ask yourself what would be the consequences if no one did it. If the consequences are small, then consider just crossing it off your list altogether.

Delegate It
Maybe it's a task that needs to get done but not necessarily by you. Hand it off to your assistant, a staff member, or a vendor. Anytime you can hand off a D-level activity to someone, you free up both your time and your focus to do more valuable work for your organization.

Defer It
Maybe this task needs to be done, and done by you, but should it happen right now? Sometimes delaying the action item is the smartest choice.

Design It Out
If you find yourself handling a recurring D activity again and again, find a way to design it out by improving the process or system to keep the task from coming up in the first place. For example, if you get the same seven customer questions, post an FAQ page with the answers on your website. Or perhaps you can preempt questions by giving new clients a "quick start" booklet that proactively answers these seven questions. Or post an instructional video on your website that gives new clients your best presentation while answering these common questions. You get the idea. While it may take a little more time to "design out" a D-level activity, if it is one that comes up again and again, a little more time up front will yield real-time dividends down the road.

no direct action or response from you because the people sending are simply including you, their boss, in the thread to cover themselves—yet you still take half a minute to scan through its contents. Regardless, it's not those few seconds that cost you; it's the multiple minutes you lose as you try to regain focus on your original task, according to a University of California–Irvine study. Multiply that by the dozens or hundreds of emails that flood your inbox each day, and it adds up to precious hours when you could have been doing something more productive.

In my company, about eight years ago we began experimenting with ways to reduce the attentional load on one another by being smarter with email subject lines. We settled on a numerical method of telegraphing the importance of an email's contents that we now call the 1-2-3 System. Here's how it works:

1 = Time sensitive and important—read and take action ASAP.
2 = Action required—read and take noted action within a reasonable time frame
3 = FYI. No action required. Scan for content when convenient.

We also make subject lines easier to scan and later search by using clear, key word–rich information that previews the email. For example, this might look like:

2: Notes from Dalloway Mtg Feb 24
2 Mark; 3 Emily: Follow up to Stetson Project Review call April 12

When appropriate, we also beef up the subject line when we forward or reply. We've found that the more information we can include at the top, the more time it saves the recipient.

Implementing these small changes has enhanced the atmosphere of my company. People are calmer and happier. Team retention is greatly improved, which is a big deal, since we all know that high turnover is extremely expensive. It's common sense. Why should someone feel they must check work messages all the time? And yet people read through hundreds of messages for fear of missing out on the one life-and-death piece of information. Yes, emergencies happen. We might have a company-wide system crash, for example. But that doesn't mean that Larry, my head of IT, needs to be constantly monitoring his smartphone for something that might occur twice a year at most. If it's that serious, our team will just call him on his cell phone.

MARK AND DIANA, WHO OWN a busy contracting business in Oceanside, California, rarely took vacations. As far as Diana was concerned, there was no point in going away. On a trip to Europe seven years ago, Mark spent every evening in their hotel room checking email and reviewing his staff's work, leaving Diana alone to wander the romantic streets of Prague, Vienna, and Budapest all by herself.

Since then, Mark has implemented the ideas in this chapter, along with the other steps of the formula I'll share with you as we continue our dialogue. With a new team in place and clear processes for them to follow, he didn't need to be electronically tied to the office 24/7. But it took time for this new reality to sink in.

Two years ago, when Mark surprised Diana by proposing a trip to Paris, she confessed to me that she didn't even want to go. Memories of that first non-vacation, and the disappointment she felt as Mark spent all his time in the hotel working, still lingered. But she decided to give Mark a second chance, and off they went. At their first layover of the trip, in New York City, Mark started to follow his old pattern of checking his email in the airport lounge. Diana watched this and thought, *Here we go again.*

But when he started to answer emails and respond to client questions, Mark got a polite yet firm email from his new office manager, Lauren, telling him to enjoy his vacation, and that the team had him covered. After Mark's second attempt to work remotely, Lauren playfully upped the ante by telling Mark if he didn't stop working on his vacation, she would be forced to "suspend his email account." She said in an email, "Mark, you're going to one of the most romantic cities in the world with your wife; enjoy your time together. We've got this covered." She reassured him that if an emergency came up they would reach out to him directly, but that his team, the team he had worked so diligently over the prior two years to build, could handle the routine operation of the business during his two-week vacation. He no longer had to be constantly tied to his laptop or reflexively answering each and every email as it hit his inbox. He was . . . free! ♦

Leverage Your Assistant

Of course, restructuring your time and decluttering your D-list is much easier to accomplish with the support of a skilled assistant— someone who knows your goals, priorities, preferences, and working style better than you know yourself. Your assistant could be full or part time, on premises or virtual. You might share an assistant with several of your colleagues or have someone dedicated to you alone. However you structure it, having even ten hours a week of support from the right assistant can free up hours each month of your best time.

Here are some concrete suggestions to get the most from your assistant.*

Know yourself. How do you like to delegate information? By text or email? By audio messages? Or do you prefer meeting

---

* There is so much more I want to share with you about finding, hiring, and leveraging a personal assistant, but my publisher reminded me that this book shouldn't be three volumes! Don't laugh—the first manuscript I turned in was roughly one hundred and twenty thousand words, which would have made this a four-hundred-page monster. One of my editors, Leah, "gently" encouraged me to cut, cut, cut. But being an entrepreneur is all about finding novel ways to do what you want that are outside the box, but inside the rules. Thus, my team and I created the Freedom Tool Kit, with detailed training videos and downloadable PDF tools posted online for you to use. One of the videos you'll find in the tool kit is a short tutorial on the five most important lessons about knowing who to hire for your assistant. You can watch this video at **www.FreedomToolKit.com**.

weekly with your assistant to hand off multiple items in one sitting? How do you like to receive updates? Verbally? Detailed emails? Or quick notes on a project-management platform? Are you an introvert who needs an assistant who will understand your need for a quiet work environment? Or do you want a lively, warm assistant who will engage you in conversation? There is no right or wrong assistant, just a right or wrong assistant *for you.*

Don't try to manage all your assistant's deliverables by email. Instead, agree with your assistant to have one spreadsheet or task-management system tool (app) where he or she puts everything. This one project list should be used to track *everything.* Make sure that your assistant—not you—owns the project list, and that your assistant puts everything you delegate to him or her on that list. This way, you can trust that nothing will slip through the cracks because you've got a single master list to which you both can refer as needed.

Record your key delegation meetings for your assistant to review. If you meet with your assistant in person or by phone to hand off multiple projects in one sitting, I encourage you to have your assistant record these sessions so he or she can review what you discussed a second or third time to catch the small details you shared.

Have an organized system to capture your delegation items for your assistant. You need a solid system to capture tasks you want to hand over to your assistant. Here's what I've found works best for me:
- In email. (I use the "categories" and "quick steps" functions in Outlook to just flag an email for her to do herself, add to an appointment calendar, add to my contacts, or discuss with me.)

- In a desk file. (This is where I put the scraps of paper or physical items that I will use to remind me to hand off to her.)
- On a written "Assistant" delegation list. (I keep mine in a notebook at the side of my desk, or you can keep track on a smartphone memo.)

You must be able to trust and train your assistant to filter your inbox. This is a tough one for many. They are afraid of what their assistant will see. My belief is that if you have the right assistant, with a clear understanding of confidentiality and a signed nondisclosure agreement (NDA; see next), they will be more than mature enough to manage your inbox with discretion and intelligence. Your assistant won't be able to handle every email you get, but with some training over time, they will be able to handle 20 to 50 percent of what comes in. This means they'll save you an hour a day—every day—by screening your inbox before you get to it.

Have your assistant sign a robust NDA. A document to sign gives you a clear way to discuss the importance of discretion. You need to explain to your assistant that they'll see things in the company that other people don't know. They must be adult about it and not gossip or share inside news.

Don't hire drama. You will spend a lot of time with this person. Simplify your life by hiring a true professional.

Once you have established a deep professional understanding and rapport with your assistant, realize that it is unrealistic to think it will last forever. Life happens. I've had a dozen assistants over the past twenty-five years in business. Some of the transitions were at my suggestion; others came as a great assistant moved or took another career path. Understanding that this is a possible outcome for any-one in this position, make one of the key responsibilities of your assistant the creation of the system of how to be a world-class assistant for you.

Ideally, doing all of these will enable your assistant to take all that they learn from you and run with it. My COO, Theresa Watson, began her career with our company over a decade ago as my assistant. Over time, she grew as a businessperson and took on increasingly higher-value roles in the company. Today, Theresa leads our leadership team, holding all of us accountable to operate daily, weekly, and quarterly in the Value Economy.

"Anyone who wants to get better at their job can benefit from these time-management skills," says Theresa, who is mother to two daughters and yet still manages to get it all done in both her work and personal lives with ease, with enough breathing room to put a hard stop on her days—most of the time. And now Theresa is passing this knowledge along to other team members, helping them upgrade their use of time and see that they aren't here simply to put in hours, but rather to create value.

Remember Sylvia's story from the opening of this chapter? Over the past five years since she became a client and began using the formula, she has radically reduced her working hours from over one hundred per week to under sixty. At the same time, she's finally taken real and regular vacations.

"I finally realized I couldn't do everything," Sylvia told me. "To grow, I needed to be willing to let my team shine. This has become even more important now that we've opened up our third school and are actively looking to scale to our fourth location."

The more effectively you use your time and train others to do the same, the more it cascades down each level of your organization, helping others on your team to thrive as you free yourself to focus on things that will help you grow faster, stronger, and better in all areas of your business. It gives you back yet more of your best time. Use it wisely.

12 Tactics to Master Your Inbox

Over the years, inside my company, we've honed our email skills still further, and now we have a comprehensive list of best email practices that will change your work life:

1. **Email is addictive—avoid that first temptation to check.** Recognize that taking that first "hit" by even doing a quick scan of your inbox almost invariably will lead you into a longer-than-anticipated run of responding to email. The best way to keep this from happening is to refrain from checking your inbox at all (for designated periods of time). Understand that anytime you open your inbox, you will be tempted to spend more time there. Instead, work offline or leave a couple of blank email windows open to use for outbound email while doing other work, so you don't have to go into your email program at all.

   This leads directly to the next several email tips . . .

2. **Set firm email boundaries and respect them.** Respect your Focus Days and Push Day focus blocks as "email free" times when you'll close your email program and do your high-value work. Coach your team about what you are doing and why, asking for their support to help you produce more for the company. I strongly recommend that you choose the first part of your day, right when you enter your workspace, to use for your Focus Day and Push Day focus blocks. Looking at the stats from our business coaching clients, odds are that if you check email early, you'll have a high proportion of your days derailed by urgent but low-value fires that could have waited one to three hours for you to handle.

3. **Understand that every time you do that one "quick" email, the interruption radically diminishes your concentration and flow on the other, higher-value work you were doing.** "But it only takes me a minute or two to do a quick scan of my inbox." Sure, but chances are that you then quickly shoot off three to five emails, which costs you many minutes to get back into your pre-inbox flow. What's more, the faster you respond

to email, the more you'll get back (see points 6 and 7), creating a vicious cycle.

4. **Leverage your staff (e.g., personal assistant, etc.) to screen your email.** The biggest excuse businesspeople give for checking email goes like this: "What happens if a key client/vendor/staff member has a problem that they need my help to solve and it's truly an urgent, important fire?" Let's get real for a moment. The average business person checks his or her inbox more than twenty times a day. How many of those twenty times uncover a truly mission-critical situation that must be dealt with? You can protect your time and your company by leveraging a staff member to screen your email (at least during certain times in the day and week) to give you solid, high-value time to focus. If there is a real time-sensitive, mission-critical emergency, they can knock on your door or call/text you to get your attention. As I discussed earlier, I can't tell you the number of business-people I know who run successful companies but are scared to have their assistant look at their email. They must receive two hundred messages a day, a good quarter of which are junk. An assistant could easily delete 30 percent of the email load, but they are uncomfortable that an employee might see something they shouldn't, like a private message from a spouse or romantic partner. It's a legitimate emotion, but I remind them that they need to be able to trust their assistant to be mature enough to handle anything with discretion. Besides, email is not the most secure of communication methods. Consider channeling these other less frequent but highly private messages through another conduit.

5. **Turn off your auto send-and-receive function (or at least reduce the frequency it downloads new email).** Also, turn off email alerts (audio and visual). You don't need to see every email the instant it comes in. Instead, intentionally check email when you choose versus when someone hits send to you. Email alerts only promote compulsive behavior that kills productivity.

6. **To get less email, send less.**

7. **To get less email, age your email before you reply.** The faster you respond, the more likely you'll get an email back. Every

email you get takes time to mentally process and to manually move, delete, or answer. Consider waiting an hour, a day, even a week before you send your response. You always can use the "delayed delivery" feature of your email program to respond now but to delay its being sent.

8. **If you're involved in a frustrating back-and-forth conversation by email due to hazy understanding on either side, just pick up the phone or speak in person.** Emails are not good as a nuanced conversation tool and shouldn't replace all conversations. If you think the topic may be a sensitive one or that the reader may be upset or offended by your email, *don't* send it. Talk with them instead (even if you then send a summary or confirming email after). One of the most important functions you perform as a leader of your company is to reduce the "FUD" factor—the fear, uncertainty, and doubt. Picking up the phone or meeting with someone face to face will quickly clear the air.

9. **In replying to a long conversation thread, pull up the key information to the top of the email.** Make it easier for your recipient to quickly get what you are communicating. Also, if you are creating a longer email with multiple items, consider numbering your items to make them easier for your reader to follow and address.

10. **Don't use email to manage your tasks or to manage your team's tasks.** Use a project list on a spreadsheet or a shared task-management or project-management tool instead. Email is a poor place to keep a running list. What comes today is washed away by what comes later today (let alone tomorrow). Simple, inexpensive project-management tools available online and on mobile devices will allow you to list, categorize, prioritize, and share your open action items. It's a worthwhile investment to prevent tasks and follow-ups from falling through the cracks.

11. **Learn your top five email recipients' preferences.** Sort your Sent folder by recipient and pick out the five people you email most. These likely will be internal team members. Ask them if they prefer wide or shallow emails (i.e., a grouped email that has more items in one single email, or one email per subject as it comes up, respectively). When are their email-free times?

What do they want and not want to be cc'd on? What are the three things they like best about how you communicate with them by email? What three things would they like you to do differently about how you communicate by email to make their life better? Then reverse the conversation and share your email preferences with them.

12. **Use powerful subject lines to streamline the time it takes for your team to process and find email.** No more blank subject lines or "Hello . . ."s. Instead, you and your team should make your subject line a clear, concise description of the email. This helps you screen messages now and search for them later. If you are forwarding the email, don't be lazy; redo the subject line so that it makes sense to your recipient, and ask that your team do the same for you. If it's an internal email, remember to add the 1, 2, or 3 to the subject line so your team knows what they need to do with the email (see page 62).

What are your A- and B-level activities? What day each week have you reserved for your Focus Day? Remember, to create the best value for your company, you need to consistently reclaim blocks of your best time. Now we'll turn our attention to how you can best fill these blocks of focus time. In chapter three, I'll walk you through how to identify your company or team's Fewer, Better, and how to leverage a one-page Action Plan every quarter to get your entire team executing on what matters most.

CHAPTER 3

Step Three:
Invest in Your Fewer, Better

To grow your business the way you want, you need to focus on less, but what you focus on must matter more. It's not about more—more hours, more effort, more control—rather, it's about better—better choices, better focus, better alignment.

Do fewer things, but make sure the things that you do matter more. Align your team around these priorities as well. To make the shift to sustainably scale your organization, you've got to make the tough choices about where to invest your team's limited resources of time, attention, and budget and which things you simply can't do for now.

This is why the third step of the formula is for you to focus your team's best attention on your Fewer, Better. These are the small number of strategies, initiatives, opportunities, projects, customers, service offerings, or tasks that truly make a difference for your company. Just as you built your Time Value Matrix of A-, B-, C-, and D-level tasks for you as an individual, your Fewer, Better are your *organization's* A- and B-level activities. These are the things that create the most value for your company.

MEDICAL PROFESSIONAL MICHELLE MEIER was in a constant state of triage. As chief operating officer of Kansas Medical Clinic (KMC), a busy multidisciplinary medical practice with a dozen clinic locations across the state and two hundred employees, she ran one of the largest independent practices in the region, managing clinics, doctors, staff, and patients for gastroenterology, endoscopy, and dermatology as well as a pathology lab and multiple urgent care clinics. She also was responsible for all human resource and regulatory aspects of an organization with many moving parts spread out over an entire state.

Her days were long, but she knew the work was important. Collectively, their clinics cared for thousands of patients. But she was frustrated that so much of her day distracted her from the things she knew would let her contribute her highest value to the practice.

> "At times it felt like I was doing the same circular dance of dealing with clinic problems and issues, but because of all the other demands on my time, I felt like I had to use too many band aids instead of getting to the root cause. Plus, I knew we were missing opportunities that we just didn't have the bandwidth to go after."

As the key person who oversaw the business side of every practice location, Michelle spent much of her day dealing with personnel problems and clinic emergencies that escalated to her, requiring her to spend hours on the phone or travel to the clinics personally to investigate. They were typical issues in a multispecialty healthcare business of that size, but with so many tasks on her plate, she couldn't give the most important, high-value tasks her full attention, despite her seventy-plus-hour work weeks.

> "My days just disappeared on me in a blur. It was one pressing problem after another. At the end of the week, it seemed like all I'd done was tread water. I knew there were things that I wanted to get to, but these things never had the urgency that the troubleshooting items did, and so I just never seemed to

be able to give them the time they deserved. I frequently said to myself, 'If only I had more time . . .'"

Actually, what Michelle needed more than anything else was a framework that would allow her to identify and focus on those fewer things that would have a greater impact and make the practice better. She had a great partnership with her boss, gastroenterologist Dr. Shekhar Challa, that over the years had made them one of the most successful multidisciplinary, multilocation medical groups in their state. Dr. Challa was the über entrepreneur whose creative brain came up with an endless stream of great business ideas. He trusted Michelle to execute on the next brilliant idea he came up with, and the next. Over the past decade, when they were smaller, that had worked; the two were an unbeatable team. But now they were no longer small, and there weren't enough hours in the day to continue to execute all of Dr. Challa's great ideas while simultaneously managing the larger medical group they had grown into. Michelle was constantly scrambling to keep all those balls in the air. ◆

YOUR TURN: How about you? Have you ever felt like you were dealing with a dozen "number one" priorities at the same time? Or that you had clear priorities, but your company or boss kept changing them on you? Like, just as you were starting to make some real headway and gather some momentum, an emergency flared, requiring you to immediately shift your attention? Or you simply were handed a new project last-minute and expected to somehow squeeze it in? And as a result, have you ever felt like you were putting in longer hours, racing through an impossible to-do list, yet standing still and not making any real forward progress on your most valuable projects?

Or perhaps you're a lot like Dr. Challa, a creative entrepreneur with a surfeit of ideas, all of which seem solid. Do you struggle to narrow your focus to the one or two best ideas that you want to implement in any given period? This is where step three of the formula comes into play. It says, now that you have been able to consistently reclaim several of your best hours, you need to invest these hours into your most important projects, initiatives, and activities. And what's more, you need a strategic structure that lets you effectively align your entire team behind your company's highest-value activities.

About five years ago, Dr. Challa read my last book, *Scale*, and something in it spoke to him. He reached out to my office, and I began coaching him and Michelle. After my first few coaching sessions with them, two things became clear. First, Dr. Challa was smart. Not just medical doctor smart, but creative, original, entrepreneurial smart. Most of his business ideas weren't just sound—they were brilliant. It was no wonder he had been able to scale his practice to be one of the most successful medical groups in the state. But it was equally obvious that they had outgrown Michelle's ability to personally manage the implementation of all his ideas. They needed to grow and groom a real leadership team in addition to Michelle. Which brings me to the second insight that quickly became clear.

For all their savvy and business sophistication, Dr. Challa and Michelle simply didn't have a strategic structure to narrow their focus each quarter to a more manageable number of priorities that they actually took to completion. Because Dr. Challa came up with so many opportunities, it became exquisitely important that they have a structure to filter these ideas so that the few ideas they ran with were their best ones. I began my work with Michelle and Dr. Challa by giving them this strategic structure to identify their company's Fewer, Better, and then to reduce this insight into a one-page plan of action every quarter.

Let's walk through exactly how *you* can do the same thing. Whether you run the whole show, lead a division or department, or manage a small team of pros, can you imagine the power of *knowing* you and your team are investing your best time, attention, and resources on your biggest opportunities and projects? I promise you'll find the simple structure I share with you to reduce your focus for the quarter to a single page so easy to use that it will become a quarterly best practice inside your company.

Ten years ago, Maui Mastermind was faced with this very same choice. At that point we had three main profit centers to the business, all hungry for resources. First, we had our live-training division that worked directly with a few thousand business leaders a year. Then we had our business coaching program, which worked one-to-one with business owners and their senior management. Finally, we had a promising new service line of online training courses that we sold directly to entrepreneurs and companies. Could we have kept all three service lines? Sure, but that would have meant spreading ourselves too thin, and at that point we were a small company with sales under $5 million per year and just didn't have the resources to do all three well.

After careful thought, using the same tools you'll find in this chapter to help you choose your organization's best leverage points to grow, we made the decision to narrow our focus to growing our business coaching program. We took the best elements of our live training and online programs and incorporated them into the business coaching program, dramatically increasing its value and scalability. However, we cut off all investments in growing the sale of live and online training programs directly to customers in favor of doubling down on the promotion and delivery of our core business coaching program. The strategy paid off, leading to years of double-digit annual growth rates.

It's time for *you* to uncover your organization's Fewer, Better.

We'll do this in three stages. First, I'll ask you to clarify your top business goal. What's the one thing that your company, division, or team is working toward that matters most? Then, I'll show you how to conduct a S-O-O-T Review™ (Strengths-Obstacles-Opportunities-Threats) to pick the best strategy to reach your top business goal.

Finally, I'll introduce you to a flexible tool called the Sweet Spot Analysis™ to help you pick the highest-leverage tactics to implement your strategy and accomplish your top goal. Let's get started.

Stage #1: Clarify Your Top Business Goal

Take fifteen minutes to get clear on the business you're working to build. What is your business's top goal? What is the one goal that you are mobilizing all your company's resources to accomplish over the next three to five years? Ask, "What business are we committed to build over the next three to five years?" Approach your answer two ways: quantitatively and qualitatively.

Quantitatively: What does your future business look like in terms of things you can measure and count? What are your annual sales? Your annual number of transactions? Your percent of market share? Your average sales per customer? Your gross profit margin? Your operating profit margin? Your retention rate of clients? Your sales per employee? Pick three to five of the most important quantitative ways to describe your future business.

Qualitatively: What does your business look like in other ways that you can't easily measure or count but still matter greatly? Who are your key customers? What is your brand? What is your market reputation? Who do you have on your team helping lead the business? Which markets do you serve? What key products or services do you offer? What impact do you have on the lives of your customers? What is your future role as the business leader? Pick three to five of the most important qualitative ways to describe your future business.

After you've combined both the top quantitative and qualitative descriptions of your future business into one single target, whittle away at this picture until you are left with a tight, clear statement that can guide your company or team's focus over the next several years. Here's an example of what your top goal might look like:

By December 31, 20XX, we've built Growth Inc. into a thriving business with $35 million in annual sales and a 20 percent operating profit margin. We have deeply penetrated four distinct verticals, with no single vertical or customer representing more than 30 percent of our business. We continue to grow at a compounded annual growth rate of 15 percent or higher.

Or:

Within 24 months, we've grown our division's gross revenues to $1.4 billion with a 25 percent operating profit margin or greater. During this time, we've successfully launched the "Tiger Platform" and built a user base of 1 million-plus active licensees.

Of course, your top goal depends on your industry, business model, and goals. The key is that you want to end up with a concentrated statement that describes the one target your team is working collectively to reach.

By the way, because you took fifteen minutes to clarify the business you are working to build both quantitatively and qualitatively, you have completed one more key component to help you reach that goal—you have drafted your enterprise-level scoreboard. (And you thought you were just dreaming on paper!) You now have a clear list of the top variables that describe your key business objective. These are the variables that you'll measure at least quarterly.* For example, looking at the first sample top goal I shared for Growth Inc., their enterprise-level scoreboard would track gross sales, operating profit margin, number of verticals they have penetrated and how deeply,

---

* You can download a free four-page PDF version of our Strategic Planning Tool discussed in this chapter at **www.FreedomToolKit.com**. See Appendix for full details.

percent of total sales that each customer and vertical represent, and the company's annual growth rate.

Now that you have a clear picture of your company's top goal, it's time to craft the best strategy to help you reach this goal.

Stage #2: Conduct a S-O-O-T Review

A S-O-O-T Review is a structured way to see where your business stands today relative to its top goal *(fig. 5)*. This tool helps you lay out the key landmarks from which to craft your company's strategy to accomplish its top goal. Here are the four components about your company to review:

Strengths: Any strategy that you eventually choose must rely on your strengths. Keeping your company's top goal clearly in mind, what are the top five strengths it can draw on to accomplish this goal?

Obstacles: Each key obstacle is a clue as to what next steps you need to take in your business. What are the five biggest obstacles that you see currently blocking your company from achieving its top goal? When you look at them from this frame, obstacles become stepping-stones to help you cross the gap from where you are to where you want to go.

Opportunities: Opportunities are where you win the game of business. What are the three biggest opportunities your company could pursue that potentially could help you achieve this goal? One guiding strategic principle is to put your best people and resources on seizing your biggest opportunities rather than fixing your squeakiest wheel.

Threats: What are the three biggest threats that could irreparably harm your business? Look at those things that, if they fell wrong, could literally put you out of business: a harmful market trend, a disruptive competitor, a change to government regulations, or even the loss of a key customer or supplier. Your goal is to take simple, proactive steps now to mitigate these dangers later. There likely will come a day when you'll either say, "Why didn't I do

5 Top Business Strengths	5 Biggest Business Obstacles
1. _____	1. _____
2. _____	2. _____
3. _____	3. _____
4. _____	4. _____
5. _____	5. _____
3 Greatest Business Opportunities	3 Greatest Business Threats
1. _____	1. _____
2. _____	2. _____
3. _____	3. _____

Figure 5   S-O-O-T Review template

something about this earlier when I had the luxury of time?" or "I'm so glad I prepared for this contingency."

Remember, a S-O-O-T Review always is relative to a specific objective or goal. In this case, you're conducting it relative to your top goal, thereby yielding important insights to help you map your way to accomplishing a specific objective. This tool helps you narrow your focus so that you can see the best path forward.

So, what is the best strategy for your company or department to reach its top goal? The best strategies have three criteria in common. First, they are firmly grounded on one or more of your key strengths. Odds are that you will be successful only if your strategy relies on things that you are very good at, so make sure you review your strategy and ask the key question: For this strategy to work, on what strengths must we rely? If, for your strategy to work, you've got to rely on something that isn't a strength of yours, and you can't buy, build, or otherwise acquire this strength, then I strongly advise you to pick another strategy. Just as the best athletes play to their strengths, so do the most successful companies play to their best abilities.

Second, the best strategies seize one of your biggest opportunities. Seizing a key opportunity is the offense that lets you score points and win the game. This may be investing heavily into a specific product or service line, market niche, or delivery strategy. The key is that any winning strategy must help you seize a major opportunity that has the real potential to yield big results.

Third, the best strategies mitigate or make irrelevant your gravest business threats. For example, if one of your biggest threats is that 58 percent of your business is with one customer, but your strategy fits for criteria one and two, then ideally it will help you grow other customer relationships so that you have some protection from the loss or diminishment of this Goliath customer.

Stage #3: Find Your Sweet Spot

What currently is your company's single biggest constraint to growth? What is the one ingredient that, if you had more of it, would help your business grow the most?

While every business has multiple limiting factors, each has one Limiting Factor—capital "L," capital "F"—that does the most to constrain its growth in the here and now. Pushing back your biggest Limiting Factor is a major leverage point to growing your company. One simple technique to grow your business is to identify and push back your current Limiting Factor quarter by quarter.

The more precisely you can identify your Limiting Factor, the easier it is to effectively push it back. For example, if you say your Limiting Factor is cash flow, you might come up with a dozen ideas to improve it, but many of them may be counterproductive because your initial diagnosis of your Limiting Factor was too broad. Is it a cash-flow challenge caused by low sales volume relative to your current core overhead? If so, you'll look for ideas to rapidly increase sales or decrease core overhead. Is the cash flow challenge instead caused by selling the wrong product or service mix? In other words, is it a pricing or gross profit issue? Or is it really an issue with your collections? Before you rush off to "solve" your Limiting Factor, you've first got to carefully and accurately nail down your diagnosis.

Here is how this works in the real world.

I WAS DOING A COACHING SESSION with Nate Anglin, CEO of Skylink, an aircraft supply-chain parts wholesaler that carries more than 250,000 parts. Headquartered in Florida, with branches in Chile, the United Kingdom, Dubai, and Indonesia, Skylink is a second-generation family-owned business. The world of buying replacement parts for airplanes is opaque and confusing. Skylink sells literally hundreds of thousands of parts, which it has to source and purchase from thousands of other companies with no central pricing marketplace. This makes finding, pricing, and selling a part a complicated, time-consuming process requiring judgment, skill, and, in many cases, sharp negotiation to get profitable pricing.

In one of our coaching sessions, Nate said something that could just as easily have come from the mouth of a thousand CEOs I've known and coached over the years: "David, we just have so many opportunities to scale this thing—how do I know which one to focus on first?"

My advice to Nate was to go back to basics. Our exchange went something like this:

QUESTION TO NATE: What really is your current single biggest limiting factor over the next six to twelve months? What's the one constraint more than anything else that currently limits your growth?

NATE: When you ask the question that way, I'd have to say it's a lack of sales capacity. We're flooded each week with RFQs [requests for quotes], and my sales and account management teams struggle to keep up with the volume of quoting they have to do. So, it sounds like we really need to scale up our sales force.

I'm always a bit skeptical about easy answers, so I pushed him to dig deeper:

NEXT QUESTION: Hold on a second. Before we jump straight to the solution for this constraint, let's define what you think is really the issue here. What I'm hearing from you is that you have so many RFQs coming in each week that you can't respond well to all of them. In fact, the real Limiting Factor for Skylink sounds like it is the inability to maximize your current RFQ lead flow right now. Is that a correct assessment?

NATE: Yes.

NEXT QUESTION: Great, then should we brainstorm all the different ways we could help Skylink make maximal use out of its current lead flow of RFQs coming in each week to quickly and profitably grow sales?

Notice the subtle change to the last question here? I've now framed the question so that Nate and I could do a Sweet Spot Analysis on Skylink's single biggest constraint to growth. ♦

YOUR TURN: What is your company's current single biggest Limiting Factor? What is the one ingredient such that if you only had more of it, you'd enjoy the biggest growth or gain for your company?

Once you have a clear diagnosis of your Limiting Factor in hand, it's time to select the highest-leverage tactics to push back this Limiting Factor. In my company, we developed the three-part Sweet Spot Analysis tool *(fig. 6)* to help you do just that.

First, brainstorm a list of all the potential ideas you have to push back your Limiting Factor. Don't settle for five or six. Push yourself to come up with at least ten—ideally, fifteen to twenty. For example, if your Limiting Factor is a cash-flow challenge caused by poor collections practices, your list of ideas could include:

- Collect more or all of your payment up front.
- Incentivize your customers to pay faster.
- Strengthen your collection systems so that you bill faster and follow up more efficiently.
- Establish clear credit policies about who you will or won't extend credit to.
- Charge a fee to your slow-paying customers so they cover the costs of slower collections.

You get the idea. The key is to push yourself to come up with as many ideas as you can that could help you push back your Limiting Factor. And the best way to do that is to come up with a lot of potential ideas.

Next, run your brainstormed list of potential tactics through two filters: what we call the Low-Hanging Fruit filter and the Home Run filter. Low-Hanging Fruit refers to a no-brainer opportunity that you're almost certain will be successful. While it may or may not have a big impact, it is fairly straightforward to implement, and you have a very high level of confidence that it's going to work. A Home Run, on the other hand, is an opportunity that, if all goes just right, promises a huge payoff for your business.

Go through each brainstormed idea on the list in turn and ask, Is this tactic a Low-Hanging Fruit? If it is, check the box in the "LH" column.

Then, in a second, separate pass, go through your list of brainstormed ideas and ask of each item in turn: Is this tactic a Home Run? If so, check the box in the "HR" column.

What you're looking for are any tactics that are both Low-Hanging Fruit and Home Runs. These are what we call your Sweet

--- **S W E E T   S P O T   A N A L Y S I S™   T O O L** ---

Low-Hanging Fruit: Solution that would be easy to implement with a
high chance of success.
Home Run: Solution that, if worked, would have a BIG impact.
Sweet Spot: Solutions that are both Low-Hanging Fruit AND Home
Runs.

Low-
Hanging Fruit

Sweet Spot

Home Run

Our single biggest Limiting Factor is . . .

Cash flow challenge caused by poor collections practices and too many
"slow payers."

What are 10+ ideas to push this Limiting Factor back?

		LH	HR
1.	Sort current clients into A-B-C buckets based on collections history.	☑	☐
2.	Move bucket "C" clients to weekly payment plan.	☐	☐
3.	Fire bucket "C" clients.	☑	☐
4.	Update contracts so that client pays for all reasonable collections costs.	☑	☐
5.	Cut off slow payers until they bring their account current.	☑	☑
6.	Create written "credit policy" of who gets payment terms and who must pay up front.	☐	☐
7.	Hire experienced collections pro to own collections calls and follow up.	☐	☑
8.	Get salespeople to help with collections—commissions only paid upon collection in full.	☐	☐
9.	Flowchart existing collection process and redesign it.	☑	☑
10.	Review aged A/R report twice a week.	☐	☐
11.	Hire collections attorney to aggressively go after all 91+-day accounts.	☐	☐
12.	Frontload collections efforts to collect more, faster.	☑	☐

Mini Action Plan	Who	By When
Solution 1: Redesign collection process.		
☐ Lay out existing process.	Tim	1-21-xx
☐ Redesign optimal process from scratch. (Frontload collection efforts.)	Tim	2-7-xx
☐ Systematize the new process and train team how to use it.	Tim	2-28-xx
☐ Launch new collection process	Tim	3-5-xx
Solution 2: Stop services for slow payers until they are current.		
☐ Identify which slow payer to cut off until current.	Lee	1-15-xx
☐ Formalize policy on when to warn, cut off, and reinstate slow payers.	Lee	1-31-xx
☐ Train staff on new policy.	Lee	2-15-xx
☐ Launch policy.	Lee	2-28-xx
☐ Formal check-in to improve implementation.	Lee	3-31-xx

Figure 6   Sample Sweet Spot Analysis

Spot ideas: the highest-leverage choices to push back your Limiting Factor. Low-Hanging Fruit are easy to implement with high odds of success, and Home Runs offer big impact if they work. Your Sweet Spots are the first and best places to focus your company's resources.

Finally, now that you've identified your Sweet Spot tactics, turn them into a mini Action Plan of who needs to do what by when.*

Let's go back to Nate and Skylink for a moment. Remember, Skylink's Limiting Factor was lack of sales capacity to fully exploit each week's existing RFQ lead flow. When Nate and I brainstormed ideas, we came up with things like hire more salespeople, better systematize the quoting process so that his existing sales team could quote more opportunities in less time, hire more purchasing agents so that they could better leverage them in the quoting process, and even create a product-purchasing platform to become a real marketplace for customers and suppliers to connect directly with one another. With our list in hand, we put each idea through the Low-Hanging Fruit filter, asking, Is this idea easy to do with a high likelihood of working? Then we used the Home Run filter and asked, If this idea works, will it have a big impact?

Curious about which idea won out? It wasn't any of the ideas just listed, each of which was either a Low-Hanging Fruit or Home Run, but none of which were both for Skylink. Instead, the Sweet Spot tactic we picked was to create a filtering system to quickly score RFQs as they came in, so Nate's team could ignore low-value quoting opportunities and instead focus their best sales attention on their highest-value leads.

---

* We'll discuss Action Plans later in this chapter. You can download a blank PDF version of this tool as part of the complimentary Freedom Tool Kit you received along with this book. This is one of the favorite tools our business coaching clients use with their teams. Just visit **www.FreedomToolKit.com**.

Nate and his key people created a simple scoring matrix based on two variables: historic capture rate (i.e., what percent of past quotes led to this prospect actually buying) and historic gross profit generated per year by this customer.

Essentially, what Skylink took advantage of was that not all RFQs were created equally, and Nate's team made the strategic decision to invest their best sales attention on their best leads. This strategy took advantage of the lead flow they already were drowning in. By scoring leads as they came in based on these two variables, their sales team could quickly filter or even ignore leads from low annual gross-profit prospects who historically had a very low capture rate (often as low as 2 to 4 percent) of actually purchasing on a quote. Instead, the team could redirect their best sales efforts onto those customers with historic capture rates of 30 to 40 percent. These later customers often generated ten times or more annual gross profit for Skylink than the lowest-tier customer leads.

It took Skylink twelve months to get this new effort effectively into the sales team's day-to-day flow. It required them to change their sales database and CRM so that lead scoring would become faster and more obvious to their sales team; retrain their sales team to change habitual behavior and instead focus their time on their best prospects while relegating lower-quality leads to remnant time; adjust which sales leads went to which sales team members so that their best leads went to their best sales people; and semi-automate the response to those lower-quality RFQs so that it took less actual team attention to respond at safe pricing.

The results? Within just twelve months of executing on this strategy, Skylink had grown their gross profit by 40 percent and increased their bottom line by 60 percent, without hiring any additional salespeople or investing more money in marketing. Simply by focusing their best talent and attention on their one Sweet Spot solution—lead scoring—they radically increased their margins. This is the essence of the Fewer, Better principle at work.

So, if you feel overwhelmed and unable to decide between so many potential opportunities and ideas, I'll give you the same advice I gave to Nate: Go back to basics. Identify your biggest Limiting Factor that holds you back from accomplishing your big goal. Brainstorm all the ways you could push back this Limiting Factor and reach your big goal. Go through your list and apply the two Sweet Spot filters. Which of these ideas is a Low-Hanging Fruit? Which of these ideas is a Home Run? Your list just got a lot shorter, didn't it?

Wondering what to do if your Sweet Spot Analysis reveals more than one Sweet Spot idea? Relax—any Sweet Spot idea is by definition a great choice because it is something that is easy to do with a high probability of working (Low-Hanging Fruit) while having a big impact (Home Run). What you really have is the choice between great idea one and great idea two. Heads, you win; tails, you win. I like those odds.

Identify Your Assumptions So You Make Smarter Bets

Invest just five minutes in taking one more simple step before you rush off to execute on your chosen idea. Ask yourself: For this idea to prove successful, what assumptions would have to prove true? In other words, pause and sketch out on paper the key assumptions you're making that must prove true for your Sweet Spot tactic to be successful.

In Nate's case, his Sweet Spot tactic had three key assumptions on which the success of his idea hinged. First was that there would in fact be a clear pattern that would allow Skylink to group all or most incoming leads into clear and actionable lead buckets. If there weren't key variables that his team could use to accurately score the RFQs in terms of highest-value leads, then the idea would have failed. Second, this lead scoring strategy assumed that his sales team could develop a practical way to act on these filtered leads so that their best sales energy would go into their best sales leads. And third, Nate was assuming that by putting their best sales energy into their best sales leads, not only would Skylink grow sales, but they would improve their margins at the same time.

All three of these assumptions seemed realistic to Nate and his team, but by clearly identifying them in writing, they were able to pause to see if it really made sense to pursue their idea before they had too much at stake. What would they have done if they didn't feel like one or more of these critical assumptions was true? They would have chosen a different path forward, or if they did proceed, they would have done it much more cautiously, paying careful attention along the way so that, if needed, they could stop efforts early before wasting too many resources on a fool's errand.

By pausing to ask and answer, in writing, what assumptions would have to prove true in order for your Sweet Spot tactic to succeed, you move into the planning and execution phase with your eyes wide open and greater odds of success. Five minutes invested to ask and answer this one extra question might very well save you and your team hundreds or even thousands of staff hours on the execution. This is the essence of the Value Economy: leveraging intelligence and strategic acumen over raw effort.

Create a Rolling One-Page Action Plan Every Quarter

You've clarified your team's top goal, conducted your S-O-O-T Review, and completed your Sweet Spot Analysis, so now it's time to create your one-page quarterly Action Plan. Why quarterly? Because the quarter is the perfect unit of time to bridge your big-picture goals and your weekly planning and daily actions. It's long enough that you can get meaningful work done to bring you closer to your long-term goals, but short enough that you can hold your focus and frequently course-correct.

Here's the key: You're now going to outline your quarterly Action Plan *on a single page*. For more than a decade, we've pushed our coaching clients to follow a one-page Action Plan. Why one page, instead of two or twenty-five? Because we've learned from our work in coaching thousands of business leaders that, in the rush of the day-to-day, if your plan is two or three pages (or more), you just won't use it on a weekly basis to guide your execution. With a one-page plan, you can see your whole plan at one glance. You'll review it every week to pull the next action steps into your weekly task list. (You'll also easily be able to review key staff members' quarterly one-page Action Plans and hold them accountable on a weekly basis.) In essence, your one-page Action Plan becomes your quarterly and weekly GPS to make sure that your team is focusing on the right things and hitting key milestones on time. Think of it as a visual cue that glues your team's best attention on those things that matter most. It's the written allocation of where your team is investing its best discretionary time, talent, attention, and money. It will help align your team on big-picture priorities so everyone can better manage their responsibilities and contribute more to the real needs of the business.

Figure 7 (see next page) shows a sample Action Plan.*

Conventional wisdom says your strategic plan is where you write down your answers; that it is a fixed-in-stone plan to accomplish your key business goals. In theory this sounds great, even alluring—a simple document that contains the secret plan to marshal your resources and smoothly attain your goals. Alas, that's just not how things work in the real world of business.

If my years of running companies and coaching top business leaders have taught me anything, it is this: **Your strategic plan is not a place for fixed answers; rather, it is a trusted process comprising provocative questions you systematically ask yourself each quarter as you iterate your way to success.** You'll ask powerful questions, explore potential answers, test those answers in the market, and willingly (dare I say, eagerly) challenge those trial answers every quarter.

---

* To download a free template to create *your* company's one-page Action Plan, go to **www.FreedomToolKit.com**.

QUARTERLY ACTION PLAN FOR: Q1, 20XX

Focus Area One: Increasing production capacity **Criteria of Success:** • Written process for how we produce our core service. • Conducted a Sweet Spot Analysis to increase our production capacity by 15+%. • KPI: Revenue generated per service team production days.	Action Steps/Milestones	Who	By When
	☐ Map out our current "production" system. Identify biggest current constraints. Conduct Sweet Spot Analysis to best increase production capacity.	Carlos	1-15-xx
	☐ Review Sweet Spot ideas and pick the winners. Create implementation plan.	Carlos	1-31-xx
	☐ Formal check-in #1: Insights? What's working? What adjustments need to be made? Update plan.	Carlos	2-21-xx
	☐ Formal check-in #2: Insights? What's working? What adjustments need to be made? Update plan.	Carlos	3-15-xx
	☐ Review status at end of quarter—capture lessons and plan to refine production system into Version 2.0 next quarter.	Carlos	3-30-xx

Focus Area Two: Hire a great director of marketing **Criteria of Success:** • Have clear, written role and candidate descriptions. • Reduce candidate profile to the 5 "must haves" and hire to those specific items. • Have written onboarding plan to successfully integrate our new hire. • Formally debrief at end and improve our hiring process for future.	Action Steps/Milestones	Who	By When
	☐ Create a written job description and candidate profile. Reduce to the 5 "must haves" for this role. Review both with key stakeholders.	Tina	1-15-xx
	☐ Create our written recruitment game plan.	Tina	1-21-xx
	☐ Launch recruitment efforts.	Tina	1-31-xx
	☐ Run our selection process and get to our finalist candidates.	Tina	3-7-xx
	☐ Create our written onboarding plan for this hire.	Tina	3-15-xx
	☐ Hire our winning candidate and run our onboarding process.	Tina	3-30-xx
	☐ Formally debrief process: What worked best? What can we do to improve our hiring process for future? Update hiring process based on learnings.	Tina	3-30-xx

Focus Area Three: Increase client retention **Criteria of Success:** • Complete retention analysis and explicitly identify the 1–2 biggest "drop points." • Retention "Tiger Team" to conduct Sweet Spot Analysis and implement ideas to increase retention. • Formally debrief at end and create Q2 plan to continue improving retention rate. • KPI: Retention score.	Action Steps/Milestones	Who	By When
	☐ Analyze current retention stats and drop points. Share results with retention Tiger Team.	Marcus	1-15-xx
	☐ Conduct Sweet Spot Analysis to increase retention rate. Pick 1 or 2 winners and create implementation plan for quarter.	Marcus	1-21-xx
	☐ Formal check-in #1: Insights? What's working? What adjustments need to be made? Update plan.	Marcus	1-31-xx
	☐ Formal check-in #2: Insights? What's working? What adjustments need to be made? Update plan.	Marcus	3-7-xx
	☐ Share results with leadership team along with formal retention game plan for next quarter.	Marcus	3-15-xx

Figure 7   Sample one-page Quarterly Action Plan

Every quarter, you and your key leaders will step away from your day-to-day business to concretely map out the next ninety days. You'll lay out your top three strategic priorities for the coming quarter and write up a simple one-page plan of action specifying exactly what you must do that quarter to grow and develop your business. Over the course of the quarter, you'll invest your team's best discretionary time into your chosen Focus Areas and execute exceptionally well on your Action Plan. At the end of the quarter, you'll evaluate your results, celebrate your victories, and clarify your lessons. Then you'll plan out the coming quarter. Over time, as you repeat this process quarter by quarter, you'll gather momentum and enjoy compounded results.

The reason why this process works so well is because it prompts you and your team to look freshly at your business every quarter, while also allowing everyone time to make meaningful progress on clearly prioritized Focus Areas. Without this clear framework, too many leaders change their focus so often that their teams are left dizzy, feeling the vertigo of too much change, and frustrated because just when they seemed on the verge of getting something big done, the leader changed the playing field yet again, forcing them to abandon projects early and wasting hours of effort. Business leaders who change things on their team monthly (or even weekly!) may just be addicted to the adrenaline of change or the illusion that this enhances their control. By contrast, stepping back once a quarter to determine your priorities and resource allocation is your best bet.

Done well, your quarterly ninety-day sprints will reward your business with two major benefits: regular opportunities to change and adapt, and the momentum of disciplined execution on known priorities. This process gave Michelle a framework to communicate effectively with her entire team about what needed to be done—with a built-in layer of accountability and clarity for everyone. Collectively, it helped the organization get results faster.

A Simple Three-Step Process to Create Your One-Page Action Plan

Every quarter, we walk our business coaching clients through a simple three-step process to create their quarterly Action Plan. With time, you'll internalize the thinking, and creating your next quarter's Action Plan will be even easier. Ideally, you'll involve your key team members in creating it. I'll have more to say about this in chapter five, "Engage Your Team." Let's get started!

Step #1: Pick your top three focus areas for the quarter.

Your top Focus Areas are the three most important areas for your business to spotlight during the coming quarter. Sure, you'll still have to take care of the day-to-day operational needs of your business, but your Focus Areas are those areas you've decided to invest a portion of your best resources that quarter, because they will help you scale and develop your business, and accomplish your big goal.

Potential Focus Areas

- Increasing your lead flow.
- Improving your sales conversion system.
- Speeding up your collections cycle.
- Making a specific key hire.
- Developing a new product.
- Progressing on a key project.

Why limit your company to three Focus Areas? Because ninety days pass quickly, and if you spread your company too thin, you'll find that you partially do several things instead of fully doing a few key chunks that actually produce value. As you know, less often can be more, especially when it's what you actually get *done*.

Step #2: Determine success criteria for your focus areas.

Now that you've picked your three Focus Areas for the quarter, the temptation is immediately to determine your action steps. Don't. Instead, pause and clarify your criteria of success for each Focus Area. What would you need to accomplish this quarter in this Focus Area to be successful? What can you actually *observe and measure* that will signal your success? This gives you a clear yardstick against which to gauge progress and paints a clear picture of what success in this Focus Area, this quarter, looks like.

To limit your Action Plan to one page, pick three or four definite criteria of success for each Focus Area, including one key performance indicator (KPI) that you'll track. Now that you've got your written criteria of success in hand, Step #3 will be easy. Most of your action steps are obvious in your criteria of success. For example, if your Focus Area is to create a new trade show exhibitor system for your road show team, then your criteria of success might include things like:

- Have a detailed master booth checklist (version 1.0).
- Have a visual diagram/pics of booth setup steps and finished layout.
- Have a clear shipping procedure and vendor contact document.
- Have a template to store online exhibitor key documentation, contract, and correspondence for each show.

Notice how obvious the key action steps are once you lay out the realistic and clear criteria of success. Your Action Plan for the quarter is going to include steps like:

- Complete a draft of the master booth checklist and get it to the road team for review.
- After reviewing road team feedback, update the master booth checklist version 1.0. Create feedback loop for the road team

to collect updates for this checklist to be reviewed after the second trade show of the quarter to create version 2.0.

- Road show team to take photos of setup and finished booth at XYZ trade show in Chicago and get them to Operations.
- Etc.

Here's another example. Imagine you are the VP of marketing for a large services firm and one of your Focus Areas for the quarter is: "Create plan for testing sale of new Bolero service offering to one vertical." Your criteria of success might include:

- Clarify the key service elements, their costs, and the relative perceived value for each component of Bolero in the marketplace.
- Compile key market research on competitors, switching costs for us to win market share, and main barriers to entry we'll have to deal with.
- Have written beta-test plan to test-market two versions of Bolero to one vertical, including key assumptions made, key variables to measure and track, and formal review steps built into plan.
- Etc.

You might be thinking, "But David, when I see your written criteria of success, it seems like each element is either an action step or milestone itself or would be made up of a few action steps or milestones." Exactly! When you get clear on your criteria of success, what you're doing is imagining it's the end of the quarter and you're looking at the actual measurable, observable, definite work that you got done in this Focus Area. What would you need to have happen to feel that you were successful in this Focus Area this quarter? By starting at the end and defining what success looks like, your action steps and way points en route are obvious. (Note I said *obvious*, not easy.)

Step #3: Lay out key action steps and milestones for the quarter.

The final step is to determine the key actions and milestones that are necessary to meet your criteria of success for each Focus Area over the coming quarter. Break down each Focus Area into three to seven action steps and milestones. While your plan should be detailed enough to guide your actions, it shouldn't be so detailed that you feel overwhelmed or lose yourself in minutiae.

For each action step, pick a specific team member to be ultimately responsible for executing that step by a specific date. While you can have multiple people contribute to a specific step or steps, you need to task one person with the responsibility and authority to get that step done and done well. This person will "own" the task. This designation of ownership is critical. It's hard to hold anyone accountable for missed milestones when it wasn't clear who really was responsible in the first place.

With this structure, the leader of any given task doesn't have to do all of the work herself; she just needs to be responsible for making sure that it gets done in the best way possible. Over time, as you become fluent in this planning process, you'll have each of your key people create their own team's one-page quarterly Action Plan. Their Action Plan is the link between their division, department, or team's targets and the most important priorities of the business as a whole. This coordinates and aligns all their efforts to get an enhanced result.

> Michelle shared: "At KMC, we started off with just a company plan of action. Once we built some muscles of how to create and execute on that plan, we introduced the practice to our key managers. We had each of them build their own team plan of action every quarter, with each of their one-page plans feeding up into our overall company plan of action. It's helped us manage tremendous growth and keep our various departments aligned."

BONUS TIP

---

5 Best Practices for Getting Results with Your One-Page Action Plan

1. **Beware of stuffing your quarter.** There can be a temptation to make all of your action steps and milestones due in the first or second month of the quarter. Resist that temptation. I've seen this more times than I can count. You've got sixteen action steps due in the first month of the quarter, six due in the second month of the quarter, and none due in the third month of the quarter. What invariably happens is that you become overwhelmed and overloaded. You get stuck and basically use that as an excuse to say, "Well, I missed all of these due dates. To heck with it. I'll just move on, and I won't do any of this stuff." It's a lot like adopting a radical diet and then, if you mess up one day, throwing up your hands and saying, "Well, I may as well just eat whatever I want now." Aim to have a pragmatic perspective about what actually is possible. Pace, plan, and balance your quarter so you don't over-stuff the first month.

2. **Avoid setting yourself up to procrastinate.** This warning is to help you avoid the exact opposite of stuffing your quarter. Setting all your due dates for the end of the quarter is a recipe for massive procrastination, and it's likely that you won't hit your goals. It opens too much of a gap in accountability between the start of the quarter and when your formal delivery dates come due.

   When I see clients setting too many due dates for the last day of the quarter, I can anticipate what will happen. They'll allow themselves to get busy with other "urgent" needs of the business, right up until the final two weeks of the quarter, when they will panic and have two weeks of frenzied activity trying to knock out their Action Plan. Just like cramming for a test at the last minute, this doesn't give your company optimal results. The key here is balance. You want due dates and milestones spread out across the quarter so that you realistically can pace yourself through the quarter and establish the accountability to reach milestones along the way.

3. **Nail your criteria of success.** I know I said this earlier, but having literally written up or reviewed hundreds of quarterly Action Plans, both for my companies and my clients, I see this mistake all the time. There's a reason that I can create a viable, doable plan in a fraction of the time than someone who's never done it before—I cheat! Here's a powerful shortcut for creating a better plan in half the time and with a fraction of the struggle: nail your criteria of success *before* you try to lay out your action steps and milestones. When you confidently articulate your criteria of success, your action steps and milestones become 80 percent obvious. Don't skip this step—it won't save you time.

4. **Ensure your team's Action Plans are coordinated and connected with the *company* plan.** The more mature your organization is, and the more experienced you are with strategic planning, the more you want to make sure that your company plan defines the big picture, your department or division plans support and feed into your company plan, and your team or individual plans feed into and support your division or department plans. You'll be creating a series of nested plans that all align with the higher-order plan.

   If this is your first time creating a formal Action Plan, I encourage you to start with just one plan for the team or company you lead. After a quarter or two of this, get your key subordinates to do their own team (or individual) Action Plans for each quarter. Not only does this facilitate meaningful dialogue with your key people about the bigger-picture objectives, it helps align your team so that all your best efforts cohere and lead to a magnified result. This process guards against one of the single biggest destroyers of business success—too many "top priorities" that drain your results.

   Alas, many companies give their teams too many priorities and goals. I once worked with a large professional services company that gave each practice leader dozens of annual goals and priorities; the entire organization collectively had hundreds. From my experiences in the business world, this is the *norm*. Don't fall into that trap. Help your team define a clear hierarchy of the top priorities and objectives so your staff can lead their respective teams to invest their best energies in your highest-value initiatives. Your collective quarterly Action Plans are how you define your respective Fewer, Better for the coming ninety days.

5. **Give your team a real voice in this process.** Bring your team into the strategic planning process. Explain your thinking on priorities; ask them for feedback; engage them with creating the criteria of success; solicit their ideas on how best to reach those defined criteria of success over the coming ninety days. Not only will your team have valuable ideas and perspective to share with you, but by getting them involved in the creation of the plan, they will be more vested in seeing the plan succeed. They'll have a deeper commitment as well as ownership—one of the most enticing spices to engage your team. By involving your team in the planning process, you will help each person gain a deeper understanding of the company and grow their business insights, which, like any muscles, get stronger through use. Over time, your team will absorb both the process of strategic thinking and also the values and priorities they see you consistently highlight as important.

 I often ask audiences I'm speaking with to raise their hands if they have or had young kids. Most hands in the room go up. I then ask, "How do you get your kids to eat healthy food?" The answers are always the same—get them involved in the cooking, model healthy eating, have healthy foods easily accessible in the house, and limit the number and types of unhealthy foods you bring into your home. I'll cover "model healthy eating" in chapter seven, "Grow Your Leaders," and I'll go into "have healthy foods easily accessible/limit unhealthy foods you bring into the home" in chapter nine, "Leverage Better Design." Right now, consider how much more willing kids, adults—anyone—would be to eat a meal they had a real hand in preparing.

The Big Rock Report

The secret to following your Action Plan is to execute weekly.

If your Action Plan is built on the quarter, then executing your plan is built on the week. Each week, review your one-page Action Plan and pull out the key steps that you need to complete during the coming week. Considering that you really have only five or ten hours of focus time during the week, you need to be very clear at the start of the week on what high-value activities you want to best complete during this limited inventory.

To help our business coaching clients operationalize their quarterly Action Plan and actually do this every week, we created a tool called the Big Rock Report. You've likely heard the descriptor "Big Rocks" before; it has become a common term in the business lexicon.* Our Big Rock Report turns this concept into a cleaner, more organized tool that you can use to execute on your quarterly Action Plan in the face of all the urgencies and distractions in your typical work week.

Here's how it works: at the start of each week, you and your key staff members will review your quarterly Action Plan, and each of you will pick two or three Big Rocks. As I use the term, these are specific action steps, tasks, or chunks of a key project that, if you did them in the coming week, would do the most to help you accomplish the key results outlined in your quarterly Action Plan. If you don't concretely identify your Big Rocks at the start of the week, odds are that any focus block you schedule instead will be wasted on low-value junk.

Each Big Rock should be something that takes no more than two hours. If it's likely to take longer, then break it down into smaller

---

* As best I can tell, the term "Big Rocks" originally came out of the work of the late Dr. Stephen Covey. I've put a link in the Freedom Tool Kit to a powerful four-minute YouTube video of his that I think you've got to watch. The video gives a concrete demonstration of exactly why Big Rocks need to be fit in first.

chunks. Why two hours or less? Because, even following the time-mastery strategies discussed in chapter two, it's unlikely that you'll consistently be able to block out a bigger chunk of time in your schedule. By limiting your Big Rocks to steps that you can complete in a one- to two-hour time frame, you'll increase your odds of getting them done.

The first part of your weekly Big Rock Report *(fig. 8)* is to review how you did on your prior week's Big Rocks. Did you get them all done? What were the outcomes? What next steps are needed? What other information do you want to share with your team on these items?

The report then lists key victories, challenges, and other updates. Finally, the Big Rock Report ends with you and your key team members reviewing your one-page Action Plan to pick your two or three Big Rocks for the coming week.

The Big Rock Report helps you escape the trap of a typical to-do list, with its overwhelming and unending supply of tasks and action steps you "have to" get done today, this week, this month, or this quarter. Stop and think for a moment about how a to-do list often is composed. It's a written or typed list of action items you own, usually with no real structure, other than as a catch-all flowing down the page and onto page two, three, four (gulp), or five. It visually treats every item on that list equally, each just owning a row on the list.

Your Big Rock Report most decidedly is *not* a to-do list. It begins with you making the decision at the very start of your week what one, two, or three action items or Big Rocks you will choose that will make the biggest impact when you complete them this week. Of course, there may be times that you need to sidestep and handle an important and pressing problem or to seize a new and valuable opportunity not listed on your quarterly Action Plan. Either way, you've pulled the most valuable, important action steps for the week off your to-do list where they were buried.

Here's one more thing the Big Rock Report does for you besides helping you better self-manage. When you get your key team members doing it, too, the format lowers the burden of managing your

—— **WEEKLY BIG ROCK REPORT** ——
Period Ending January 21, 20xx

LAST WEEK'S BIG ROCKS

	Big Rocks	Comments
☑	Formal debrief of Sand Hill project.	• Biggest insight was that because we agreed to include the two on-sites as part of the implementation contract, the client was thrilled. • We have already generated two strong referrals. (I'm following up on them now.) • I have also scheduled a 90-day follow-up with client to make sure they stay happy and to ask for next round of referrals.
☑	Follow-up and schedule assessment presentation with Core Inc.	• Scheduled for February 7th. • Already in contact with Lee from Engineering to get his help on technical portion.
☑	Make 20 outbound stage one prospecting calls.	• Made 23 outbound calls; 3 stage two appointments set; 2 "timing issue" prospects to follow up with next month.

BUSINESS REVIEW

Key Victories:
• Sand Hill project—client thrilled. Gave us 2 strong referral prospects.
• Was able to set assessment presentation with Core Inc. for Feb 7th.
• Tanya made an incredible save with Mirror Tech to bring them back to negotiating table. Way to go, Tanya!

Key Business Challenges:
• Trying to match up travel schedules with Engineering to accompany me on Core Inc. presentation. They are feeling very full. Working on it, but any help would be appreciated.

Key Updates:
• New pre-call direct mail package made a real difference for my stage one prospecting calls. Three of the prospects I talked with specifically commented on the quality/value of the package.
• Tried out Paula (new sales admin) on scheduling stage one calls for me. Didn't work well. Will try a different scripted opening next week to see if that helps.
• Reminder that Tech World conference is 3 months away. We need to get trade show team together sometime in next 2 weeks to get organized.

NEXT WEEK'S BIG ROCKS

1. Global Finance Inc. presentation on 19th.
2. Make 20 outbound stage one prospecting calls.

Figure 8 Sample weekly Big Rock Report

key team. In one standardized format, you can see what they felt was most important to get done this week. You can see if they were accurate and optimal in their choice of priorities, and if not, the report prompts you to have a coaching conversation to better direct their attention onto the things that matter most. You have a clear accountability loop: Did your team complete their Big Rocks this week? I love how the Big Rock Report gives me a fast and direct insight into my direct reports. Considering it takes you and your key team members only five to ten minutes each week to fill out, and it takes you only a few minutes to read several reports, this simple tool yields a big return. Plus, people thrive and perform at their best when they can see the progress they are making. You can use the list of your team's victories as a reminder to help them celebrate or, at the very least, acknowledge, the progress they are making. And the challenges they list become a place for you to see how you can help remove obstacles and coach them to grow.

Focusing on your Fewer, Better is an approach to business that urges you to put your best time and attention into your highest-value activities. In this chapter, you learned to identify your company, department, or team's Fewer, Better and how to turn this strategic insight into a quarterly one-page Action Plan. And you learned the power of the week and the Big Rock Report in executing your plan. Now it's time to move to the final step of the core Freedom Formula: how to build the strategic depth into your organization needed to sustain your gains.

CHAPTER 4

Step Four:
Develop Strategic Depth

Three years ago, my company was hosting an awards dinner for our business coaching clients. There at the banquet were the CEOs and owners of over a hundred companies from around the world. One of the final awards we gave that evening was to a quiet woman named Tammy, who, along with her husband, Mark, owned a successful commercial and residential flooring company in the Midwestern United States. Tammy's company had grown by more than 300 percent in less than thirty-six months. As she came up to receive her award, I asked her to share a few words. What she said has stayed with me to this day:

> "While I'm proud of what our team accomplished growing the company, the biggest impact of the work we've done hasn't been the growth. Earlier this year, my father was hospitalized and needed my help to be there for him for an extended time. Before we started doing this work, I would have had to choose between being there to care for my elderly dad or having my company fail because I wasn't there to run it for an extended time. The impact of this work—and it has been work to follow the program—was that I got to be there to care for my dad. I didn't have to make a choice between my business or my dad; I got both."

Tammy wasn't the only one wiping away tears. We all understood the pressure and the relief she felt being able to trust that her business had the depth to run and grow for a few months without her attention while she did what she needed and wanted to do for her father.

Look at all the people who work for you. Odds are at some point over the next several years that one of them will have something happen in their family or personal life that requires them to step away for an extended time to deal with an extremely difficult situation. Strategic depth is what allows the rest of you to cover for this person, just like you know they would if the roles were reversed.

Strategic depth is built on sound business systems and structured approaches that allow you to capture, organize, store, and access key know-how. It's also both the formal and informal ways you train, cross-train, and grow your team over time, so that your company, department, or team has the durability to withstand the loss of a key player—temporary or otherwise. Strategic depth gives your company both the staying power and scalability to compound your results by building on a secure base.

What's more, strategic depth protects you from the stress, fear, and anxiety of being totally reliant on yourself or a key team member. It gives you the peace of mind that comes with knowing you and your team won't face the excruciating situation of having to put work needs in front of your most important family and personal needs.

A Cautionary Tale

IT WAS 6 AM and still dark out. The outside temperature was 40°F, but with the damp fog, it felt even colder. Elizabeth Cauldwell, a senior VP with one of the world's largest consulting companies, arrived at her office like she did most mornings, an hour earlier than everybody else. Elizabeth's company employs seventy thousand people and has five hundred offices around the world doing business in over one hundred countries.

Elizabeth specializes in risk management for large, multinational clients, and in her world of risk management, she is a rock star. She has been in the industry for over twenty years and has risen to be one of the most valued consultants at her firm, charged with leading a key ongoing engagement with one of its largest clients, a Fortune 50 multinational. The client has come to rely on her competence. In fact, it's not a stretch to say that if Elizabeth retired or moved to a competitor, her current company would face steep odds against retaining this critical, high-profile account. We're talking millions of dollars of bottom-line profit that in a very real way lives and dies by the value Elizabeth creates.

Of course, she is not the only team member servicing this massive client, but she was the only one the client mentioned by name as a negotiating commitment in order to sign on over a decade ago. Back when her firm was wooing this client, the message was clear: no Elizabeth, no contract. As part of the original deal, Elizabeth was pulled off all her other projects and given over to just one client—this client.

Let me explain something; Elizabeth works. And she works and works. No wimpy seventy-two-hour work week for her; she regularly puts in 100-hour work weeks servicing this incredibly demanding and complicated ongoing client engagement. Despite getting in to the office by 6 AM, she doesn't get home until after 9 PM. She works most weekends, and even when she doesn't work, she informally works. When her family came into town to visit, Elizabeth snuck away from the office to have dinner with them—but take a full day off? Couldn't do it. There literally was no break in the workflow, and this has gone on for over a decade. The reality is, she's doing the work of three people (if not more.) Her analytic skills have saved her client tens of millions of dollars and helped them intelligently hedge billions in exposures.

Of course, you could read this and say, "I wish I had my own Elizabeth. In fact, I want an army of Elizabeths." But as a business owner, I see this and it makes me want to cry, or at the very least cry out. Why would an employer set up the culture and systems to allow this, or in Elizabeth's case, tacitly encourage this? It's insane. It's inhumane. It's not sustainable. And to be blunt, it's bad business.

They literally have put one of their most valuable eggs in one basket, and then for over a decade, they've unwittingly jeopardized that basket with 100-hour work weeks. If she got hurt, her company never would be able to cover her absence for any extended time without a significant degradation of work quality. If she were to be romanced away by a competitive firm, she'd be the wedge for this new employer to woo away this massive client. It could cost her employer millions in lost profit, not to mention the reputational blow. ♦

Elizabeth's story is a great example of why the fourth and final step of the Freedom Formula matters so much. **To sustain the progress you've made by focusing your best talent and attention on your highest-value projects and initiatives, you've got to move beyond a potentially disabling reliance on any one individual, whether that person is an Elizabeth or *you* are your team's Elizabeth. You've got to build strategic depth.**

Imagine if one or more of your key people, or one of their relatives, faced an unexpected health issue. Or imagine their spouse got transferred to an out-of-state office, and your key team member gave notice to follow to the new city. Or they were recruited away by a competitor. Or even just that they burned out and decided to retire. What would be the real impact on your company, department, or team?

It's naïve to think that it could never happen to your organization. Given enough time, the odds are close to 100 percent that at some point it will happen, and likely it already has multiple times. To sustain the gains you generated through applying the first three steps of the formula, your company, team, or department must be strong enough to handle the sudden, unexpected loss of any key team member, whether this means you or your Elizabeth. I call this process "building strategic depth."

Following the formula, you'll take small but critically important ongoing steps to cross-train your team and systematize key functional areas of your business so that each key role has a backup with clear systems and centralized documentation. Over time, you'll encourage a culture in which it's everyone's responsibility to back each other up. This protects everyone and is a nonnegotiable if you're going to sustain the real rewards of applying the formula over time.

If Elizabeth's company hadn't been so short-sighted, they'd realize that her working 100-hour weeks wasn't a boon, but really was a bomb, ticking in the heart of their premier client team. This bomb was at risk of being triggered by burnout, health challenges, relationship needs, defection, or plain old retirement. Elizabeth's firm laid a sucker's bet with no backup or hedge. They let Elizabeth's star performance gild over a very real vulnerability.

By contrast, after building strategic depth, you'll help your Elizabeth get great work done but in a sustainable way. This means helping to carve out what she does that is most, most important and supporting her with more staff, structured systems, and resources that will allow your Elizabeth to run longer and greatly reduce the risk to your company. Besides, what kind of company do you really want to be building? In my value hierarchy, there is something wrong with a firm expecting its team to work two or more full-time jobs simply because it's that or leave the company.

But strategic depth is about more than just playing defense to protect your organization from the risk of losing a key person; it also is about playing offense. Done well, strategic depth gives you the stable base for explosive growth.

Let's go back to Kes Andersen, owner of Pathfinder Signs, whom you briefly met in chapter one. As you recall, essentially every business day for eight years, Kes had been rising before dawn to check in with his installation teams to ensure they had all they needed to do their work for the day. After speaking with his two field managers, Kes would start his morning ritual and then head into the office for another long day of work.

When he became a business coaching client two years ago, I asked him how his family felt about his long work hours, especially those 4 AM calls.

"Oh, they're just used to it by now," he said. "It's amazing what we can become resigned to when we think there is no way for something to be different."

I asked him this very direct question: "Are you willing to do the toughest thing in the world if it will make your company better and your family life richer? Don't say yes just yet, because what I'm going to ask you to do is to face your real reasons for getting up at 4 AM every morning. You may think you're doing it because you have to, but you don't. In fact, you getting up that early every day to check in is actually hurting your business."

You'll recall that Kes was able to acknowledge his fear of not being in control. In our early conversations, we discussed his fear as the real driver of his behavior around how he managed his teams. I asked, "Are you willing to face that and do it differently?"

Kes quickly said yes, he wanted to get out of those 4 AM daily calls, but he didn't think he could. He said, "I hate those 4 AM calls, but I don't see any way around them. As it is, we've had to tell several of our biggest customers that we can't take on more business from them because I'm concerned we couldn't do the expanded work up to the same quality standard we've become known for."

With a little more conversation, we mapped out a plan for Kes and his team to build the depth his production crews needed to be able to produce independently of him. At the same time, we drew a line in the sand and said that by October 15 of that year (ninety days after we started working together), not only would he be out of those 4 AM calls, but we'd do it in a way that would make his company stronger and more scalable.

Kes's first step was to meet with his key team, including Cesar, his production manager, and his two field team managers. He started by acknowledging the root of his getting up so early every morning was fear that if he didn't, things wouldn't be done the right way. He explained that at this point, the three managers collectively knew more about the field installation of large outdoor signs than he ever did, and that the situation was caused by his own discomfort with feeling out of control. He owned the problem and explained how Pathfinder literally had turned away millions in new business because he was concerned the company didn't have the capacity to take on that new business the way they had been doing their production. He asked for their help, and they quickly assented. They all wanted to take Kes out of the daily loop. They saw that it was not the way things really should be, but they, like Kes's family, had been resigned that he likely wasn't going to change.

First, they processed out the entire production flow, from signed purchase order through the permitting process, to the sign manufacture, all the way through the final sign installation by the field crew. They laid out the steps and common pitfalls they had to avoid, capturing this data on an eight-foot whiteboard in their office. They got clear on who was responsible for each step, what information would be needed, by whom, and at what steps. They outlined some simple visual controls into the process so their production team could self-manage. When they were done, in theory, those 4 AM calls no longer would be necessary.

For the next two weeks, they tested out their process, with Kes still in the flow as in the past. But then, as agreed upon in their meeting, he turned the whole thing over to Cesar to run, with Kes available for the next thirty days in the early morning if they needed him.

It turned out that Cesar didn't want to get up at 4 AM, and every time he was needed that early in the morning, he used the occasions to tweak the system to preempt it from happening again for that reason. For example, one morning when one of the field crews called him about how to get into a gated community where they were putting up a new sign for a local developer, Cesar and his team realized that they needed to keep a central list of all the entry codes for the various homebuilders they served, so next time the field crew would have that information in a data field on the work order. Also, Cesar began meeting with his two field crew managers at 3 PM the day *before*, to go over the next day's assigned installations last thing in the day.

Kes and his team hit the agreed-upon ninety-day target. The real victory for Kes wasn't being able to eliminate the morning check-in calls, or even the fact that their new system expanded their production capacity by 25 percent with no additional staff. The biggest victory was the lesson it taught Kes about the real cost of his compulsion for control. He realized that to exercise that kind of tight-gripped control, he had to be there, every morning, day after day, year after year, to maintain it.

When I asked Kes what he thought it had cost his company to wait on doing this important work, he shared,

> "Delaying building in strategic depth literally cost us millions of dollars in business. Remember, I was turning away business because I just couldn't see how we could produce the work to the standard I wanted. And the thing I realized was that I was the bottleneck. My fear meant we underserved our customers who had to find other vendors, even when they knew we were the best value in town in our niche. Plus, now I can do the highest-value things that I'm really on the payroll to do instead of getting trapped doing other people's jobs."

The retooling of processes that Kes and his production team accomplished wasn't simply to protect the company in case Kes wasn't on the phone each morning to help problem solve. The real payoff came from the way the combined work of improving the design of their production system and the cross-training of his team collectively increased their production capacity by 25 percent. This in turn allowed them to take on large chunks of new business. Today Kes is scaling his sales force, laying the foundations for an expanded account executive and outside sales team. He's also expanded into a totally new market and is about to branch into selling to a new vertical. These are things he never would have done if it wasn't for the confidence and capacity growth Pathfinder Signs enjoyed from the earlier stages of work to deepen their depth.

Strategic depth isn't just about having an insurance policy to protect your team from a key loss. Done right, strategic depth is the offensive platform that gives you the extra capacity to focus your best attention on seizing new opportunities and scaling.

Let's dive even further into the nitty-gritty of how you build strategic depth into your company and team that will help you both play defense (protect yourself from the loss of a key person) *and* offense (have the capacity to handle explosive growth).

Think of strategic depth as a three-legged stool. The first leg of the stool is your team itself: the human hands that drive your organization and actually do the work and create value. Your team is at the core of your business. Their skills, their drive, their discernment, their judgment and innovation are critical ingredients for your organization's future. But your team by itself is not enough. People come and go; life happens. That's why a critical part of the team leg of your stool includes the ongoing training and cross-training you do company-wide to build depth to your bench.

The second leg of the stool is composed of the systems that you develop to give your business structure. These systems formalize best practices and share proven approaches and tools company-wide. They include the step-by-step instructions to start a new client project, the checklist your marketing team follows to make sure they don't skip a key step when advertising, and the interview scripts and question templates your recruiting team uses when talking with a prospective new employee. Collectively, this structure empowers your team to get their best work done with less time, effort, and variation. It also ensures that your best thinking and ongoing innovations get captured and propagated throughout your organization, rather than just stored in the head of any one individual.

The third leg of the stool is the culture within which your team operates. Think of your organization's culture as an invisible guide that shapes behavior and subtly influences what and how your team sees, approaches, and thinks about the situations they encounter at work. By creating a culture that buys into the need for strategic depth to protect and empower all stakeholders, your organization will stay the course in creating and training your team on the internal systems that work so well.

The First "Leg" of Strategic Depth: Your Team

Every business needs talented people to help make it successful. My insistence that your business's success be independent of any one person does *not* mean your team is unimportant. On the contrary, the only way to build a sustainably successful organization is to have great team members who consistently perform for your company. It's critical, however, to ensure that your company doesn't rely on the presence of any one individual. You can't allow your company to risk a fatal point failure should one of your team members need some time away from the business for whatever reason. Instead, make key team members responsible for creating the systems to do their individual jobs and groom their successors and backups. Invest heavily in cross-training your team members; extend that notion of a stool to create a deep bench to cover for each other's functional responsibilities.

The team leg of your stool doesn't just mean hiring and trusting great people; it also embodies a full, ongoing commitment to train and cross-train your team so that you develop your people quarter by quarter, strategically cross-training them to cover for each other. Of course you want a talented, committed team member for every key role in your company, if not for every role. The key is to stabilize this potent leg of the stool with the two other legs.

Far too many companies build their results on the one-legged stool of "team." They find extremely talented people and let them work freely to get great results. A one-legged stool works, for a time.

I hardly need to say that the problem with balancing on a one-legged stool is that it is inherently unstable. Rarely can a one-legged stool survive an unexpected shock.

Take an honest look at your company. Have you built and developed a team with members who can cover for each other? Do you have the strategic depth to keep the company operating strong even after the loss of a key team member? This goes to the heart of the formula. In order to sustain the gains you've made by focusing yourself and your team on those Fewer, Better activities in your company that truly create value, you've got to have the structure and team to carry it forward, even in the face of a tough team member loss.*

Strategic Depth "Leg" Two: Your Systems

Systems are the foundation of how great work gets done in your organization. They are the reliable processes and procedures that empower your business to consistently produce an excellent result for your clients or customers. They're documented best practices that increase your company's efficiency and reduce costly mistakes. Systems include documents and processes such as the checklists your fulfillment department follows to ensure that all orders are shipped correctly, the orientation process for all new clients when you begin working together, the standardized contracts you use with all your new vendors, and even the checklists you use before you bring any new hire on board. Your business systems include any company know-how captured in a tangible format (versus locked in the brain of an individual team member) that enables the business to reliably achieve. Essentially, systems are any tools you've created to get consistently great results in a functional area of your company.

---

* I'll go into greater depth about how to develop your team in part two, "The Five Freedom Accelerators."

The Two Layers to Every Successful Business System

Every successful business system has two layers: the process layer and the format layer.

The *process* layer consists of the step-by-step procedure you've created—the recipe for a given result in an area of your business. Does your system accurately capture the steps of the process so that when you follow it, you consistently get the desired result? It does you no good to formalize poor processes. You want your systems to capture your best practices and winning moves, making it easier for your company to replicate and scale those successes.

The *format* layer addresses how you package and present your system to your team. Is your system easy to use? Is it transparent so team members intuitively understand how to use it? Can it be automated so much of the work happens technologically versus manually? Done right, systems make life easier for your team and success more predictable for your business. (See the next page for twenty-five example formats to use when capturing a system.)

Having a solid process isn't enough. You have to package that process in ways that your team actually will use. How do you know if your system has a good, usable format? Ask one simple, unambiguous, incontrovertible question: *Is your team using it?*

Your team members want to do a good job. If your business systems are simple, intuitive, and effective, they will use them. If they're confusing, complicated, bloated, or cumbersome, they'll ignore these systems and even create their own "cheat sheet" hybrid versions instead. But such homespun, individual hybrids normally aren't scalable. In fact, they usually work only for that one team member and only as long as the volume of your business stays relatively level. Plus, even if this private shortcut works, rarely is it ever captured in a way that the rest of your business can use. And when that team member goes, so does that know-how.

To get the format layer right, closely observe the way your team members use, or don't use, your systems. Don't argue, don't preach, don't cajole—simply observe. Take their behavior as critical feedback to refine and improve your systems. Remember, those systems are meant to leverage, empower, and simplify the lives of your employees, so don't fall in love with any specific system. Rather, fall in love with the result it's intended to generate.

---

25 Effective Formats to Package Your Systems

Here is a quick list of 25 potential formats for you to package your systems to make them easier and more effective for team members to use.

1. Checklists
2. Scripts
3. Worksheets
4. Step-by-step instructions
5. Software that automates a process
6. Databases of key information
7. Pricing lists
8. Templates and samples
9. Common Q&A sheets
10. Spreadsheets with built-in formulas
11. Printer-ready art files
12. Filing system (paper or electronic)
13. Preapproved vendors lists
14. Standardized equipment and parts
15. Online communication tools for effectively sharing information (discussion forums, wikis, whiteboards, social networks, etc.)
16. Delivery timetables
17. Job or role descriptions
18. Instructional videos
19. Project management software with reusable project pathways
20. Reporting templates
21. Organizational charts
22. Preapproved forms and contracts
23. A timeline or master calendar
24. Document workflows mapped out or embedded in software
25. Complete enterprise management software

For example, my company, Maui Mastermind, produces multiple high-end business workshops each year for our business coaching clients. To make sure each of these events runs smoothly and creates maximum value for our participants, we created a live event "screenplay" as if the events were a theater production. Which props go where? What handouts need to be given to participants during the first, second, and third part of each day? What are the audiovisual needs for each segment and for livestreaming the workshop? This screenplay allows my team to consistently produce five-star business training events, while ensuring flexibility should a key staff member need to miss an event for personal reasons.

As you can see, systems include the processes and procedures—the recipe if you will—for how a reasonably skilled team member can get a specific result for your company completing a given task or function. Systems also include the tools you develop to help a team member get that desired result faster and more easily and consistently. They also include your formal ways of documenting and storing key institutional knowledge like client contact history and vendor contract details. Finally, systems also include the automation and larger-scale tools you leverage in your business, such as a formal enterprise resource-planning tool.

Build Your Master System

Years ago, when I was hard at work building my first successful business, my partner and I came up with the idea of creating a company that would be independent of both of us. We laid out our dream on an oversized sheet of yellow poster paper (which I still have in my archive), calling it our "Business System." When we abbreviated that two-word phrase, we ran into a little trouble, so we quickly added the word "Ultimate." Now we had the acronym "UBS."

Our Ultimate Business System was the collection of processes, procedures, checklists, and other systems we would spend the next five years refining. In fact, in our company, UBS became both a noun and a verb. We'd say things like, "Great idea to lower costs, Paige. Will you please add that to the UBS so that other team members can use it?" Or "Samuel, will you please UBS that process so we don't have the same problems next time?"

UBS-ing became a discipline and an obsession in our business, and it's one I strongly urge you to adopt for your company. It's a philosophy of capturing winning processes and best practices into repeatable, scalable systems. It's also a clear framework within which to organize and house your growing collection of business systems.

Bear in mind, we are *not* talking about a policies and procedures manual. After surveying thousands of business people, I've come to one firm and irrefutable conclusion: no one uses a manual, especially after the first thirty days on the job. Policy and procedures manuals are generally written once, updated rarely, and used essentially never. UBS-ing is an ongoing discipline and commitment. Too often, businesses invest time and money into creating systems that no one uses. Why? Because the policies and procedures manual comes like Moses with his stone tablets from on high, usually from someone who is several steps away from the actual work the system defines. For employees, it feels more like red-tape rules than the best possible approach. **At their best, systems aren't about constraining behavior so much as they are about capturing and disseminating best practices and effective tools.** This means you must get your team involved in creating, or at the very least giving helpful feedback about, the systems they use.

Your UBS is the organized collection of tools that captures the actual, everyday know-how of your business in a searchable, accessible, and editable way. These tools are held inside a simple structure of file folders, generally on a cloud-based system, and include things like your checklists, spreadsheets, proposal templates, training videos, and sample marketing pieces.

Without a UBS, it is likely you'll have a hodgepodge collection of files spread on dozens of different team members' computers or, even worse, locked informally in their heads. When Juan creates a better version of a process, without a formal UBS these improvements likely just stay with Juan. When Sarah figures out how to do a key function, she may write a few notes for herself on yellow Post-its stuck on the side of her desk. If she ever were to leave the company, all those notes would get swept into the trash can and all that valuable company knowledge would be lost.

Your UBS is a way to start gathering your systems into one place, making sure that your whole team has access to best practices and key institutional knowledge that previously was trapped in a few key people's heads. The UBS concept also is the best way to start the dialogue about systems inside your company. Your ultimate goal is to make your UBS a living, breathing way of doing business in your company—an ongoing practice. You'll know you've won when you regularly hear your team say things like, "Did you add that to the UBS?" and "Great solution to that problem—can you UBS it?"

4 Steps to Build Your UBS

Here is a simple four-step process to start building your UBS in the next ninety days.

Step #1: Create your UBS's organizational file folder hierarchy.

If you had to cluster all the functions of your business into five to nine main folders/areas, what would they be? (See an example in *fig. 9*.)

If you ran a service business, your UBS folders might look like this:

1.0 Marketing
2.0 Sales
3.0 Operations
4.0 Human Resources
5.0 Financial
6.0 Leadership

YOUR "UBS"

The System of All Your Systems

Your "UBS" is your "Ultimate Business System." It is your master system for how you organize, store, access, and refine your systems. Your goal is to make your UBS a living, breathing way of doing business in your company. You'll know you've won when you regularly hear your team say things like, "Did you add that to the UBS?" and "Great solution to that problem; can you UBS it?" This is not something you'll do in one sitting, but rather it is a way of approaching your business that you'll engage your entire team in owning over the long term.

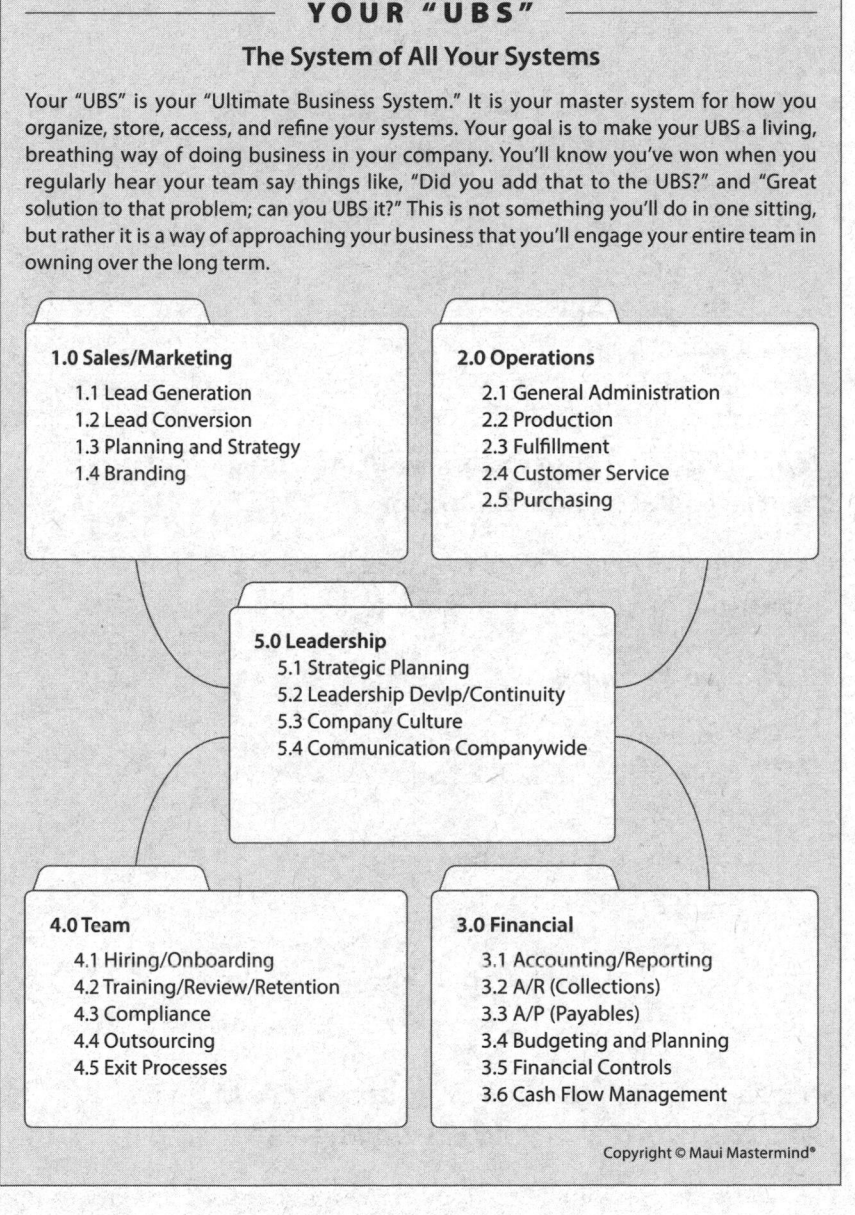

1.0 Sales/Marketing

  1.1 Lead Generation
  1.2 Lead Conversion
  1.3 Planning and Strategy
  1.4 Branding

2.0 Operations

  2.1 General Administration
  2.2 Production
  2.3 Fulfillment
  2.4 Customer Service
  2.5 Purchasing

5.0 Leadership

  5.1 Strategic Planning
  5.2 Leadership Devlp/Continuity
  5.3 Company Culture
  5.4 Communication Companywide

4.0 Team

  4.1 Hiring/Onboarding
  4.2 Training/Review/Retention
  4.3 Compliance
  4.4 Outsourcing
  4.5 Exit Processes

3.0 Financial

  3.1 Accounting/Reporting
  3.2 A/R (Collections)
  3.3 A/P (Payables)
  3.4 Budgeting and Planning
  3.5 Financial Controls
  3.6 Cash Flow Management

Copyright © Maui Mastermind®

Figure 9 Sample UBS (Ultimate Business System)

If you own a manufacturing company, your UBS folders might include:

1.0 Marketing and Sales
2.0 Production and Purchasing
3.0 Quality
4.0 Engineering
5.0 Administration
6.0 Human Resources
7.0 Finance
8.0 Leadership

Step #2: Pick one area to start with, and break that one area down into five to seven subareas.

For example, if you ran a service-based business and chose "4.0 HR," to start with, your subareas might look like this:

4.0 Human Resources

4.1 Recruitment and Hiring
4.2 Onboarding and Orientation
4.3 Training
4.4 Benefits and HR Admin
4.5 Exiting

The key is to start with *one* area of your UBS and build from there.

Step #3: Populate this one area, and its five to seven subareas, with any of your existing systems.

Get yourself and your team looking through your hard drives and see what systems you already have. You'll be surprised at how many of these systems will be known to only one person. You might be horrified to discover how many out-of-date versions of documents, spreadsheets, processes, or tools are still being used regularly because someone didn't know there was an updated version.

You might find job descriptions and position recruitment ads, interview sample questions and candidate debrief worksheets, or quarterly and annual review templates. Generally, what I hear from coaching clients when they do this process is one of two things. First, they are shocked by how much of the key work their team does that simply has gone undocumented. They realize how vulnerable they are to the loss of a key person and how much valuable business know-how is tied up in the heads of their team members. Second, some of them are floored by how many good tools their team members individually have created and stored in the one-person silo of their hard drive. They recognize that these tools need to be centralized and shared.

As you look through your team's computers and files to gather existing systems and tools and put them into your new UBS, this is a perfect time to identify which tools are outdated or inadequate, which work well, and which tools and systems you desperately need.

Save to your UBS only those documents and tools that you want your business to actually use going forward. (You can store anything no longer current in an archive folder in each section of your UBS on the off chance you need to access it later.)

Rename all files you put into your UBS so that they are obvious and easy to search for later. Think "search" and "key words" here. Don't necessarily name a file based on what the person who created it thinks it should be; establish your naming system based on terms a new user of that file will use to *search* for it. Optimize your naming of files for ease and transparency of finding them. Standardize your key naming conventions (or start to, at any rate). Are you going to call this type of report a "scoreboard" or "dashboard" or some other term? Is it a "new client intake form" or a "new customer start worksheet"? Is it a "standard employee agreement" or a "new team member contract template"? The difference is not trivial. Team members will look for a tool by searching your UBS. If they don't find it after two or three tries, or a few minutes, whichever comes first, they will assume the tool or document doesn't exist and re-create it themselves. Now not only is your team member wasting his or her time duplicating from scratch the earlier work, but also your UBS will be degraded, as it will have two versions of a specific document or tool in it. This in turn will dilute any future improvements or updates—some refinements will go into one document, while others will go into the other.

By naming your files to make them intuitive and easy to find, not only will the team use the right tools, but also your systems will get the benefit of any refinement your team members make as they actually use your systems in performing their day-to-day jobs.

Step #4: Pick one or two systems to build this quarter for this area of the business.

Ask, "If we could only build one or two systems in this area of the business in the next ninety days, which would be most valuable to create first?"

Notice that as you involve your team in doing these four simple steps, you have a chance to talk with them about the value of systems and how they benefit each team member and the company as a whole. Share with them your commitment to having a systems-driven culture within the company, and ask for their help in taking the first key steps to start this process.

Each quarter, repeat steps two to four to build and sustain your UBS. Over time, this process is like magic, and you'll find that you consistently make your business more and more scalable and less and less reliant on a few key staff members (including you).

Systems and controls cannot be a fad, but must instead be an ingrained way of doing things inside your business. If you start the process and don't see it through, your efforts will wither and you'll lose credibility with your team. They must see why systems and controls matter to the business, to you, and to them. And they must see you staying the course by making those systems and controls a fundamental part of your business.

I've created a ten-minute video for your team to watch that explains the value and best practices of the UBS. You can access this free resource at **www.FreedomToolkit.com**.

Find Your Optimal Balance Point

Every system takes an investment of time, attention, and money to build it. Is it worth the investment? That depends on the importance of the process, task, relationship, or responsibility you are considering systematizing.

Imagine it as a set of balance scales. On the left side of the scales, you have fewer systems. This helps you remain streamlined, efficient, and flexible. But the fewer systems you have, the greater price you may pay. A more chaotic workflow requires more attentional energy to ensure things don't get missed while doing your best work, and makes it harder to cross-train team members for strategic depth.

On the right side of the scales is the company, department, or team that is heavily vested in systems and has them for everything. This helps people stay organized, moderates the work quality across performers so that you consistently get better work from your players, and enables you to reduce reliance on any one staff member. These systems come with a price as well. First there is the cost of time, energy, and attention to build, train on, store, refine, and update your systems. Just writing out a process or creating a better tool to do a function isn't enough—you've got to get your team to use it, which can directly equate to a dollar cost. Beyond this direct cost, too many systems can overly formalize or even suffocate a team.

Maintaining the right balance of systems and structure is a dynamic balance. For my company culture in Maui Mastermind, we invest heavily in systems and cross-training the team to be able to back each other up. That works for us. When we've had people in key functions out on personal time or even lost them, the investments we've made in crafting, refining, and organizing our systems have been invaluable. You'll have to find the right balance within your organization.

Here are a couple of important truths about systems and the systematization of functional areas of your business. First, you'll never be able to systematize everything. The fantasy of having a business so well systematized with proven processes and procedures for every task, function, scenario, and decision is just that—an illusion. The business world is just not that clean. It requires creativity, flexibility, discernment, and judgment. Even if you were able fully to process out all aspects of a functional area of your business, the world is changing so fast that today's systems will need to be refined, adjusted, and even retired next month, quarter, or year. **Systems need to be seen as a living, breathing, cultural commitment rather than a book of knowledge that you'll never finish. Systems are an approach to business, a commitment to a way of doing business—not a manual with all the answers.**

The second fundamental truth of systems is that they are expensive. Every system takes time, attention, and money to create, train your team on its use, manage and coach them for its deep acceptance, and then refine, update, and retire it over time. Given this cost, some things in your business life just don't deserve to be formalized or systematized.

Be strategic about what you choose to systematize. What is the value of a possible system you're considering creating? Ask the following questions:

- How valuable is the output of the system? Is that value only accrued when the work is done with exacting precision, or would good enough still yield your intended result?
- What is the risk you run by not investing in its creation? What is the consequence you risk if you *don't* have this system?
- How frequently is this system needed? Is this a once-a-year task? Or is it done weekly or even daily?

- How obvious or transparent is this process? Is it intuitive and easy for a relatively capable new team member to step in and just do it? Or is it complex, with layers of nuance and required judgment? The harder it is for a new team member to follow, the more valuable it would be to systematize and structure it, to accelerate that employee's ability to master it.
- How expensive is the function? Does it take your priciest talent? Would systematizing it bring the same or better result with less-expensive inputs and team members? Is the cost of a mistake when running this process great? If so, then weigh the value of systematizing it, both to lower the level of talent needed to perform part or all of it and to reduce the risk of having to scrap or redo subpar work.
- How important is the quality of the work output of this process? The greater the need for high quality, the more likely you'll want to leverage refined systems for that outcome.
- How long does this process take? One thing refined systems are great for is speeding up the time it takes for a repeated process to be completed. A small investment to optimize a process on the front end can yield recurring dividends on the back end.

It's likely that once you assess the value of each potential new system, you'll still find you have too many systems you want to tackle at one time. It can be overwhelming. Draw on the four-step UBS-ing process. Start with *one* area of your UBS and simply begin by loading that one folder and subfolders with the systems you already have. Then ask yourself what one or two systems would prove most valuable for your company, department, or team to create or refine over the next ninety days. At the end of the quarter, come back to this question and pick one or two more systems to work on in the coming quarter. Over time, not only will you compound progress in systematizing your area of the business, but you'll also be able to engage your team in this process. This will accelerate things, as now it's not just one person but instead multiple people championing systems in your organization. Plus, your collective fluency with absorbing and using systems will grow over time.

Remember Elizabeth and her hundred-hour work weeks. What would it have done for her company if they'd given her enough support so that she had the time and tasking to systematize and cross-train her staff as she went? This would include capturing in a shared format the historic information of the client relationship, documenting her best practices and insider shortcuts that she learned working with this demanding client for over a decade, and sharing the tools and templates she created that helped her get such great results with this client.

This would have provided Elizabeth a framework for training other staff members on how to work with this client. Would this have been an investment for her company to make? Of course. Yes, it would have raised the cost of the staff needed for supporting this client. But think what all of this would have done for Elizabeth's company. First, they would have had real depth to cover if she ever got sick or when she later retired. Next, the support would have made for saner hours for Elizabeth, which would have extended her longevity with her company. Finally, this would have created other points of contact and connection with this client that would have anchored them to the company beyond just the relationship with Elizabeth. The company would have been in much better position.

The only way to sustain your commitment to building strategic depth over time is to make it part of your business culture. This leads us to the final leg: culture.

The Third "Leg" of Strategic Depth: Your Culture

The third and final leg of your stool is your company culture. Your culture is the informal way that your people see, prioritize, and approach doing things in your business. It is essentially the hidden hand that shapes your team's behavior without them even thinking about it. Many companies and teams leave culture up to chance, but you can shape culture intentionally so that it supports and even drives the success behaviors you desperately want from your team.

Obviously sound systems and intelligent internal controls are two major ingredients to building strategic depth. **But what happens when a novel situation comes up for which you don't have a system to detail how you want your team to respond? This is where your company's culture can save the day.**

Your company's culture is the sum total of the absorbed values and unstated "way we do things around here." If it is built wisely, it becomes the third key ingredient that gives your organization the strategic depth to thrive. I've saved an in-depth discussion of using culture as an accelerator for the Freedom Formula for chapter eight, "Cultivate Your Culture." Meanwhile, here's a preview of how role-modeling company culture starts at the top.

LONG BEFORE HE HELPED CO-FOUND famed travel website Price-line.com, entrepreneur Jeff Hoffman had built a travel software business called CTI. Already successful, CTI had reached $5 million in sales and had just been named one of *Inc.* magazine's fastest-growing small businesses. But Jeff was never one to rest on his laurels. To take his company to the next level, it was critical they get a new travel software program released on time. It had to be perfect. It had to surprise and delight the marketplace with its ease and speed of use. It had to be something that no one in the travel industry had seen before.

Jeff was checking in with his development team, who had camped out in a conference room where they were working day and night to hit their release date. Jeff popped his head in the room and asked this crew, "Is there anything I can do for you to help you meet the deadline?"

One of the junior team members, a bit of a wiseguy, said, "Yeah, Jeff, can you pick up my dry cleaning for me?"

A hush fell over the room as everyone waited for Jeff to react. People were expecting Jeff to deliver a verbal smackdown to this impudent young programming whiz. How dare he disrespect the CEO like that? But, to their amazement, he simply said, "Sure, give me the ticket."

Jeff's reasoning was that the best thing he could do for his business at that moment was keep his talent in that room, working on the product, so that they could meet their looming release deadline and wow their waiting customers. If you have to run a few errands so your company wins, then that's what you need to do—ego and personal glory be damned! His team watched Jeff's behavior and understood that it was all about doing everything you can to serve those who are creating value in the company. CTI tripled sales to more than $15 million in the next twenty-four months, which led to a successful sale of the company to American Express for an eight-figure payday.

Ever since, when Jeff speaks at large CEO conferences, he's quick to share this story with his audience.

"Build a culture and environment where really talented people want to work," he advises. "And then go get their dry cleaning!" ◆

Test Your Strategic Depth—Take a *Real* Vacation

In my late twenties, I went on a two-week rafting trip with my dad and my brother, Alex. We were in the wilderness of Canada with a group of twenty other participants being guided down Class III and IV rapids in one of the most stunning expanses of nature I'd ever seen. On that trip, I met Roy, an extremely successful entrepreneur who had made his fortune developing real estate in San Francisco. This was about four years into my first real start-up, and I spent several nights around the campfire asking Roy to share his experiences that had allowed him to scale his company and wealth. He shared lots of great suggestions, but one night I pushed him to share his most important insight that had allowed him to succeed on such a large scale.

Roy got quiet for a moment, reflecting on his forty-year business career. I inched forward on my camping chair, leaning forward to make sure I didn't miss a word of what he was about to say. Finally, he turned to me with his answer. "David, you want to know the one thing more than anything else that has made the biggest difference to my business success . . . it's this trip," he said, looking around the campsite.

"It's what, Roy? I don't understand."

"It's this," he repeated, passing his hand in a circle around the area we sat in.

For two days I kept asking him to share what he meant by that cryptic phrase, but he kept quiet when I asked, smiling but not saying any more. Finally, when I couldn't take it anymore, I said to him, "This is driving me crazy. What did you mean by, 'This trip is the one thing that helped me be successful'?"

Roy relented and explained that in the early years of his company, he worked long hours just like all of his peers. What he came to realize was that he cast a pretty big shadow in his organization. When he was around, people deferred to him. While this gratified his ego, it hurt his company. It stunted the growth of his team and severely limited their potential contributions.

"I make sure that each year I take enough extended vacation time away from the business so that my team has the space and need to step up," Roy told me. "And every time when I come back, I find that my best people have used my absence as a spark to grow. This has been the key practice that has allowed me to grow my business to where it stands today."

I've never forgotten that trip or Roy's counsel, given to me two decades ago at a time in my business life when I was just starting to enjoy greater success. To this day, I make sure to schedule in ten weeks or more away from my business. Not only does this give me the time to recharge and make memories with my family, but it helps my business grow beyond me. Every time I leave the business, I gain new clarity about which tasks or responsibilities still are partially or fully reliant on me. It gives me the surge of focus and energy to reduce these reliances and build depth into my systems and team to cover these responsibilities during my time away. I also encourage my leadership to take time away for the very same reasons, including that it helps us progressively root out and deal with critical reliances on them. Over time, this has powerfully shaped the culture of our company. Building and using systems, cross-training team members, and creating strategic redundancies is just the way we do business.

Building strategic depth into your organization is a progression, not a light switch you suddenly flip one day. It's not a binary yes/no, but rather a spectrum that you slowly progress through over the course of several years. You won't set this up all at once; rather, it's a cumulative process that takes place over time. And the best way to ensure that your team keeps living this commitment to create strategic depth is to absorb it as a part of your company culture.

Congratulations for making it through all four steps of the core Freedom Formula. You now recognize that you are not paid for time served, but rather for value created. You know that to create your best value, you consistently must reclaim blocks of your best time and attention, and then consistently invest these reclaimed blocks into your A- and B-level activities that create the most value. What's more, you also understand that you need to align your team behind doing the same thing—consistently investing their best time into the company's Fewer, Better. You've learned how to do this planning each quarter and to reduce this to a one-page plan of action for the coming ninety days. Finally, you now know how to sustain these gains by building the strategic depth that you need into the very bones of your company. Over time, these four steps collectively will create remarkable breakthroughs and your organization will enjoy rich results.

———————————————————————

In part two of this book, we'll explore another essential question: How can you make the formula go faster? I'll share with you five accelerants to help you and your team get breakthrough results faster. If you're ready to speed things up so that you can enjoy the rewards of the formula sooner, just turn the page and let's explore the five Freedom Accelerators.

PART II

The Five Freedom Accelerators

CHAPTER 5

Accelerator One:
Engage Your Team

Imagine for a moment that every member of your team wasn't an employee, but rather they were a volunteer. How would this lens change how you saw them? Interacted with them? Led them? Here's the thing: Your best people are *all* volunteers.

Think about it for a moment. Couldn't your best people easily go to a competitor or a new company and quickly get hired, likely for more money than you are paying them? Aren't they getting calls from an army of recruiters with siren pitches of brighter skies and warmer waters? Of course they are. Your top team members are in fact paid volunteers. You and your company are a *choice* for them.

What keeps them with you, then? Is it simply inertia—the fear of change and their comfort with the status quo? Or is it a sense of being part of something important, doing work that matters and helps others? Is it because of the compensation package you provide them? Or the challenging work that they love wrestling with and find inherently interesting? Is it their relationships with their coworkers, customers, or vendors they interact with? Or their desire to grow professionally? Maybe it's the flexibility you offer to fit work and home lives together in a healthy way? For your best people, it's likely a combination of all of these factors.

Obviously, there is no one reason, but just as obviously, if all that is keeping your team working in your company is the single, tenuous thread of inertia, then you'll lose them the next time some interpersonal office drama or outside event "snaps" that string.

You must tie your best people to your company with as many of the threads and cables of connection as you can. In fact, you need to be as strategic and purposeful about retaining your best people as you are about retaining your top customers. And it is in this area that business leaders have a lot to learn from the world of nonprofits.

IT'S A TYPICAL SUMMER SATURDAY AFTERNOON in Fredericksburg, Virginia. The temperature outside is a blistering 94°F, and the humidity drenches the air. Thirty-two members of the Crossroads Church's welcome committee are out in the parking lot of the small strip mall where their 16,000-square-foot church is located. The volunteers are picking up trash and broken bottles and sweeping the 214-space parking lot. This week, like every week, is their chance to make their Sunday home a special, safe, and welcoming place for members and guests alike. They are all smiles as they work and sweat in the hot sun and heavy air.

I know this because their pastor, Joel Lowery, is a friend of mine. Fifteen years ago, Joel worked for a while as my assistant. During that time, he shared with me his and his wife's, Christina, dream of founding their own church. As he worked setting up meetings, screening calls and emails, and arranging for my travel, Joel kept one eye clear on his real goal—to start his church. His first steps were small, attracting a core group of passionate congregants to meet weekly in his home for Bible study. Yet, somehow, out of this core group, the seeds of his 654-member church took root and flourished.

> "During the time I was working for Maui Mastermind, I was learning. When you taught business owners how to build systems-driven, owner-independent companies, I was learning how to build a sustainable, pastor-independent church."

While Joel may have picked up some important business lessons during the years we worked together, his success has something compelling to teach any business leader who wants the same type of commitment and mission-driven engagement for their company. ♦

What would it mean for your business if you treated every employee as if they were a volunteer? If it were your job as a leader to help them find the meaning and passion in their work the way the thirty-two members of Joel's volunteer welcome committee do each Saturday?

In the United States in 2017, 77.3 million adult volunteers donated 6.9 billion hours of free work with an estimated value of $167 billion.[1] In the European Union, 93 million people do volunteer work of some sort each year. Worldwide, it's estimated that over 900 million individuals volunteer each year, and that this volunteer work has an estimated value of $1.3 *trillion*.[2] These are people who aren't being paid and yet still show up to help a cause or group they believe in.

Contrast the volunteer world with the work of for-profit companies, and the statistics are startling. A Gallup daily tracking survey published in January 2016 revealed that 68 percent of employees are not engaged at work,[3] and 51 percent of workers are actively searching for a new job.[4] A Glassdoor.com survey showed that a majority (51 percent) of employees would *not* recommend their current employer to a friend! A Deloitte University Press article shared that 87 percent of companies cited culture and engagement as one of their top challenges.[5] Gallup's State of the American Workplace report revealed that 51 percent of US employees are "not engaged," with an additional 16 percent of employees "actively disengaged."[6] Essentially, what Gallup found was that three out of four employees aren't engaged at work.

What does this mean for you? Simple—you're likely only getting a fraction of what your team is capable of producing. What's more, many of your best people may be connected to your organization by the barest of threads, a hair away from being recruited away by another company.

If you want to speed up your results using the Freedom Formula, then you must retain and engage your team to do this important work *with* you.

What Your Team *Really* Wants

According to a recent study reported in *Harvard Business Review*, your people want "Career" (having autonomy, a role that leverages their strengths and helps them grow and progress), "Community" (feeling respected, cared about, and recognized or seen), and "Cause" (feeling like they're making a difference, that the company's mission and their role are doing good in the world).[7]

See how similar this list of desires is to what people say about why they volunteer:

- I belong here.
- I care about this organization.
- I believe in what we do.
- What we do matters in the world; it makes a difference.
- I find it personally satisfying and fulfilling to know that I played a part in this.
- I feel good about myself being the kind of person who wants to give back.
- This is my team; these are my people.

All too often, we think that what retains our team and motivates them to perform is simply the money. Of course money matters, especially because people have responsibilities and economic needs, but in my observation money is more often about fairness and respect than the actual dollars. For right or wrong, money often is interpreted by a team member as a proxy for how valuable or worthwhile an organization considers him or her to be.

You almost never win on money. Pay too little, and your talented employee feels unappreciated and disrespected. Pay too much, and you can ruin a team member who now feels spoiled and entitled. I've made both mistakes and have seen many of my business coaching clients do the same.

Instead, remember that when it comes to money, the best you can hope for is to find the right neighborhood. Rarely will you find the perfect house in that neighborhood, but if you're in the wrong part of town, either too high or too low, you won't have a long-term fit.

In my experience, here is what your team *really* wants:

- **Respect**: They want to know they are held in a positive light and esteemed, that they are seen by their peers as capable, integral, and valuable.
- **Autonomy**: They want to be able to use their strengths, make decisions, and get things done.
- **Growth**: They want to learn and grow, to feel that they are progressing in their career.
- **Connection**: They want to feel a part of something that matters, with a community of peers they feel good about.
- **Impact**: They want to feel that what they are doing daily is making a difference and helping the world in a real way.
- **Money**: They want to feel like they are being compensated fairly and that they can care for their family and personal needs.
- **Flexibility**: To the degree it makes business sense, they want a balanced path between work and life, without silly formality stopping them from seeing their kids' plays or graduations.

Notice how our expectations of work have fundamentally changed. Your employees want more than just a paycheck, more than even just security. Study after study shows that money matters, but only as a second-tier need, and that once it has been fairly dealt with, the other needs far outpace it in importance to your team. Let's turn now to the important work of how you actually give your team many of these other, nonmonetary rewards of working with your company.

Give Your Team a Voice

People want a sense of control or efficacy in a situation, to be able to influence and impact. When you give your team a real voice in how the business operates, at least in their area of the business, you give them the ability to make a difference and to be heard, seen, and affirmed.

How does this concept work in the competitive world of for-profit business? Look no further than entrepreneurial doctor Pariksith Singh, MD.

DR. SINGH BEGAN HIS FAMILY CARE PRACTICE back in 2001 with a single office in a building that formerly housed an Ace Hardware store. In the early years, his practice grew slowly, as he added an office here and a location there. Two years after he founded Access Health Care, Dr. Singh gathered his leadership team together for a meeting. When they all were assembled, he shared with them his vision for their practice. He shared from his heart about how he wanted the organization to aspire to five-star quality scores, empowered patients, near–100 percent patient satisfaction and operational efficiency, and better health outcomes. But when Dr. Singh told his leadership team his defined vision for the practice, how many people on the team do you think agreed with him?

The answer? Not one. Not a single person on the team he had assembled to run the healthcare company he had founded was interested in his vision for Access.

"So then we argued, we wrestled with one another, we went back and forth, back and forth, and we never really could agree," he says now, reflecting back on that time.

The leadership's overall vision remained a point of contention for years, and in that time Dr. Singh gave up on trying to articulate a vision for the company—because his team always seemed resistant.

For a while he even thought it might not be necessary to have an overall vision. After all, the practice was growing. But he felt like they could grow faster and deliver even higher quality, so he made the decision to bring in an outside coach to facilitate a strategic-planning retreat for his leadership team.

"Let's talk about where we want to take Access Health Care," said the coach, addressing the fifteen-person leadership team that had assembled for the planning session. "What are your thoughts?" Notice that the coach didn't start by asking Dr. Singh for his vision; instead, he started out by asking Dr. Singh's team for their input. "Where do you think we should take Access? What kind of future for the company excites you? What big goals do you think we should set for the practice?" he asked each person in turn.

Some members of the leadership team started sharing their ideas. One person said she thought that every office should be a patient-centered medical home. It was a lofty goal, and one that would require a great deal of work. Dr. Singh was surprised—not that this member of his team held such a high goal for the company, but rather that she appeared to be saying the same thing he'd been saying all along. Turning every office into a patient-centered medical home would mean excellent patient engagement, good communication, high-quality care, and evidence-based medicine. It was everything that Dr. Singh had wanted, though the team member was voicing it in her own words.

Other team members chimed in, sharing in their own words what they felt was important, and as they did, a picture began to emerge of a patient-centered practice that provided an exceptional quality of care. They went further and laid out the specific credentials they wanted to earn from their regulatory body, and one team member even said, "I would like for us to hit five stars this year." Dr. Singh looked on, amazed. Here was his team, saying what he had tried so hard to get them to accept all along.

Their coach continued to guide the team on topics of utilization management, IT, digital strategy, inventory—everything. One by one, everyone's specialty was brought up and addressed, and everybody had their goals. By the end, they had put it all together into one comprehensive plan. Now they had something that was everybody's vision; everyone was a stakeholder, and everyone knew what they wanted the company to be.

The process didn't end there. Quarter by quarter, their coach was in contact with each leader about the particular aspect of the plan that he or she owned. He emailed the chief quality officer to inquire about quality scores. He checked in with the appropriate person about the company's patient-centered medical home designation. And as they moved forward, everyone was kept current on everyone else's progress because it moved them toward their joint goals. If there was a failure in reaching a goal, then everyone knew the cause. It was openly shared and addressed, because everyone was a stakeholder.

The energy at Access changed. Suddenly, everyone made concerted efforts to help one another, and they all were focused on shared success because they considered themselves owners of a collective vision. It wasn't some vision handed down from on high, but rather an emergent vision that they had a real voice in articulating.

It was at that first coaching meeting that Dr. Singh gleaned his single most important lesson about leading his organization. It's a lesson that has been crucial for much of his success since then. In his words,

> "If it's top down, [your vision for the company] won't work. It's got to be bottom up. Everyone on the team needs to have ownership."

On that single day, the company went from having one person in the top leadership role to fifteen people devoting themselves to formulating an ambitious vision. Over the next decade, Dr. Singh and his team scaled Access Health Care into a $168 million medical group with one hundred and fifty locations across the state of Florida and over one thousand employees. ♦

From the outside, it is clear that what his team wanted was a real role in articulating the vision of the company. They didn't need to have it their way, but they did need to have their viewpoints solicited, heard, and valued. This is what your team wants, too. Giving your team a real voice means that you ask for their help and meaningful participation in this work of growing the organization. It means asking them for their thoughts, ideas, and feedback. And it means listening to their answers and giving their ideas real consideration. Whether or not you agree with their ideas or perspectives doesn't matter; the central theme is that you must give them respect and a seat at the table.

Through this approach, you'll gain a much deeper buy-in and commitment level from team members, no matter the ultimate vision and strategic plan you collectively agree on for the company. **Remember, to crush it in the Value Economy, you don't just need your team members' hands to do the work; you need their heads and hearts, too. This isn't soft "make people feel good" goo; it's a hardcore business best practice.** Having coauthored a book with Dr. Singh and keynoted a number of conferences with him, I've talked with his team—from the doctors who work there to the executives who lead departments.[8] His team not only is engaged; they are committed to the business and its mission. Their staff retention and team member engagement are something most CEOs can only dream of.

A Simple Pattern to Give Your Team a Voice

Here is a winning pattern to pull ideas from your team and begin the process of engaging each member.

First, pick an area of your company to work with, such as your marketing team, leadership team, or operations group. Ask the group to decide on one of the biggest limiting factors that holds the company back in this area. Notice I didn't ask you to get the perfect answer, just one of the limiting factors. We want to set your team up to succeed, so if they agree on a limiting factor that you know to be important, but not the most important, accept their answer for the moment.

Next, lead your team through a Sweet Spot Analysis (see chapter three), where they ultimately pick one or two ideas to push back this limiting factor. Clarify the plan and steps to implement each of their chosen Sweet Spot solutions, including who owns each step and by when it will be completed. Agree on how your team will report back to each other on how implementation of these ideas is going. Will they give updates on their Big Rock Reports? Or perhaps make this an agenda item for a follow-up meeting in thirty days?

Then, make sure you—as a leader in the organization—model the behavior you want to encourage them to show. Check in with key team members. Celebrate victories and help to overcome obstacles. Along the way, at strategic moments, help your team gather insights and lessons. When the ideas they chose are solidly in place, repeat the process on the next limiting factor or key opportunity to seize. Perhaps on this next time through, you will let another team member lead the process from start to finish.

But, David, you may say, *that's too much work. I don't have the time to do that. Why can't I just tell people what to do? Or sell them on my ideas?* Well, let me ask you, do you have the time to replace your best team members? This includes the time to recruit and onboard a replacement player while dealing with all the disruption to the organization in the several months this process will take. Can your company afford to let your team drift, giving their best work to activities outside of your business that they feel are more personally gratifying? Plus, are you really too busy to do this? Remember, this isn't about you personally producing more; it's about you leading your team to be more engaged so they produce at their best. It's amazing how small moves like this can compound. Giving your team a real voice takes time. But in the end, it accelerates your pace to reaching your company goals.

If giving your team a voice is so productive, why don't more business leaders do just this? In my experience, it boils down to two things: fear and inertia. Fear of losing control; fear that no one will do it as well as you or care as much as you; fear of not feeling important or not being needed. And the status quo that lulls so many business leaders into simply perpetuating today how they behaved yesterday. But if your real goal is to grow your business as fast as possible, sustainably, then you need to get past these fears and break free of your inertia, because they are traps that hurt your company and limit you.

"I WAS WORKING AN AVERAGE of eighty hours or more each week," said Patrice, co-founder and CEO of a large professional education company, hosting over one hundred continuing education conferences each year in North America and Europe for ten thousand primary care physicians. The business was thriving, but Patrice still felt uncomfortable stepping out of the day-to-day. She felt compelled to work long hours, well past the point when the business really needed her to do this.

> "My husband and I did take vacation time, but we did conference calls, worked on content development for future conferences, and handled staff issues when away. If I were being honest about it, our vacations were more like working remotely. Sure, the locations were pretty, but the fact that we still felt so tied to the business really pointed out a flaw in how we were growing the company. The biggest thing holding our company back was ourselves."

I remember talking with Patrice at a business conference my company hosts each year in Maui, and as we sat and ate lunch together, I challenged her on the real cost of holding on so tightly in her business. From the outside looking in, it was clear that Patrice and her husband, Rob, had done the hardest work to build a great business that profitably delivered real value to the market. They had built a solid leadership team, so why not give this team a bigger voice and role in the growth of the company?

Something about that conversation stayed with Patrice, and she and her husband made the concrete decision to engage their team, leaning more heavily on them and trusting them to own more in the business. Initially, this was uncomfortable for Patrice. She was used to jumping in and solving problems. In her heart was a desire to help and serve, but what she came to see more clearly was that her old way of leading her team had stunted their growth, and the company's, too.

Patrice started with a small, handpicked group of her key leaders. Slowly, over the course of twelve months, Patrice grew her ability to intentionally let her key team take on and own more—more of the decisions, more of the problem solving, and more of the responsibility for key outcomes in the business. At the same time, she and her leadership team clarified what information and safeguards needed to be formalized so that Patrice could feel that the business was well cared for, which reinforced her willingness to let go of even more direct control of the business's daily operations.

None of this happened overnight. There were plenty of moments when Patrice caught herself jumping in with answers instead of first asking her team for their observations and insights. Building an empowered organization takes time and requires deep buy-in from key team members that cascades down over time. As her leadership team felt Patrice's trust in them to generate ideas, make decisions, and solve problems, they stepped up to own more functional responsibilities in the company.

In the second year of this process, this feeling carried over to how her leadership team in turn led their subordinates. That's when things really started to click. When her core team's colleagues saw how engaged and effective they were being, they broadened this system of engagement to include more teams, then divisions, until, a little less than two years later, the whole company was engaged in building the company. They also got more strategic about which parts of the business to invest in more and which parts to step away from. The end result was a business that was more profitable, more sustainable, and more enjoyable to own.

"We now work twenty to thirty hours a week, enjoy eight weeks of real vacation each year, and earn far more income," says Patrice.

In fact, the more Patrice and Rob have stepped away from the day-to-day business and empowered their team, the stronger and more profitable the company has become. ♦

Too many businesses never tap into even a fraction of the true talents of their team members. What a catastrophic loss—one that their leaders may never even understand. But not your business. Make sure you engage your team in building your company with you. No longer will it be you driving them forward. Instead, you'll get their help in doing it *together*.

Make Your Mission Real

FACTS Engineering is a highly specialized manufacturing firm that makes control devices for other manufacturers. Founder Ron McVety, an electrical engineer in St. Petersburg, Florida, initially launched the company out of his garage, but over the past quarter-century, Ron and his team have grown the business into a market leader in its niche. From the very start, Ron set out on a mission: to make automation easy and affordable. Today his company makes three hundred different products, serving multiple industries.

When I first began working with Ron in 2015, he and his COO, Rick, had built a solid team, but they still were the glue that held it all together. They were the only ones with all the pieces. They were used to doing everything themselves, carrying all the institutional knowledge about customers and strategy in their heads and doling out information on a need-to-know basis. Processes were fragmented, and department leaders often wasted time with overlapping efforts. Business was good, but it could have been better. There was a sense of isolation and lack of trust among members of the leadership team that heightened stress and hurt the company's performance.

"When we were a smaller company, [we] could get away with running things ourselves," Rick shared. "Back then we had our finger on the pulse of pretty much everything. But now we're ten times larger, with more products, overseas manufacturing partners, and without realizing it, our old ways of running things were holding the company back."

Rick and Ron held a series of company-wide meetings, taking the entire company, in waves, through an intensive multiday training program. The program challenged people to see themselves, each other, and the company in new ways. Old resentments were dissolved, leaving the entire team with less stress and a clear sense of purpose. Then Ron backed up that start by investing in the ongoing coaching and development of his entire leadership team. Each month we worked with that leadership team, and quarterly we stepped off-site for a day to objectively review progress and plan out the coming quarter. Ron's team pushed the formula throughout the organization, getting individual departments to create their one-page Action Plans and redesigning their work weeks so that all key team members had six or more hours a week of uninterrupted focus time in one- to two-hour blocks spaced throughout the week.

Today the entire company understands FACTS's mission, what's going on in each department, and how their individual Big Rocks fit into the overall picture. This improved connection to the mission of the company helps team members feel part of the larger story. When the company wins an industry reward, the team feels a sense of pride and ownership.

One direct result of this connection to the larger narrative is how it pulls out the best in their entire team. For example, two years ago, FACTS began work on their new line of control boards—the P1000. This new product line was a massive breakthrough, akin to the new iPhone of their industry. They had set an aggressive target date of September 2017 to introduce the P1000 to the world, which was a year earlier than they originally believed they could finish the product.

Because the entire company understood the importance of this new product line and how it fit into the longer-term vision of the company, the team moved heaven and earth to accomplish this goal. The quality team invented a new test-fixture process that sped up the testing of parts. Then they created a batch-testing sampling process to speed up testing even further while reducing costs. The production team figured out a streamlined packaging system to again speed up the process and reduce costs. Furthermore, the entire leadership team volunteered to spend an intensive ten-day period in Taiwan with their key suppliers there to find ways to speed up the development cycle and ensure they met their aggressive launch date.

In the end, every department proactively found ways to shave days, weeks, and dollars as they collectively chased the company's ambitious goal. And on October 3, 2017, three days late but essentially a year early, they launched the line.

> "Not only did we learn technical solutions to problems we had to overcome, but more importantly, our leadership team really matured in this process," Ron shared. "This experience cemented for me, and for our team, how much we could accomplish when the full team was behind something. Today, our profits are higher than ever, but the real reward out of this experience has been to see the team become more confident and engaged than at any time since we launched the company thirty years ago."

Growing your company is hard work, and to do it you need the talents, insights, and creativity of your team. And the fuel that fires the best of what's in people is meaning. Meaning drives emotion. Emotion drives behavior.

Leaders create the narrative through which all stakeholders interpret the business and their relationship to it. It's your job to help your entire team make the direct connection between what they do and the value your company creates in the world. Why is it that you are even in business at all? Try to look beneath the obvious answers like, "We make analog control units for manufacturers" to the more emotionally compelling and broader reason you are in business: "We make automation easy and affordable." It's your job as a leader to find creative ways to consistently connect what your team does to this deeper mission.

Here's how I've done it with Maui Mastermind. Yes, we're the premier business coaching company in North America for owner-run businesses with annual revenue between $1 million and $50 million. But what we really do is help business owners fall in love with their companies again—for the lives their businesses impact, the value they create, the people they employ, the profits they earn, and the freedom they enjoy. That's why our leadership team works hard to continuously share stories of our clients' successes inside our company. It's important that each of our team members understand that they are not just updating a website, organizing a conference, making a sales call, or paying our vendors. Instead, each of them, in a very real way, is helping a business owner who used to feel trapped in a "good" business grow faster and increase their company's strategic depth so that everyone on their team benefits.

On Monday morning conference call huddles, we'll often ask a few of our coaches to share a client success story. On monthly company-wide web meetings, we invite a different client to attend and share his or her story of how working together in the coaching program helped them succeed and touched their lives and the lives of their employees and their families. At quarterly live events, we harvest stories of the impact of the program on the lives of our clients and their respective teams.

The attention we invest in capturing and sharing stories of how collectively our team has touched the lives of thousands of clients and their employees helps our team connect its work with our mission. And in a very real way, we all know that helping our clients has directly and indirectly improved hundreds of thousands of lives. It's likely one of the greatest forms of service we each will have in the world outside of raising and loving our families.

YOUR TURN: What is the deeper mission that your company is engaged in? What is it that you *really* do for your customers? Have you effectively shared this message with your team? Do each of your team members understand how what they personally do each day connects to this deeper purpose? It's your job to help your team make this all-important connection.

Share the Formula with Your Team

Are you ready to fully engage your team? Go back to the four steps of the Freedom Formula discussed in part one of this book. Only this time, intentionally travel through all four steps in lockstep with your team.

Work with your team to collectively break your organizational chains about what the givens are for how you work and where your time and attention really go. Challenge the status quo and create an opening that there just may be a better way of doing things as an organization, a way that would allow each member of your team to do their best work and still have a life. Where filler and low-value work come last, and you collectively take a good, long, hard look at the influences and limiting beliefs that have been driving behavior in your organization. Discuss what it could mean for them if you were to confront the limiting beliefs that your organization has absorbed without even realizing it. How would this transformation impact your team members? Their families? Your customers? Your suppliers and vendors? And how would all of this feel for them? Would it be worthwhile to attempt? Notice that at this point you are not trying to convince and persuade; rather, you are trying to introduce some new possibilities and create a doorway to take the next step.

Once you've created an opening, drive the wedge deeper by helping your team members individually reclaim even just a few hours a week of their best time and attention. Support this seemingly simple step by structurally building in a Focus Day for each of your key team members. Even if it's only one two-hour block every Tuesday, that reclaimed block of their best time each week gives them a taste of what they can accomplish with uninterrupted focus time. Coach your team to build their own Time Value Matrix so everyone understands what their A-, B-, C-, and D-value activities are. Encourage them to block out a focus block at least an hour long each Push Day. And agree on some simple ways you can support one another in protecting the vacuum of your focus time so that you more ably use it for your A- and B-level activities. A big part of this is to have the hard conversations about expectations and your culture of communication inside your company.

Once you start gaining some momentum on consistently creating focus time, get more strategic and discerning about what you invest that time into doing. Involve your key staff in the creation of your team's quarterly one-page Action Plan. Coach your key team members to create and use their own one-page Action Plans. Start using the weekly Big Rock Report to connect your Action Plans to your week, and cheer one another on as you execute on your rolling ninety-day plans of action.

Finally, sustain the change by building the systems and internal controls that formalize your processes and procedures, allowing your team to consistently get great results in specific functions with less time, energy, and attention. Get serious about cross-training your team and growing your people so you have greater depth. Intentionally craft your culture so that your new and improved way of working together becomes part of the new givens in your company.

The bottom line is that if you want to go faster, you've got to engage the full buy-in and support of your team. Your team—their talents, best abilities, creativity, and energies—is the fuel that rockets your company forward faster.

In the next chapter, I'll share one superpower that will best help you develop your team. I'll guide you in exactly how to develop and deploy this superpower to create breakthrough business results.

CHAPTER 6

Accelerator Two:
Become a Better Coach

If the first half of this book was about how you personally can use the core formula to create more value for your company and career, then this last half is about how you can leverage your team to go faster. One of the most powerful tools at your disposal is for you to become a better coach to your team. You may not always have a lot of control over who is on your team, but you do have full control over how you work with them to help them perform at their best. And it's here that we all have something important to learn from the world of professional sports.

In that high-stakes, high-pressure world, managing talent can mean *billions* of dollars. The top ten professional sports leagues in the world generate over $45 billion of revenue each year.[9] Top sports franchises like the Dallas Cowboys (NFL) or Manchester United (English Premier League) are each valued at over $4 billion. Then there are the players themselves. The average NFL player earns $2.1 million,[10] with the five highest-paid players averaging $48.8 million for the 2018 season.[11] In the English Premier League, the average player earned $3.5 million in 2017,[12] with the five highest-paid players earning an average of $19.7 million for the season.[13] And this is just their salaries. With so much riding on the results of these players, teams collectively spend hundreds of millions more on facilities, medical care, support staff, and coaching. It's therefore easy to understand why franchises pay top coaches so much. For the 2017–18 season, the top ten NFL coaches earned an estimated average of $8 million.[14] That same year, the ten highest-paid English Premier League coaches earned an average of $9.7 million.[15]

Top coaches live and die by their ability to achieve concrete results through growing, grooming, and leading their teams. Great coaches find ways to harmonize and align. They draw out the best performance possible from their players—over a season and even a playing career. Likewise, your ability to speed up the Freedom Formula relies in large part on your success coaching your key team members to be active contributors toward your collective goals.

My first taste of great coaching came in 1986 when Australian native Ric Purser became head coach of the US Men's National Field Hockey Team. Recruited from Victoria, Australia, Ric moved to the United States to take over a struggling national team program. He was a former star center forward who had been coaching for thirty years. He worked with me and a generation of junior national team players in the United States, developing us into competitive international athletes. It was quite a ride. After Ric retired from coaching, I had other coaches, both when playing for the United States National Team and for the years I played semiprofessionally for foreign club teams. I've experienced firsthand the transforming influence of great coaching, both on me individually and on the teams I played for and against. I watched weaker teams blossom under great coaching, and I winced when top teams I played on wilted under poor coaching. My hockey years were quite an education in how the right coach could develop and draw out the best collective performances from his or her team.

When injury ended my playing career in 1995, before what would have been my first Olympic Games, I shifted into coaching, becoming an assistant coach at Ohio State University. During my years playing internationally, I also had to support myself, and I'd done this by coaching, both men's and women's teams. I knew nothing about how to recruit athletes to a Division I program, organizing the complicated logistics of a playing season, or guiding student athletes through their years at college. But I did know how to coach hockey.

At the time I joined the Ohio State coaching staff, the team was coming off another losing season, and the next season's prospects looked even worse, with nine of the starting eleven players being freshman or sophomores. As an assistant, I was tasked by then head coach Karen Weaver to work individually with each of the student athletes to increase their skills and performance on the field. My first year with the team, we blew away expectations and enjoyed one of the strongest seasons in the team's history, including a top ten NCAA Division I national ranking. The next year, my last with the team, we again enjoyed another winning season and a top twenty national ranking.

For the past two decades, as I've collaborated with business owners and their top executives, helping them scale and mature their companies, I've worked to transfer my coaching skills from sports to business. I've watched our clients blossom with great coaching, and their companies enjoy an average annual growth rate five times higher than the average privately held US company. **When it comes to making your company grow and mature faster, becoming a better coach to your team is one of the most powerful skills you can cultivate and employ.**

In this chapter, I'll share with you the bottom line of what my combined career as an athlete and coach—and entrepreneur and business coach—has taught me about being an effective coach. I'll give you the solid foundation you need to bring out the best in your team. Let's start by getting clear on your top responsibilities as a coach.

The Four Coaching Responsibilities

You have four main responsibilities as a coach.

#1. Recruit Great Talent

One of any coach's most important jobs is to gather together great players. While the subject goes beyond the scope of this book, I do want to share with you the one commonality shared by great business leaders who've taken talent seriously: they spent a lifetime building a deep bench of relationships they could tap to bring talent to their team.

Avoid the careless attitude that the talent hunt is something to engage in only when you have a specific job opening to fill, or, worse, as something the HR department is responsible for handling without your purposeful collaboration. Instead, constantly be on the lookout for great talent wherever you go, and keep careful notes on who the top players are or one day may be. Work to cultivate ongoing relationships that later can lead to important hires. Recruiting expert Geoff Smart, author of the *New York Times* bestseller *Who*, shared this with me:

> "Top CEOs and corporate leaders all know that the best way to find A-players is through their relationships. They constantly are asking people in their network who they should meet and get to know as potential future A-player hires. They do this over their career, not in the two months before they need to fill a key position. In fact, in our comprehensive studies on hiring best practices, 77 percent of the industry leaders we interviewed said they sourced their best hires through referrals from their personal network. The best ones work to build a rich web of relationships to tap into to source talent."

The next time you go to an industry trade show, either traveling or working with vendors or suppliers, keep your talent antennae up. When you find someone you see is extraordinary at what they do, find ways to keep in touch with them and begin building a real relationship. This could be sending them a handwritten card, reaching out to them by phone, or even inviting them out to a meal from time to time to reconnect. Even if you never hire a single one of these people, all of them are potential talent scouts, whom you can tap to help you find other talented A-players.

#2. Get the Best from Who You Have

Of course you'd like to gather a team of superstars, but let's be real for a moment—you may not have the luxury of time or budget to recruit a full roster of experienced, highly skilled top performers in your industry. Even if you did, it would take years to gather and integrate this team. Which is why one of your core responsibilities as a coach is to get the most from your current set of players.

Great coaches put their players into the right roles and task them with clear responsibilities. They somehow balance the egos of their "stars" in such a way that these players lift the team, versus dragging other people down. And they consistently get great performances out of a medley of solid, but hardly startling, players.

YOUR TURN: Pause for a moment and consider your team. Are you currently positioning your players for the greatest collective performance? Do you have any team members whom you've shifted into a role that actually limits their contribution? Have you let lower-value work and nonproductive demands steal your best producers' time and attention? How could you make a few course corrections with how you deploy and protect your team so that you create more value from your current roster of players?

#3. Develop Your Talent and Build Depth

The difference between having a great season and building a successful, long-term program lies in developing the individual team members you have, especially your less-seasoned members who have the potential to be future stars.

How do you help your employees grow professionally, build skills, and acquire a rich experience set to bring to new situations and novel challenges? Great coaches help their players identify specific skills and the progressions to master those skills. They give team members exposure to learning projects and progressively greater responsibilities, along with the feedback to use these experiences to develop.

But more than just working one-to-one with their key direct reports, great coaches also build a winning program. That program is made up of a cross-trained team, sound business systems, and vibrant company culture—aka the three legs of the strategic depth stool discussed in chapter four. These three elements combine to environmentally shape your team over time in a way you never could person by person.

#4. Have an Uncompromising Core

The final responsibility of a coach is to stand for something. While flexibility and creativity help you find fresh ways to deploy your team and healthfully absorb and leverage change, the best coaches all have an unchanging core—an approach or vision of how the game should be played—to which they hold firm.

For Steve Jobs, it was design. He wanted to build extraordinary products, which meant they had to be elegant, beautiful in both form and function.

For Bill Gates, it was his obsession with absorbing the best of the best of other software products. Rarely were Gates and Microsoft first, rarely were they initially best, but over time, their relentless learning, iteration, and refinement repeatedly made them the best, especially with their integrated suite of business applications. There is a reason 1.2 billion people use Microsoft Office, and that reason started with Gates's commitment to his core.

With my business coaching company, my uncompromising core says we must eat our own cooking. If we truly are going to be the best business coaching program in the world, then we need to leverage our own methodology and structure. We must be a product of our own program. That point of view has led to over a decade of double-digit growth for us and a client success rate that is the envy of our industry.

YOUR TURN: What is your uncompromising core? The place at your business's center where you won't compromise? It's your job as a leader to plant this flag and relentlessly, stubbornly, and creatively hold your team to it.

The Mechanics of Coaching a Key Team Member

Coaching takes time. It's a deep investment. To do it well, and to handle all the other responsibilities your company tasks you with, requires you to narrow your focus to the few people you will invest more into. Over time, you'll gain more momentum and move faster as you task the people you coach with coaching and cultivating a small group of people to grow themselves.* Start small, perhaps identifying just three key players you will invest your limited time and attention in developing. Use some focused time to brainstorm how you see each of these key people growing, both within your organization and perhaps—gulp—even beyond it. What are their strengths, and how can you better leverage them to reach the company goals? What are their weaknesses, and are these things that they can outgrow, or should you as a leader find ways to "coach around" any potential drawbacks via the roles you assign and supporting players you give them? What experiences could you supply that would best help them and your organization?

Talk with each person individually about how they see themselves and their career. While you may see them a certain way, do they agree? Does how they see themselves align with your outside perspective? If not, what can you both learn from this incongruity? What matters most to them, both personally and professionally? What gives them joy and brings them rich satisfaction at work? **The best coaches help their players find a role that optimizes their individual contributions and inspires them to feel part of something bigger than themselves. They coach their players to find**

---

* I'll specifically address developing your leadership team in chapter seven, "Grow Your Leaders."

the right balance between performance today and growth for even greater capability and contribution tomorrow.

If you have ever had a boss you loved working for, it's likely that he or she took the time to know you and set you up to succeed within the organization. This is precisely what great coaches do for their players.

Be sure to meet regularly with each of your key players, biweekly or monthly, for a formal coaching session. While you'll likely have many other interactions with them, these regular sessions push you both to invest the time, attention, and energy to help them develop and get the results you've tasked them with. If you're meeting with them biweekly, then thirty minutes is plenty of time. If you're meeting with them monthly, set aside forty-five minutes to an hour.

How to Structure Formal Coaching Sessions

Having a consistent structure makes it easier to coach your key team members and increases the impact of those sessions. Here's a proven format for these coaching conversations.

#1. Get an update.

Begin every coaching conversation by asking your employee for updates on the one or two most important projects they have been working on since you last talked. I encourage you to get all of your direct reports using the Big Rock Report discussed in chapter three. Not only will this give you context for what they are working on, it also will give you insights into what they see as their priorities, victories, and challenges.

If you are receiving a weekly Big Rock Report from them, rather than just asking for a generic update at the start of your coaching session, be prepared with a few comments or questions based on what they shared since you last met. For example, you might say, "I read on your Big Rock Report that you met with your team to redesign the staff scheduling process. How did that go?" Or, "I was really happy to see that your team hit the deadline for submitting our bid on the Rockwell project. I know you had a really tight time frame on that. Were you pleased with the way things went? How did you cel-ebrate the milestone with your team?"

If you don't have a Big Rock Report or its equivalent from your employee, ask him or her to give a rough three- to five-minute update at the start of your meeting. While they give you that update, be sure to take notes. In addition to getting a quick context, these first few minutes offer you a chance to create accountability, both for past commitments they have made and for future items you want to cap-ture and follow up on later. It also gives you an opportunity to spot and celebrate progress. It's been my observation that many business leaders struggle with helping their team see and *feel* the progress they are making. The best coaches know that focusing on progress not only motivates your team to stay the course, it also reinforces the behaviors you want to see more of. By contrast, if you focus on their failures, you'll actually be reinforcing that wrong behavior. If you've ever been river rafting, you'll know what I mean.

Before we had kids, my wife, Heather, and I used to go white-water kayaking. One of the principles we learned early on was that when you're going down a rapid, don't look at the rock you're try-ing to avoid. When you look at it, without even being aware, you often reposition your body in such a way that you'll end up steering directly toward the rock. Instead, you should keep your eyes focused on where you want to go.

That might seem counterintuitive; you might think that if you want to avoid the rock, you need to keep your eyes on it. But I can tell you from experience—keep your eyes on the rock, and you hit the rock. So in business, as in running a river, focus on where you want to go and the behavior you want to see from your staff.

#2. Lay out and stick to an agenda.

Yes, you need an agenda for each coaching session. Top coaches know that to maximize their limited coaching time, they need a concrete plan for every minute of practice. What are the key two or three things that you'd like to focus on during the coaching session?

Tell the team member what items you have on the agenda and why, and then invite them to add their own items. Ask, "Is there anything else that you want to make sure we cover today?" If they bring anything up, be sure to cover it, either during this session or at a later time you set to specifically discuss it.

I want to caution you to restrict yourself to no more than three items. If you give your employee seventeen different things to work on, it's going to be overwhelming. Great coaches focus at any one time on a few coaching points, but they make sure that these coaching points matter. Less is more in this scenario. Stick with the one, two, or three pieces of guidance that will make the biggest impact.

#3. Review key deliverables.

Presumably, in previous coaching conversations, your employee promised certain deliverables. Now is the time to close the accountability loop and check in on progress. It's important that you not rely on your memory to track what your direct reports' ongoing projects are. If you're busy running a company, there's a good chance you'll lose track of what individual employees are supposed to report back on, so write that down. Top coaches know how chaotic and fast moving life can be and keep careful notes on all their most important athletes, logging their progress and capturing ideas to help them develop faster and perform better. Personally, I keep a journal with tabbed pages for each of my five main direct reports that I'm currently coaching within my company. Many of my coaching clients prefer to use cloud-based apps, but I still like the physicality of pen and paper. The key is to decide on the tool you'll use and go all in on using it. Detailed notes allow you to get specific. The more specific you are, the more effective your coaching will be.

#4. Determine next steps.

Formally identify any key action steps that you'd like this team member to report on next time you meet. Also, you'll want to schedule your next coaching session.

Be sure to consider each of your key team members individually when setting meeting frequencies. Remember that different employees thrive with different levels of coaching. For an employee with a high level of autonomy and big demands on her schedule, you may choose to do a formal check-in just once a month. By contrast, an employee who has less experience or struggles with accountability might make more progress with shorter check-ins weekly or biweekly.

#5. Send a meeting recap.

After the coaching session ends, your employee should send a quick recap of what you agreed to during your meeting: who promised what, by when, and how they will close the loop. Closing the loop usually involves notifying the other person when a project is complete. Be specific about how that notification will happen—via email or a project management tool, in person, or in the next coaching session.

Notice I said your employee should own this recap, not you. Why? Two reasons. First, you are busy. You have enough pressure and obligations as it is. Delegating the workload frees up your time. Second, you can establish an important feedback loop to make sure that your team member understood the action steps that you discussed. If something's missing or misunderstood in the recap, you can spot the miscommunication immediately and quickly clear things up. That said, you still should keep your own recap notes for future reference.

Your employee should send the recap out as soon as possible, ideally within half an hour after the coaching session ends. The sooner they write the recap, the clearer the communication will be. Requiring a rapid recap also reinforces the importance of accountability, showing how serious you are about execution and following through on promised deliverables. Ask them to schedule in five to ten minutes to do the recap right after you meet.

If you follow these five steps, your coaching sessions will become measurably more productive. You will reinforce desirable behavior, develop clearer communication with team members, and see better follow-through on commitments made. In the long term, this process will help you grow your key team members and accelerate your team's progress toward important goals.

Ask, Don't Tell

One of the biggest coaching mistakes is to think that the coach's role is simply to tell her team what to do. The best coaches grow their players, and the best way to do this is by giving them progressively increasing challenges. Great coaches let their players struggle right on the threshold between what they confidently know how to do and the next stage of what they want to grow into. It's on this capability frontier that the biggest gains and growth occur.

Yes, it is faster and easier to just tell an employee what they need to do, but that doesn't lead to rich growth. In fact, over time, autocratically telling your team what to do and how to do it diminishes their capabilities. Your goal isn't to groom a team of glorified gofers whom you direct in detail. This sends the message that you just want their hands, not their minds, and certainly not their hearts.

When you ask questions that help elicit insights and action steps from your team, they grow. They also own the next step, since it was their idea, and this ownership pulls the best from them. Furthermore, this scenario enhances their capability as it demands more from them than merely following instructions.

When a team member comes to you with a challenge or problem, restrain your reflexive response, which is to give them "the" answer. Instead, let them own solving their own challenges:

OWNERSHIP QUESTION: What do you think we should do here?

Ask the reason for their initial response. If sensible to do, challenge them to go deeper:

PROBING QUESTIONS: What do you think is really at cause with this problem? What do you see as most vital about any potential solution to this challenge? What do you think are the most important variables to keep clearly in mind as you solve this? What would you do if you couldn't do your initial suggestion? Why? In what ways is this solution superior to your first initial answer? How might this be a worse answer?

If sensible, push them for additional answers. Finally, encourage your team member to integrate their thinking by asking:

OWNERSHIP QUESTION: Considering all you've just shared about the situation, what do you think we should do now?

Often, it's the synthesis of two or more of their answers that yields the best results, and what they really need from you isn't an answer or even an ear, but rather a prompting to fully consider all aspects of their problem. Think of this as a "steel sharpens steel" conversation, in which your role is not to give them answers, or even to have the answer, but to help them think through the situation fully and find their own path forward.

Drip, Don't Drown

I remember when, years ago, my wife and I had a new home built for us. The house was lovely, and when we moved in the landscapers put in new trees and shrubbery. They were very clear that each day we needed to water the roots of our new landscaping so that the plants would take hold. "Make sure to give them just the right amount of water," they told us. "Too little, and the roots won't grow deep; too much, and you'll wash away the topsoil because the earth only can absorb so much water at a given time."

It strikes me that our employees are a lot like those new trees and soil. If we water them with feedback too infrequently, they'll wither from lack of attention. But if we try to shower too much feedback and input on them at any one time, we'll overwhelm them and they may shut down. One of the key elements of being a great coach to your staff is to time your feedback. The best advice I have for you is to drip input; don't drown your team at any one time.

I see this mistake all the time. Business leaders want to help, and they have so many great ideas and suggestions—sometimes coupled with a compulsion to share them all in one sitting with their employees. I remember one CEO I coached who was a sponge for new ideas. He read multiple books every month, listened to podcasts, and had a mind that just never shut down. When I first began working with him, I watched him overwhelm his leadership team with dozens of "brilliant" ideas every quarter, but with little depth or follow-through. His staff's reaction to being swamped by the volume of suggestions and changes he wanted them to make was to wait him out. They nodded their heads but never seemed to act on the ideas he shared. They knew that the new ideas he had today would be replaced by other ideas the next week or month. So, they gave lip-service nods of agreement, and then ignored his input.

One of the first things I worked with him to do was to see the impact of flooding his team with ideas and input, and the adverse impact it had on the company's performance. Then together, we filtered his ideas down to the very best one or two to share with his team. He learned to give his team a real voice in how to implement these filtered best ideas effectively. Once he had a key idea in motion, his next assignment was to make sure he didn't wash away the soil by flooding his team with more ideas; rather, he learned to keep coming back to these Fewer, Better ideas and support his team on executing them. Eventually, he recognized that one idea they implemented exceptionally well was a magnitude more valuable then skimming the surface of hundreds of ideas that never took root. Over the past three years, his company has enjoyed the greatest years of growth in its history, tripling operating profit.

Frankly, this was one of the hardest lessons for me to learn as an entrepreneur myself. My mind always raced with ideas. I wanted to help my staff and add value to the company, so I jumped in and frequently flooded my staff with too much input all at one time. The older I've gotten, and the more entrepreneurs and CEOs we've coached, the more I've come to realize that less is more. I now filter my coaching suggestions and input to just the most essential one or two coaching comments at that time. I'll capture the ideas I don't share for a later time, but most I never share. I've learned that one or two coaching insights that get real buy-in and rigorous execution are worth hundreds of casual coaching comments I could have made. And you know what? My company and the businesses we coach are thriving. By every metric of effectiveness we track, we've seen that sharing a smaller number of essential coaching touches, dripped out over time, yields a far greater return than a deluge of input in one sitting. You will enhance and develop your players to make the biggest gains and enjoy the greatest growth, not by giving them more, but by focusing on just a few things at a time, and making sure each of these few things matters more.

YOUR TURN: How are you getting your team to perform better? Do you give them small, highly specific coaching suggestions that your players can consume in one bite, and then find creative ways to keep reinforcing these most important fundamentals in fresh ways? **Your real goal isn't to feel smart; it's for your players to absorb, integrate, and own the very most important ideas for themselves.**

Gentle Pressure Applied *Relentlessly*

While you may not be able to get an employee to buy into an idea initially or to absorb and apply a key suggestion, gentle pressure consistently applied over time can work miracles.

I WAS COACHING THE OWNER of a small regional chain of retail stores. The owner shared with me that because they carried such a wide selection and varied product mix, it took the company an average of three years before a new sales associate was fully trained. Later in the coaching conversation, it became clear that one of the biggest limiting factors for the company was finding and retaining strong sales associates.

When you're coaching experienced, highly capable people, many times your most important coaching impact comes by helping them challenge some of their accepted givens that no longer serve them. With this business owner, the given that was holding her back was the accepted belief that it took three years to fully train a new retail sales associate. Challenging closely held beliefs is delicate work, and often in these situations the best coaching strategy is to inject doubt or the seed of an alternate possibility, and to allow that seed to grow at your player's own pace. You'll nurture the seed by drip, drip, dripping attention on it over time, all the while being careful not to push too hard.

One of my early exchanges with the owner went something like this:

> COACH TO RETAIL CHAIN OWNER: I know that in the past it's taken you three years to train a new sales associate. But based on what I've seen in other companies and industries, I'm sure you could do it faster. Play out a thought experiment with me for a moment. How could you get a sales associate fully trained and selling effectively in 180 days or less?
>
> OWNER'S INITIAL REACTION: Impossible. We can't do that. We've tried everything to shorten that cycle. It just can't be done.
>
> COACH: Okay, I get that it just can't be done; at least, you haven't come up with a viable way—yet—to do it. Let's set that aside for the moment. May I just ask you, if there *was* a way to make this happen, what would the impact be on your company?
>
> OWNER: It would be huge. It would take so much stress off the system, and we could sell so much more.

This owner went on for a minute, listing off all the benefits to the company if they could figure that out. She then ended with, "But it just isn't possible."

COACH: Okay, right now you haven't figured it out. Will you do something for me? Just play with the idea, let it be a seed in the back of your mind, and when you least expect it and you have a flash insight, write it down and share it with me, okay? I'll bring it up again in a few months—would that be okay with you?

Two months and four coaching sessions later, when I brought the idea up again, I was met with an implacable wall: "Impossible." Again, I didn't try to brute-force the wall.

COACH : I get it. The timing for the solution isn't just yet. Keep stewing on it. I'm sure you'll get an insight about how it might be done at some point. I'll check back in with you on it down the road, okay?

Finally, five months later, when I asked her about it, I got a very different answer:

OWNER: I've been doing some deep analysis. It turns out that 80 percent of our revenues and profit come from roughly 20 percent of the products we carry. In fact, 10 percent of our products account for over 70 percent of our profit. That got me to thinking, what if we simplified our product mix and eliminated as much as 40 to 50 percent of what we've historically carried that we just don't sell much of. After all, we still could order these things if customers asked for them, but by getting them off the showroom floor, not only would we free up a lot of cash that has been tied up in inventory, but it would cut our training time for new sales associates substantially . . .

Together we laid out a pathway to shrink the products the chain carried, standardize the "custom" packages they designed for customers, and modernize their training process—all with the goal of shortening the learning time for a new sales associate from three years to under 180 days. When they finally implemented the changes over the next several months, they found something interesting: they were able to reduce the training time to get a new sales associate fully ramped up and effectively selling to less than 120 days! ◆

Great coaches drip, drip, drip on their players until eventually key seeds that were planted months prior take hold and break through the surface and into bloom.

There is one more thing that "drip, don't drown" also means: drip your celebrations into the daily, weekly, and monthly rhythm of your organization, rather than making them just a once-a-year event. One of your core jobs as a leader is to be a catalyst to bring out the best in your team. Well, any team wants to feel they're making positive progress toward their key objectives. Your job is to help them see this progress. This isn't just about motivation and engagement, it's about helping to focus your team on the things that are working and that you want to see more of. Whether you highlight victories at your next staff meeting or send out a team update biweekly, or just congratulate an individual performer as you're walking through the office, the best leaders train themselves to spot the behaviors and progress they want to see more of. It is a powerful leadership habit to form.

"Liked Bests" and "Next Times"

Have you ever received feedback that just didn't help? I'm guessing it was generic, abstract, and infrequent. Contrast this with a time you got important feedback that made a true impact on helping you improve and get a key result. I'm guessing that this powerful feedback was specific, concrete, and timely.

Part of your job coaching your team is to model for them how to give feedback and gain insights from your week, month, and quarter. Here is a simple tool one of my business coaches shared with me twenty-five years ago when I was just starting out as an entrepreneur. It has made a huge difference for me in growing multiple companies, and I've shared it with thousands of business leaders over the past decade. It's called Liked Bests and Next Times.

Whenever you need to debrief—whenever you're looking for feedback or insight—ask yourself two questions. What did you like best about the project, performance, or activity? For example, we recently hosted a two-day conference for business leaders about how to increase profitability. After the event, I wrote in my journal on my flight home my Liked Bests for the event.

I Liked Best . . .

- How my staff promoted the event, resulting in one of our largest events to date.
- How the check-in team was so prepared and got all of the attendees into the ballroom and into their seats for an on-time start.
- The three live interviews we did with coaching clients who agreed to share their personal experiences of what has worked best for them in applying the ideas from the event.
- The social we hosted at a local English pub.
- The private one-to-one coaching sessions my staff arranged so that first-time conference participants could talk with one of our staff members about how to best apply what they learned at the event to grow their companies . . .

The second question to ask is, "What would I do differently next time?" You aren't asking, "What went wrong?" or "What did I screw up?" Instead, you're asking, "What did I learn? What insights did I gain? And how specifically will I apply them next time to get an even better result?"

Positive framing is a crucial part of this tool. My Next Times list for this conference was relatively short:

Next Time . . .

- Create a short, pre-event briefing video that attendees can watch to prime themselves to have even better insights from the event.
- Have an attractively printed post-conference summary checklist of key concepts participants can take back to their companies with them.

Imagine you were part of the team that put on the event. How would you feel after hearing a long list of the things your boss had noticed you did that went exceptionally well? Would you be more or less likely to repeat these good things in future? And how receptive would you be when your boss then shared just a few concrete Next Times? This pattern of capturing Liked Bests and sharing just a few specific Next Times is incredibly effective. One added benefit of doing this consistently with your team is that you're subtly modeling for them how to debrief their own projects and performance so that they take an active role in their own growth.

YOUR TURN: Pick a recent project you or your team worked on. What did you like best about how you or your team performed? What worked well? What specifically would you want to do differently next time? When you go to share these with your team, don't just tell them your thoughts; first ask them what they liked best about how the project went. What one or two specific Next Times do they have for themselves? After hearing their ideas, share yours. Some even may overlap, helping you appreciate where your thinking is aligned.

See how simple this is? It doesn't require a cumbersome debriefing document, just two questions. What are our Liked Bests? What will we do differently Next Time?

Here's a useful tip when using Liked Bests and Next Times. You'll likely be tempted to share too many Next Times—be careful about this. As with new ideas, one Next Time that actually gets implemented is infinitely more valuable than a hundred Next Times that go undone. You can see how really long lists of Next Times tend to do more harm than good: they're overwhelming, they create a sense of failure, and they're impractical to implement. In other words: Drip, don't drown.

When you need to have a tough talk with someone, do it right away. I call this having an "adult conversation." There will be times in your business life when a staff member behaves in a way that simply must be addressed. They'll send an inappropriate email or say something harsh to another team member or vendor.

When a situation arises that must be dealt with, don't delay. Yes, it may be prudent to gather your thoughts, let emotions cool, and even to get input from someone else yourself, but you need to deal with the situation in a timely fashion. I've watched too many business leaders stick their heads in the sand and wait for things to blow over. This can kill the spirit of your team because—trust me—everyone is watching to see how you as a leader handle the situation. Do you let principles or personalities rule? Does your best self step up and talk professionally and clearly, or does the frightened part of you cause you to duck the situation altogether? Or does your reactive self explode and say harsh things in an unprofessional manner?

When the time comes for an adult conversation, remember these three guidelines. First, adult conversations should be held in private. You may want a third party there, but you wouldn't want to have it out in the middle of your place of business. Second, focus on behaviors, needs, and expectations, not on blame, justification, or punishment. Third, have your adult conversation after the initial emotions have cooled and heads are clear, but don't wait so long that it feels like the matter wasn't addressed in a timely fashion.

Coaching for Development Versus for Results

A key distinction that will help you be a more effective coach is to ask yourself, "Am I coaching this person for results, or am I coaching them for development?"

When coaching for *results*, your emphasis is on current performance. Results coaching tends to be shorter, with a clear focus on accountability for key action steps, deliverables, and performance metrics. If the team member runs into trouble, you tend to give him your best input on how to deal with the situation rather than let him struggle and perhaps generate a suboptimal result.

Coaching for *development* emphasizes the growth of the employee and developing the capabilities and experience set that enhance future performance. These coaching sessions tend to be longer, with more time given to help the employee struggle through and reach her own conclusions.

Both kinds of coaching sessions matter. It's just important to get clear on what type of coaching you want to emphasize with a particular team member or in a specific situation. I've mentioned Theresa Watson, whom I hired over a decade ago as a remote admin when she lived in Dallas. Quickly it became clear that she was astute, accountable, and hungry to learn. Less than two years later, she took on a bigger role for my company in operations. Three years after that, she was leading operations. Today, as mentioned, Theresa is our company's COO. What a loss it would have been to our company if we only had coached Theresa to perform her first role. Instead, when we spotted her talent, we made the intentional decision to develop her skills over time. We looked for experiences she would require to grow, and we matched her up with one of our best coaches, Patty, who worked with her one-to-one for several years. We consistently pushed Theresa into business situations that were progressively just on the edge of her abilities, and coached her through the struggle as she figured out her own path. Initial situations included how to handle sharing bad news with a client. Later they included how to negotiate on mid-level vendor contracts. In the past few years, they have been more about how to hold a department of the company accountable and coach that department's leader to get a great result themselves.

YOUR TURN: Make a list: Who are the team members in your company for whom you are responsible to coach for current results? Who are the team members for whom you are responsible to grow and develop? With this clear understanding, what do you like best about how you currently are coaching your team? What one or two specific things will you do differently going forward based on this new insight?

The Capability Spectrum

You've likely seen it: an employee who was thrown into the deep end of a situation without the skills or experiences to handle it. Perhaps his boss didn't want to micromanage; perhaps his boss was just so busy that she felt she didn't have a choice; or perhaps his boss just never gave it any thought.

The next time you are ready to delegate a responsibility to a staff member, first pause for thirty seconds to ask yourself this powerful question: On a scale from 1 to 10, how capable is this team member with this specific task or responsibility?

If your team member—let's call her Maria—has never done this before or has very few skills or experiences in this area, score her low, perhaps a 1, 2, or 3. If she has done it many times and has a deep reservoir of experience in this area to draw from, you'd likely score her an 8, 9, or 10.

How would you delegate to Maria if her capability score for a specific function was a 3? Would you let her just go do it herself? Of course not. Ideally, you'd walk her through it or perhaps have her shadow you or another experienced team member through the process. Then, as her capability score climbed to a 5 or 6, and if the stakes were survivable, you'd let her try things out herself, with a safety net under her. If Maria's score was an 8, you'd merely make a clean handoff to her and let her own the task or responsibility herself, closing the accountability loop through your normal processes, perhaps with a quick email, note on the project management tool, or bullet point on her Big Rock Report.

Not only does identifying where Maria's skill set stands on the capability spectrum help you know how best to delegate to her, it also helps you predict her response to how you manage her on this task or responsibility. If you manage her closely and give clear directions about how to do each step, and even stand next to her and watch her do key steps, her reaction will be predictable. If Maria's score is a 2 on the spectrum, she'll view this as great management. Wow, you really gave her the support and coaching to help her succeed. If Maria's score is a 9 on the spectrum, she'll resent your micromanagement and likely start looking for another boss who respects her abilities.

It's too easy to just shoot off an email or assign a responsibility during a meeting without even a moment's thought about the capability of the recipient in relationship to that specific deliverable or responsibility. If you're not sure where their skills fall on the Capability Spectrum relative to a specific task, ask them: "On a scale from 1 to 10, how confident do you feel about handling this specific task or project?"

As I've shared, I've got three kids: Adam, Matthew, and Joshua. In my struggles to be a better parent, one thing I've come to understand is that treating all my kids the same is not only unfair, but also just plain dumb. Each of my kids has different needs. **The best coaches don't treat their players equally. They treat them *equitably*. They tailor their coaching to pull the best performance from each player.** You need to meet your employees where they are at and adjust your style to help them and your company generate the best collective outcome possible. By pausing briefly to determine where your team member's skills are on the spectrum, you'll more effectively be able to adjust your management approach for the best result and relationship with that team member. You will be setting your team up to succeed.

BONUS TIP

Learn How to Be a Great Coach by Hiring a Coach Yourself

If you want to become a better coach for your team, hire a great coach for yourself. A business coach is an experienced entrepreneur or executive who's been where you want to go and can give you the outside perspective and counsel to build a more successful business—without having to go through all the painful trial and error yourself. Just as a coach does for a sports team, a business coach's role is to help you focus, plan, execute, learn, and regroup so that you make consistent progress toward your most important business goals.

Too many business leaders build their companies in isolation, lacking the outside perspective and feedback from an experienced coach. What's more, they don't have anyone in their business lives to challenge their thinking and to question their assumptions. Sure, you may have lots of subordinates, but it's asking a lot for a subordinate who depends on you for his or her family's financial support to really challenge you with the things you don't want to hear, but desperately need to hear. As star CEO Jack Welch put it,

> "Good coaches provide a truly important service. They tell you the truth when no one else will."

Besides modeling to your team your willingness and personal commitment to grow professionally, engaging a coach for yourself will shorten your learning curve to becoming a better coach yourself.

THE TIME AND EFFORT ECONOMY SAYS: You can figure it out for yourself. You don't have the time or budget to waste. Given a little trial and error you can make your own way forward.

THE VALUE ECONOMY SAYS: Leverage outside expertise. Model proven coaching patterns that work. Hack the system and go straight to the things that work best.

Here are my top tips to get the most out of your business coach.

- **Pick a coach who has a deep experience set and knowledge base to draw on.** The whole idea of leveraging a business coach is to help you avoid a lot of the expensive trial and error that many business leaders endure. While many of the situations you come up against in your business (be they about managing your team, growing your sales, creating your next products or services, or controlling your expenses) may be new to you, your coach can draw on his or her past experiences, plus the relevant experiences of all the companies they've coached before, to clarify the best path forward.

- **Pick a coach who can articulate and explain things to you in simple, step-by-step language so that you can integrate what the coach shares and put it to immediate and effective use.**

- **Meet frequently with your business coach—but not *too* often.** Every two weeks is optimal: often enough that you get effective accountability (monthly generally is not often enough for this), but not so often that you have no time to get things done.

- **Share your performance numbers—candidly.** Yes, it can be scary to share your KPIs, revenue, gross margin, and operating profit figures with complete candor, but by being open you will get valuable outside perspective and feedback. Don't sugarcoat *anything*. Your coach won't judge you. Her real desire is to help you grow and succeed, and to do that, she needs accurate data.

- **Don't just focus on one-off challenges—look for systematic, global solutions.** Solving a challenge is great, but solving a challenge in a way that improves your team's strategic depth is even more valuable.

- **A coach is more than a mentor.** Mentors are great resources to help you grow, but mentoring tends to be an informal, ad hoc relationship. There is something different when you work with a coach. The relationship is more formalized, with clear accountability and deliverables both ways. A coach is responsible for crafting a progressive plan to help you reach defined goals, whereas a mentor is a great sounding board in which you, the mentee, are responsible for driving the relationship. Ideally, you'll have both: a coach for structured work and accountability, and numerous mentors who can share ideas and contacts

to help you progress. Just don't think one replaces the other—
it doesn't.

- **Pick a program, not just a coach.** You want and need more
  than just a great coach; you want a solid, proven coaching *program*. The best coaches have a formal process that has been
  designed and validated to help you reach a specific result. It's
  been my observation that a structured program, rigorously
  adhered to, will yield you far greater results than working with
  a business star who merely says he'll be your coach. Remember,
  structure plus talent almost always outperforms isolated talent. In effect, the right coaching program makes sure that your
  coach balances both you and your company's immediate day-
  to-day operational needs with your longer-term development
  goals. If your coach just helps you deal with your current challenges but doesn't give you a clear map to mature both yourself
  and your company, then any progress you enjoy will be brittle
  at best.
- **Give your business coach permission to hold you accountable.** The right business coach always will be in your corner, and sometimes this means being the one person in your
  business life who calls you out. Your employees can't fully do
  this, because you control their paychecks and professional
  advancement.
- **Don't rationalize or explain away reality—even if you win
  the discussion, reality will still win the war.** I smile when I
  think about all the exceptionally smart and articulate business leaders I've coached over the years who, at one point or
  another, thought they could explain away a challenge or situation with a well-rehearsed argument. Reality is what reality is,
  and the objective facts are the objective facts. Your coach will
  help you cut through your own rationalizations and fantasy
  thinking, helping you take full responsibility and accept the
  objective facts on the ground. And from this place, together
  you can come up with an effective plan of action to harness
  those facts to reach your business goals.
- **Let down your ego and accept your business coach's help
  and insights.** You don't have to posture or look good. Your

coach has seen just about everything you are dealing with and has worked through it. Let your coach save you time, energy, emotion, and money by helping you learn from his or her experiences, versus painful and expensive trial and error.

- **Consider leveraging outside coaching for your top leaders, too.** According to a 2015 survey conducted by PricewaterhouseCoopers with over 15,000 respondents from 137 countries, the average return on each dollar invested in coaching was seven times the initial investment.[16] Given the impact your key people have throughout your company, consider strategically using outside coaching.

Coaching key players is a key leverage point to help you advance in the Value Economy, but you'll be limited if your team has only you as the sole coach. You simply don't have the time or attention span to be the only leader. To help your team go further and faster, you need to learn to grow other leaders in your organization who will in turn coach their direct reports for the greatest contribution and impact. In the next chapter, I'll share my best ideas on how you effectively can grow other leaders who will truly own their functional areas of responsibility, which in turn will radically accelerate your company's success.

CHAPTER 7

Accelerator Three: Grow Your Leaders

IN THE UNITED STATES, the world of residential contracting continues to be a disjointed vertical filled by hundreds of thousands of small companies with no clearly dominant market giant. In this world, John Gwaltney and Bryan Miller, the owners of Outback Deck, are a rarity. They have managed to blast right through the million-dollar revenue mark, which caps over 90 percent of these small contractors, and are steep into their scaling curve. But it wasn't always that way.

Initially, Outback Deck was one of several service lines that John and Bryan operated in their contracting company, Virtus Family. Outback offered decks, porches, and patio additions, and their other divisions offered general contracting, remodeling, and renovation services. Collectively, the family of companies was stuck at $3.5 million in revenue, with John and Bryan doing all they could personally to push the company to the next level.

This is when my team first began coaching them. Initially, we focused on the four core steps of the formula. We helped John and Bryan get consistent control over a portion of their best A- and B-time; schedule their Focus Days and set aside a focus block on their Push Days; and apply the four D's to offload or diminish their D-level work in which they'd been drowning.

When they got their heads out of the raging river of emails and fires that used to be their world, we next determined exactly what were the Fewer, Better for their company and roles. Turns out that their various divisions were not created equally. A simple analysis revealed that their Outback Deck service line and brand was their clear winner. It had the best margins, deepest competitive moat, and most promising future. They could be just another general contractor, or they could be the premier company in their region for the outdoor living-area niche (aka decks, porches, and patios). They chose to go all in with outdoor living, and what a difference this has made. The year before we began working together, they were profitable, but the trend line was that even though they had increased sales by 12 percent, their operating profit margin had *declined* by 26 percent. Part of this was caused by the wrong mix of service lines (i.e., decks vs. remodels), but another part resulted from the overwhelm John and Bryan felt as they were pulled in so many directions leading their company. The growth they had enjoyed was actually like giving oxygen to a fire; it caused the flames to flare, and the operating environment in their business was tense and stressful. After John and Bryan got clear on their Fewer, Better, it became much easier to focus their company and staff on a smaller span of projects and initiatives, each of which had a much higher return.

"Our coach actually wrote up our first quarterly Action Plan for us," Bryan shared. "It felt like magic. 'Wait a minute,' we said. 'Are you telling us that we don't need to do 247 different things this quarter? That all we need to do is focus our best discretionary time on these three Focus Areas?' It was liberating. The next quarter, while our coach gave us counsel and accountability, John and I created our own one-page Action Plan. In the past, when we had done planning, we came up with complicated, long documents that still were fuzzy and hard to implement, let alone share with our team."

And share with their team they did. By the third quarter, John and Bryan were bringing key staff to their quarterly offsite retreats, giving their team a clear voice and vision for what they wanted to do.

Their team stepped up and began taking the lead on building the internal systems and structure to operate the core of their business better, so that John and Bryan could focus more of their personal time on growth—where they could contribute some of their highest value to the company. With the four steps of the formula running well, John and Bryan began looking for ways to speed up their engine and grow the company even faster. This is when they started growing other *leaders*, not just delegating to functional managers.

The combination of their stronger core and the sharing of the leadership roles in their company has accelerated Outback Decks to escape velocity. Each successive year we've worked together has witnessed a new high for them. This was made possible because John and Bryan didn't merely produce more. They didn't just delegate tasks and responsibilities. They tapped into real ownership and the creative energies of their team by growing other leaders within their company. No longer was it just the John and Bryan Show. Their leadership team had stepped into the spotlight and shined. ♦

The third freedom accelerator is to groom and develop a real leadership team of capable, empowered peers. Building your leadership team draws on Accelerator One—Engage Your Team—as it requires you to give your leaders a real voice and help them connect to the deeper mission of your work. It taps into the skill set of Accelerator Two—Become a Better Coach—using the techniques great coaches employ to help shape behavior and develop players over time. Accelerator Three builds on One and Two, helping you break through the limitation of your own personal leadership attention by developing other leaders who are independent voices championing the growth of your company.

Let's be clear: I'm not talking about just turning more over to your managers; rather, I'm talking about grooming real leaders. What's the difference between a manager and a leader? Managers organize, delegate, explain, and hold accountable. Managers get *today's* work done well. Leaders empower others to fully own a functional area of responsibility. They build *tomorrow's* capabilities by developing, grooming, and inspiring. Managers implement on defined objectives; leaders wrestle with and decide on those objectives and the strategy to accomplish them.

Manage better; incremental growth is likely. Lead better; compounded growth is virtually assured.

The Time and Effort Economy counts on managers who get things done by personally putting in long hours and getting their employees to do the same. The Value Economy, on the other hand, requires leaders who not only get their employees to focus on the right things, but also those who groom a successive generation of company leaders.

In 1956, researcher George Miller published a paper in *Psychological Review*. The paper, which since has become one of the most highly cited articles on the limitations of working memory, shared what Miller called the "magical number seven, plus or minus two."[17] Essentially, human beings have a storage limitation of only seven items of information in working memory, plus or minus two, at any given time. Any more than that, and you behave just like a modern parent, trying to carry in all the stuff your kids left behind in your car: you pick up a bundle, but when you reach your capacity and try to pick up that last jacket, you drop your son's shoe. When you bend over to pick up the shoe, you drop your daughter's lunchbox. Ultimately, if you're anything at all like me, after a minute or two of comical dancing, you'll resign yourself to making two trips.

As human beings, we deal with attentional limits the same way: we "attention shift," or move things in and out of our working memory, just like the overloaded and frustrated parent does when carting in his or her kids' stuff from the car. Attention shifting is cognitively demanding, and as the parent does, we often drop things in the transitions. When it comes to leading your company, if you're overloaded with too many things at once, you make choices, intentionally or otherwise, of what you will leave on the ground and what you will carry on this trip inside the house. Not only is this ineffi-cient, but each trip increases the odds that you'll drop something. Plus, it's *exhausting*.

I'm sure you've experienced a day when you had to handle what seemed like a hundred different decisions and were overwhelmed by details. You went home drained. If this were to continue for a longer period—say, your career at a job—you'd never be able to do your best work. The design of that environment would be suboptimal. Trying to brute-force your working memory by consciously trying to be more efficient at multitasking—which is really nothing more than rapid micro-switching between activities or focuses—is still Time and Effort Economy thinking. Even at its best, your gains will be limited.

To accelerate the growth of your organization and fuel the results you want to achieve, you need the talent, creativity, and best attention of a cadre of leaders. Each of your key leaders becomes an extension of what your company really can accomplish when it invests its best attention on those things that matter most. For example, John and Bryan wanted to put their best attention on growing sales. Before they could do that, they needed to grow their structures and staff inside of their operations so that the leaders they empowered to run that part of their company could do great work.

The Four-Letter Word That Traps You in Endless Days of Doing, Doing, Doing

If twenty-plus years coaching business leaders has taught me any-thing, it's that John and Bryan's behavior before they began working with Maui is the norm, not the outlier. The overwhelming majority of business leaders pay lip service to the importance of empowering oth-ers. So why do so many of these bright and otherwise capable leaders get stuck with everything on their plate? It's simple—F-E-A-R.

In chapter one, I shared with you how many business leaders fear the loss of control that comes with truly handing off functional ownership of a business area to someone else. "After all," they say, "I've tried this before, and it didn't work." So, rather than look at the *way* they handed off to their subordinate or the *way* they undercut or failed to support their subordinate after the handoff, they simply declare, "This doesn't work."

These leaders fear that their team might make a mistake. They fear that their team won't be able to handle some nuanced variable on a job. They fear the feeling of not being needed by their team, of feeling unimportant. They even fear the uncomfortable feeling of not having direct control over a person or activity. And this fear behavior causes many business leaders to hang on too tightly. They delegate, but they do it poorly. They either hand off with strings attached— "Do this step, but then come back and I'll make the decision about what to do next"—or they simply dump and run.

I know this firsthand. I used to do these behaviors for over a decade until a team member of mine, Stephen, confronted me about it: "David, you say you want people to feel empowered, but we all know that when you hand us something, you don't want us to do it our way; you want us to do it your way. So, we've all learned just to wait until you tell us exactly how you want it. If you ask us to take a shot at it, we just go through the motions. Why should we bother coming up with fresh ideas or putting our best work into it when we know that no matter how we do it, you're going to correct us to do it the way you wanted from the start?"

It took a lot of courage for Stephen to take me to task like this, and it was eye-opening. He was absolutely right. So, I started to hand off by dumping the task on someone else's lap and not looking back. I found it so hard to manage my own fear of losing control that my strategy to manage my personal anxiety was just not even to look at it once I handed it off. But this meant I wasn't taking into consideration my team member's capability level at this specific responsibility.

Clearly, both of these behaviors were horrible ways to lead an organization, and both were driven by fear. It cost my company millions; it cost my team frustration, dissatisfaction, and lost growth opportunities for over a decade; and it cost me hours and hours of my best time as I was trapped doing the work that my team, with better leadership, was more than capable of handling.

Understand this: The compulsion for control can be one of the biggest chains that traps you in endless days of doing, doing, doing.

BRIAN ANDERSON, OWNER AND CEO of Hostek.com, a server management company founded in 1998, described controlitis this way:

> "For fifteen *years* I worked sixteen to eighteen hours a day, seven days a week. Looking back, I don't know how I did it. I just felt like if I wasn't there managing sales, support, and operations, things would just fall apart. It was me and a small team of helpers whom I had to manage closely."

Over the past seven years that my team has coached Brian, he has implemented the formula, and the process just worked, with Hostek enjoying seven straight years of double-digit growth. What I want to highlight, though, is the impact of growing your leaders inside your company. During one particularly intense stretch in 2017, Hostek opened up two new data centers, one on the East Coast of the United States in April, and the other in Europe in October. But now, because Brian had built a team of other leaders who owned areas of the business from technical support and operations to sales and systems engineering, Brian was able to focus his best time during this same six-month period on the acquisition of a UK hosting and server management company. In fact, his team was so strong by this point, that the day after Brian closed on the purchase of the UK company in November 2017, he and his wife, Dayna, enjoyed a week-long European vacation, with Brian's team handling the initial integration while he was gone.

"If you would have tried to tell me back during our start-up years that I'd ever find people who cared as much as I did about the business or who were as capable as I was in doing things for the business, I would have told you it wasn't possible. What I've come to learn is that not only can I find people who care as much as I do, but they are more capable than I am in their areas of specialization. For example, our operations manager, Jeremy, is far better than I am at running our company day-to-day. He makes better decisions, has better follow-through, and gets more from the team than I ever could. If I could go back to that younger me back in the early 2000s, I'd tell him that the only way to enjoy the growth I wanted for the business and to have a rich personal life was to learn to stop trying to manage it all myself. Hire and grow great people to lead areas of the business, and give them room to be great." ♦

One of the most important questions you can ask yourself is, "Am I growing this person to own this functional area of responsibility, or am I merely delegating a task for someone else to carry out my plan?" You want leaders who are intimately involved with setting goals and creating their own plans to execute them. While you'll need to ensure that the goals they set fit into the larger business context, rather than merely delegating tasks, strive to give your leaders autonomy and agency. This is heady stuff to a competent team member, and it affirms your trust and respect in their abilities.

The same holds true with letting your leaders help design the accountability structure that they will use to self-monitor their results and be accountable to you. In chapter five, we talked about the importance of giving your team a real voice; this need is even more critical when it comes to growing real leaders inside your organization. You empower your leaders by giving them clear objectives and defined expectations. As long as they are performing well and playing within mutually agreed-upon boundaries, let them lead. Ask them how you can support their success. Flip the script so you find out from them how you best can help them build on their successes. Let them direct your help. Over time, you'll see them replicate this process with their team members.

The "ask, don't tell" skill discussed in chapter six becomes critically important when it comes to you growing other leaders. How you handle things when your leaders come to you for help is the critical moment that either pushes them back to being a doer you must closely manage or empowers them to step up and own the responsibility. Do you rush in and immediately offer "the" solution to the problem, or do you help them come to their own best conclusions by asking questions?

As I shared, this was a hard lesson for me to accept. When I was being domineering in how I delegated, I felt I was serving my team and adding value to their lives. What I came to realize was that I was pushing my future leaders back into their old, comfortable roles because I liked the feeling of having the answers. It made me feel important. It made me feel safe because, not surprisingly, I liked my answers and ideas best of all. Of course I did. They were mine!

A couple years after Stephen confronted me on my behavior, one of my business mentors, Stephanie, gave me the missing ingredient I needed to fully change my behavior. She asked me to write down a single question on a 3-by-5-inch index card and display it prominently on my desk. She instructed me to pause and review the question anytime one of my team members came to me for help. This single question was the seed for helping me break free of my compulsion to control. The question was this:

I don't know; what do you think we should do here?

So simple, and yet so profound. Still, I struggled with it for about two more years before I broke my old habit and began to use this question as my default. Before that, I was the know-it-all who might have had confident answers, but just never saw the way my jumping in undercut the initiative and ownership of my leadership team. I learned that my desire to have the right answer and save the day was one of the biggest limiting factors stunting my company's growth.

YOUR TURN: The next time one of your team members brings you a problem, pause and ask the preceding question. Let that question remind you to push your leaders to grow to solve their own problems. You're there to support them and help them both broaden and sharpen their thinking—not simply to give them the answers. **When the leaders you are coaching wrestle with the ideas and struggle with the decision, they grow.**

What do you do if you think their solution is way off base? You simply coach them to find a better solution. Ask solution-oriented questions: "Why is it you think this is the right solution? What do you think is the real cause of this situation? What do you think matters most about this situation? Does your initial idea for how to handle this really solve that core issue? How does X [the variable they are not seeing] factor into this decision? If you couldn't do this, then what would you do?" Not only does this tactic help your team member develop as a business person and leader, but you are role-modeling an important leadership pattern. You'll be amazed one day to overhear Ming coaching her direct report Carlos through the same process to solve his own problem, just like you once upon a time did for Ming.

Does this take more time? Of course. Is this less emotionally satisfying for you? Perhaps initially. But is it more emotionally rewarding for your staff? Yes. Is it more effective in growing other leaders who take the initiative and are fully bought-in to execute on their ideas? You better believe it. Letting your leaders own their own answers not only helps them grow faster but also deepens their commitment to the answers. In essence, what you're doing is turning real-world situations into incredibly robust learning opportunities.

Here's the best part: Leading this way is not only better for your company, it's easier! Talk about a Value Economy win-win—better for your organization, easier for you. Now you get to focus on your own areas of maximum value generation for the business instead of rushing around trying to do everyone else's job. Meanwhile, your highly skilled leaders are proactively looking for potential trouble spots before they flare into fires. They are finding ways to seize opportunities and shift resources to accomplish the bigger-picture goals of your business.

Create a Development Plan for Your Key Leaders

Accelerator Three can lift a company, department, or team to the next level.

You've already identified the key people you want to coach. Here is a coaching pattern that I've found to be incredibly effective in helping to develop your leaders quarter by quarter. For example, imagine you chose your VP of Marketing, Lettie, as one of the leaders you want to grow. What do you imagine Lettie's role with the company might look like twelve months down the road? Thirty-six months from now? What are the most expensive gaps in her capabilities that would hurt or even stop her from contributing maximally over the next twelve to thirty-six months? These gaps could be skills where she is currently weak, or experience sets she lacks, or even behavioral patterns that hold her back.

After you've brainstormed this list, pick what you consider to be the two or three most valuable choices for her to work on in the coming twelve months. For example, you might observe that while Lettie is very good at navigating tense vendor and team issues when emotions get hot, she too often finesses conversations where being more direct about boundaries, behaviors, and expectations would serve her and the company better. So, your list of potential growth areas for Lettie might include, "Growing your ability to have direct, nonfinessed conversations with internal and external team members, especially early in a project when you are setting expectations and defining boundaries." When Lettie gets better at this skill, she will have greater flexibility to match her approach to the situation and players.

Using the Action Plan format from chapter three, ask Lettie to come up with a simple, one-page plan for how she will grow herself in this specific area over the next ninety days. Ask her to start with her criteria of success for this period. What would it look like at the end of ninety days if she successfully improved in this specific area? Ask her to detail her action steps for how to accomplish this. With Action Plan in hand, make sure you regularly check in with her about her progress on her plan during formal biweekly or monthly coaching sessions. Celebrate victories. Add one or two select coaching suggestions if appropriate. At the end of the quarter, repeat the process for the following quarter. This simple process will help Lettie grow, and it also will be a great opportunity for you to grow your coaching skills.

"Can't Do; Won't Do; Don't Know How"

Here is one more powerful tool to help you work with your leaders. A good friend of mine who built a regional chain of convenience stores with $80 million in revenue shared it with me four years ago. It's called Can't Do; Won't Do; Don't Know How.

- **Can't Do:** This is a skill or activity that this particular team member simply isn't suited for. No amount of training or ongoing coaching is going to overcome this deficit. Your best choice is to see if you can shift or adjust his role to leverage this person's strengths and make his glaring deficit irrelevant to his role.

    For example, one of my coaching clients has an incredibly talented operations leader named Bill, who is smart, innovative, reliable, and proactive. You give him a spreadsheet, and he'll make the numbers dance. Give him an impossible logistics problem, and he'll find an innovative and profitable way to solve it. But Bill is simply tone deaf when it comes to empathizing with other people. Had to go to your great aunt's funeral yesterday? All Bill wants to know is did you finish up your project list before you left for the memorial service.

You can coach Bill to avoid some of the glaring social gaffes from his lack of emotional intelligence, but he simply shouldn't be in a role where social skills and empathy matter most. By selecting the right role for Bill and supporting him with team members whose abilities complement his own, my coaching client is able to leverage the best of Bill to run his internal operations.

- **Won't Do:** This implies that the person is capable of doing the activity or responsibility, but for whatever internal reason, this person simply doesn't do it. Assuming you've had a clear, adult conversation with this person, generally a Won't Do team member needs to work for another company, the sooner the better.
- **Don't Know How:** This is when you have a willing team member who simply lacks the skills or experience set to handle a specific task or responsibility. This person needs training and support to learn how to succeed at this specific function.

Can't Do; Won't Do; Don't Know How gives you a conceptual model to better interpret team member behavior. It's an especially powerful tool to share with fledgling leaders you are grooming, because many of them lack the leadership experience that you've internalized over your years of business.

Great Leaders Raise the Accountability Bar

You know that the most effective form of leadership is by example. Great businesses are built on teams that take full ownership of individual responsibilities. If you want to raise the accountability bar throughout your company, here are seven time-tested tips on your role in doing just that:

- **Be on time, all the time.** Being on time is a simple behavior that symbolizes to your team that you take your commitments seriously and live with integrity. It is one behavior with a huge return on investment in terms of modeling accountability inside your company. Too many companies implement respect in a hierarchical manner. Your time is *not* more important than a subordinate or a customer's time in their eyes. Being on time shows respect, and it makes a big difference to the receiver. Of course, you can rationalize why you didn't meet a stated deadline and no one will challenge you, but they will model the behavior you show them. So, model the highest standard.
- **Clarify your commitments in writing at the end of every meeting.** One of the biggest reasons things get missed is because they weren't handed off cleanly to begin with. Many times the receiving party doesn't know exactly what they've been asked to do, or in fact may not know that they've been asked to do something at all. Not only does a written follow-up ensure that you've captured all your action items, it's also a powerful way to role-model how you want your team to behave. Wherever possible, number the commitments so that they are absolutely clear. Also, guide your team to employ this same skill with their staff. Companies that successfully execute use this best practice.
- **"Close" the accountability loop.** It's one thing to meet your commitments, but it's another to make sure that the other parties involved realize that you've done so. So, consistently close the loop.
- **Clearly state what you can't commit to so that you don't lower the accountability bar in your company by missing a "phantom deliverable."** These are things that the other person *thinks* you committed to, but you didn't. As a leader, you need to exhibit great communication by making explicit any phantom deliverables you see come out of a meeting. That way, if you can commit to that deliverable, you do so, and if you can't, you clarify that you are not committing to it.

- **How you own your failures is as important as how you model your successes.** You're human and you *will* mess up. To think otherwise is not realistic. How you own your missed deliverables is incredibly important to the culture you are building. Do you make excuses? Sweep them under the rug? Melodramatically beat yourself up? Don't! Instead, show your team how mistakes are a part of being in business and often can lead to profitable insights. When you make a mistake, publicly take responsibility, share what you learned and how you'll apply it, and implement a better solution going forward.
- **Most breakdowns in accountability come from incomplete or poor handoffs.** At the moment any deliverable is created, it needs to be assigned to someone who will be responsible for seeing that it is completed. I call this assignment a "hand-off." As a leader, you need to ensure that every handoff clearly details who is responsible for what, by when; what success in meeting that deliverable will look like; and how he or she will be held accountable for that deliverable.
- **Be aware of your stress behaviors.** It's been said that adversity and pressure don't so much make the person as reveal the person. What you do at stressful moments leaves a magnified impression on your team, your customers, your vendors, and your investors. Let stress be a trigger for you to take a deep breath and behave at your best.

Building your leadership team is an investment that takes time, but, done well, it is richly worthwhile. It helps you retain your best people by giving them the opportunity to grow professionally. It helps your company by maximizing their contribution to the business. And it helps you blow past the expensive attentional limitations of personally trying to be the sole leader in your area of the company. This is why it is such a powerful accelerator to help you stay in the Value Economy and accomplish more with less time and personal effort.

BONUS TIP

Leadership Growth Self-Check

Here is a quick self-quiz you can use to gauge how you're doing as a leader. Be ruthlessly honest in answering these five questions. Let your insights help you accelerate your ongoing growth as a business leader and the success you enjoy.

1. In general, are you doing fewer things each week, with the few that you do mattering a whole lot more to the company?

   Hint: Do you get that you aren't the best person to do everything and, instead, have you narrowed your focus to those limited few activities that let you contribute your best value to the company? Remind yourself as often as needed that a frenzy of chaotic activity is not the hallmark of a great business leader—rather, it is a symptom of an immature one.

2. Does your team have more strategic depth today than it had last quarter?

3. Are you growing your next generation of leaders to be strong, capable business leaders for your company?

4. Do you regularly ask your team, "What do you think we should do?" instead of just reactively solving their problems and doing their work for them?

5. Do you find yourself regularly frustrated by your team's inability to "get it" over time?

   Hint: Meaning that they get the strategy, the business context, the culture, and the company priorities that you're trying to share with them. If most of your team isn't "getting it," then you have to own that the one commonality with the whole team is *you.* How can you change your approach? What hasn't been working in the past and what else can you try? What small things had some positive impact that you can build on?

The bottom line is that when you grow other leaders, you accelerate the growth and strengthen the foundation upon which your company is scaling. Each leader becomes a seed of future growth, and this growth accelerates as they in turn grow other leaders.

In the next chapter we'll look at the invisible hand that shapes behavior when there is no one looking or when there is no literal system or training for how to handle a situation.

CHAPTER 8

Accelerator Four:
Cultivate Your Culture

You now are well acquainted with the four-step formula for focusing your company's best time, talent, attention, and resources on your Fewer, Better. You have a clear understanding that the right kind of growth comes from value created, not from hours logged. Together we've explored ways for you to speed up the process by engaging and coaching your team and growing your leaders. **Your company culture is the key integrator that pulls all of these elements together and makes doing these things just the way people in your company behave.**

Culture is the invisible hand that shapes behaviors and decisions when you aren't present to help directly guide your team. It's the sum total of the absorbed values and unstated "way we do things around here." It takes what once were conscious behaviors and absorbs them into the default behavior of your team over time. "After all," culture says, "how could I have done anything else? Of course, that's what I did/how I saw it/how I approached the situation." Culture makes certain perspectives, decisions, and behaviors automatic. It is a filter that shapes what we see, what we *don't* see, and how we interpret things. It shapes decisions and behaviors at an almost unconscious level. **If you have created a culture that's focused on creating value, then culture can become one of your most powerful engines to accelerate and sustain growth.**

The Most Successful $130 Billion Bank That You've Probably Never Heard About

WHEN BOB ENGEL JOINED COBANK* in 2000, the bank saw itself playing a holding game in a shrinking market outside of its direct control. The culture of the organization was unhealthy. Years of internal gerrymandering of performance bonuses, and fiefdoms built by favorites, had left a deep mark in the psyche of the organization.

> "When I came onboard I knew I needed help, particularly an immediate need to grow earnings and increase capital. Before I started the job, I made my first key hire, which was to bring Brian Jackson in as our CFO for much-needed financial knowledge and discipline as well as to gain access to the capital markets. I remember the first few days on the job. Brian and I met individually with many of the key staff. We asked the same questions of each of them: How did they see the organization? What did they think needed to be done to get CoBank back on track? We got totally different answers from everyone."

That last comment from Bob needs to be repeated because in unhealthy or immature company cultures, you'll often hear this over and over: "We got totally different answers from everyone."

One of the most compelling reasons to focus on your culture is because it is the hidden fabric that binds and aligns your team to one collective vision. This is what pulls people together. **Culture guides your individual team members, business units, and departments so that their actions, objectives, and approaches cohere with the bigger-picture company strategy.**

---

* I want to thank Jason Jennings, a fantastic author and speaker, whom I was interviewing for an *Inc.com* article. Jason had written about CoBank in his bestseller, *The High-Speed Company*, and he introduced me to Bob Engel in spring 2018. One of Jason's books is on my "Top 10" business and leadership book lists, posted at **www.FreedomToolKit.com**.

"It was obvious to me that CoBank needed a North Star. We needed a single guiding light that every member of our organization could look up and see at any moment of their day, a light that was compelling and guided their actions in the same direction."

But what was this North Star going to be? Bob spent several months on the road, talking to customers, staff members, directors, and his leadership team. He realized that their North Star couldn't just be "We're a bank that provides capital to agriculture," which was how the bank saw itself. CoBank needed a broader vision for itself:

"We needed a compelling 'why' to bring our team together. We couldn't differentiate ourselves based on size or customer count—we were only $20 billion with a shrinking customer base. Let's face it, we couldn't make our money any greener, we couldn't compete on scale with a charter that mandated we cover all fifty states, and we simply didn't have the resources to compete with technology."

What they did have, as Bob explained to me over several long conversations, were three key sustainable advantages. First, as a member of the Farm Credit System, CoBank was a "government sponsored enterprise," which meant they had the implicit backing of the US government to access liabilities to fund loans of varying terms—a huge advantage over banks that need to gather deposits through a costly branch-gathering system and hedge fixed-rate loans. CoBank also had the sole authority within the Farm Credit System to lend to infrastructure industries: generation and transmission, electric distribution, telecommunications, water, and wastewater. Their second key advantage was their ownership structure. CoBank was a cooperative bank, which meant that their 2,500 customers were actually their shareholders, the same shareholders that elected directors who understood the business of the customers. That cooperative structure allowed Bob to take a long-term view of success without being held hostage to quarterly earnings and share price. The third key advantage came in the form of the employees at CoBank—in spite of an unhealthy culture, they had a deep understanding of their customers' businesses.

But how to turn around how CoBank saw itself? Bob used these early conversations with employees, customers, and other stakeholders to define a broader mission of service to rural America. CoBank would "know more and care more about rural America than any other bank."

> "Our niche was serving all of rural America, making rural America a better place to live, work, and raise a family. This was our calling. I realized that if we were to live our mission of serving rural America, that we had to be there for them, in good times and bad. And when I spoke with customers in those early days, I was horrified to learn they sure hadn't found us to be dependable, especially in bad times. I vividly remember a meeting in Texas where one of our customers vented his anger and sense of betrayal when we up and closed our Lubbock, Texas, banking center in the middle of the night. No warning, nothing, one morning the office was just gone. And I had to sit there and take it because he was right. We had screwed up."

For months Bob stayed on the road, speaking with customers, listening to and absorbing story after story of where CoBank had lost its way:

> "I listened, and after seeing the pain our past choices had caused, I told audience after audience of customers, 'Never again.' I promised them that never again would CoBank jump in and out of a market. Never again would CoBank be a fair-weather friend or lose sight of its mission to serve rural

America. I let them know that from this day forward, we would remember who we were there to serve, for this generation of rural America, and the next, and the next."

Slowly, this message started to take hold in the minds of the CoBank employees. Which is when Bob and a key addition to his team, Phil DiPofi, introduced another way the bank was committed to serving rural America—through capturing and sharing knowledge:

"I was very clear that the only way we could truly differentiate ourselves and serve rural America was by knowing our customers better than anyone, and offering them knowledge, not just money."

Bob, Phil, and the CoBank team created the Knowledge Exchange Division with several Centers of Excellence focused on the industries they served, sharing information and ideas that their customers could tap into to drive success in their respective businesses. There was no cost to customers; this was an investment in the future of rural America. CoBank hosted customer meetings nine times a year as well as many industry-focused conferences, inviting their customers to join them and some of the world's leading experts in agribusinesses, infrastructure, rural healthcare, finance, leadership, and politics. Over the course of his career, Bob was relentless in finding ways to reinforce CoBank's mission, both inside his organization and outside with customers and other partners who cared deeply and had a stake in the future of rural America. He traveled throughout the country, talking with staff and customers in big groups and in small, intimate forums. His message never changed:

"We are here to serve rural America . . . What our customers do to improve the quality of life in rural America, in our nation, and in much of the world is not replicable . . . We will serve by not just providing dependable capital but by sharing information and knowledge with our customers they need to be successful . . ."

As CoBank's successes began to build greater confidence and financial capacity within the organization, Bob realized there was a need for another key component of his bank's culture: sharing the bank's success. CoBank created a program that allowed every employee to contribute $500 annually to a cause that mattered to them and encouraged them to combine that with a paid day off to be of service to others. The Board adopted a policy to contribute up to 1 percent of annual net income, almost $10 million annually, to charitable causes in rural America, with much of the contribution done in partnership with customers.

"Over time, we became an indispensable part of our customers' lives, both through the lending we did as well as through serving their local communities in new ways. I think in a very important way, CoBank played a real leadership role in helping rural America see itself differently. In the early years, I saw that our customers were afraid of the future. They felt the pressure of foreign competition from Brazil, Argentina, and China, and many had narrowed their vision. What CoBank helped them to see was that it was these foreign markets that would be responsible for their greatest growth potential. Rural America has deep advantages in arable land, access to water, infrastructure, and technology that gave them a huge head start over these foreign competitors. More than anything, CoBank gave them confidence."

And what was the outcome of this single-minded commitment to CoBank's calling? For Bob's entire seventeen-year career with CoBank, while this transformation in culture was going on, CoBank enjoyed seventeen consecutive years of earnings growth, growing from $185 million in net income to nearly a $1 billion when he retired. Remember, this period included the tech bubble, 9/11, and the economic meltdown and Great Recession, which swallowed banks. Today, CoBank is one of the most profitable companies, let alone banks, in the world, with annual profits of over $1 million per employee.

Let's be clear: CoBank did not have it easy. When Bob took over, CoBank was struggling with what the future held—or if there was a future for CoBank at all. Bob shared with me how there were weeks when the regulators said CoBank was below its capital requirements and threatened to restrict lending if the bank didn't immediately build capital:

> "There were days when we had to sell good loans so we could maintain sufficient capital to get us through the short-term. Brian Jackson and I went hat in hand to Wall Street and raised hundreds of millions of preferred stock to give us the resources to survive. There was nothing inevitable in the CoBank story; it could have ended very differently. But it didn't, and that was in large part due to the deep commitment of our directors and employees throughout the bank to our vital mission to serve rural America."

How can you plant the lessons from the CoBank story as a powerful seed to help your organization massively accelerate its way to its key goals? First, CoBank had to get rid of the culture cancer that had grown within the organization. This meant making the hard decision that some employees just couldn't be kept on the team, no matter how long they had been there or how many internal allies they had secured. The organization simply couldn't accept the cost to the culture. Next, Bob had to rally a core of believers who fully bought into the culture and vision he was committed to create at CoBank. Finally, Bob had to dive deep into the business until the mission became clear, and then find a powerful way to distill and communicate this mission throughout the organization over the long term. ✦

Your team doesn't want to just serve time at work; they want to do something meaningful. It's your job as a leader to help them connect their work with a deeper meaning and coherent narrative.

YOUR TURN: What is the unchanging core of your company? What is its driving mission—the purpose of your business—that will remain consistent over time? If you already have a stated company mission, decide if it still is valid or if any revision is warranted. This timeless core of your company is the heart of the culture you are committed to build.

Five Simple Steps to Begin Building Your Culture

Remember, your company culture gets built—bit by bit—over the course of years. It took Bob Engel and his team at CoBank a decade to transform their culture. Here is a five-step process to start this important work and take control of how your company's culture is evolving.

Step #1: Clarify your company's core values.

Your company's values are the filters through which you want your team to make any tough decision. How do you want your team to treat a customer in an emotionally loaded moment? How do you want your team to make a decision about how to prioritize an over-full to-do list? How do you want a team member to respond when they see out-of-bounds behavior from a coworker? All of this should be clear from your company values.

EXAMPLE: My company's values include:

- We do what we say we'll do and hold other people accountable to the same standard.
- We eat our own cooking. We are a product of our own coaching program.

Notice that we use short, simple statements to make our values clear *behaviorally*. This has proven to be an effective way to lay out our company values and one that many of our business coaching clients have modeled.

Take the value "We eat our own cooking." When our tech leader, Larry, is faced with too many requests from internal team members all asking for tech resources to fix or advance their key projects, he draws on this core value to help him decide where best to focus and invest our company's limited tech budget of time, attention, and money.

He asks, "If I were coaching one of our clients, how would I make this decision?" The answer is easy: "I'd prioritize our developer time by our current company priorities, not by the volume or force with which a team member or department makes their specific request." The value lets Larry make a smart and appropriate decision without having to enlist our COO, Theresa, to play traffic cop or "ultimate decider."

The same holds true for our other values. For example, if our operations manager is dealing with a difficult hotel where we are hosting one of our quarterly business conferences, and the hotel wants to change our arrangement, she looks at our values ("We do what we say we'll do and hold other people accountable to the same standard") and holds firm to our written agreement. What if the agreement works against our interests? Well, of course she'll try to find a win-win amendment to that agreement, but in the absence of being able to do so, we'll follow our values and do what we say we'll do. That may hurt us in the short run, but I'm a big believer that in the *longer* run, by operating consistently within a clear, intentionally chosen set of values, your company will be much stronger and more successful.

Step #2: Create a written draft of what you want your company's culture to be.

Over the next thirty days, set aside a few forty-five- to sixty-minute blocks of time to just journal what you want your company's culture to look like. What behaviors would you like to be the norm at your company? Ideally, what would someone be able to observe about how your team has internalized your company values in their day-to-day jobs? Review your list of company values and ask, "What would it look and feel like if our entire team was living this specific value?"

EXAMPLE: For our company value of "We eat our own cooking," my brainstormed list includes:

- Our entire team uses our coaching app to fill out their weekly Big Rock Report every Friday afternoon or Monday morning.
- We regularly ask ourselves and each other, "What did we learn from this experience, and how can we use what we learned to improve the company?"
- We systematize processes and functions as a standard way we do business, and all of these systems are organized in our cloud-based UBS.
- We measure our company success not just through the filter of growing our gross revenues and operating profits, but also by the increase of our strategic depth.

By documenting behavioral cues that you and your team would like to see each other do when living the company values, you make those values concrete, which is a key step in crafting your company culture.

Next, ask, "What would an outside observer ideally notice about the *feel* of our company if they spent the day in our offices?"

EXAMPLE: At Maui Mastermind, I would answer,

Our culture is intentionally informal, and we've chosen to be a low-drama workplace. We believe that business and life bring enough challenges on their own, so we set the norm that it's not okay to artificially create more drama through games or immature behavior. In our company, we talk in respectful tones with each other. Where possible, we give people realistic time frames to get things done. We encourage the team to turn off work at night and on weekends so that they can have a life. We are quick to cover for each other if a family situation like a sick relative or a health emergency comes up that we need to deal with. We've got each other's back. These are all parts of our culture.

YOUR TURN. If I were visiting your company for the day, what would you want me to observe about the way your team behaves? What behaviors would you want me to see that illustrate the way your team has absorbed your company culture? Your answers will give you a picture of what you want your culture ideally to be.

Step #3: Get a reality check. How does your company currently live up to your vision of what you want your culture to be?

Sure, you want your culture to be a certain way, but have the courage to describe objectively what your current culture is today. No need to judge or rationalize it; just get clear on your starting point. You'll use this feedback to redefine and develop your culture over time.

Start by talking with your key team about how they perceive the company culture, both what they wish it were and what they see it to be. Gather their thoughts and input—give them a real voice. This is a process that unfolds over several months; it's not just a "sit down, one-time" event.

Step #4: Concretely do three things every week to reinforce the company culture you are committed to build.

Your action list could include:

- Send out a company-wide email retelling the story of a victory that reinforces a key cultural element.
- During a meeting, highlight an example of a great team member behavior.
- Look for and share small, company-wide occurrences that symbolize deeper values you want the company to absorb.

- Consistently role-model the behavior you want them to internalize.
- Ask a team member how they would make a decision they are dealing with if they were doing it "the company way."

Step #5: Revisit your ideal and actual company cultures, and repeat step four again and again until over time the two are essentially the same.

Involve your leadership team in the process of defining and modeling your optimum culture. Encourage them to look for ways to intentionally influence your culture. This process takes time, but when you get your culture right, it accelerates everything else.

BONUS TIP

Ten More Tips to Get Your Culture Right

Culture turns your best behaviors and approaches to business situations into intuitive, patterned behaviors for your team. Here are ten more tips to cultivate a vibrant, winning culture.

1. **Look for everyday, symbolic stories that transmit the values of your company and share these stories at every opportunity.** If you see Mario, a client support rep, creatively solve an issue in a way that delights your client, share this story internally with your team again and again. The best of these stories will be absorbed into the mythology of your company and shape its self-perception for years to come.

2. **Intentionally seize moments to take an action or make a decision that illustrates the best of how you want your team to behave.** Maybe it's always calling your customer by name as they walk back into your store, letting your team see you write a thank-you card after a sales call, or recapping who owns which action steps after a meeting and by when. Your company's culture is built by the accumulation of thousands of small decisions and examples that you model over and over and over. There are no throwaway moments; your team watches and absorbs *everything* you do.

3. **What you do at stressful moments in the business has a magnified impact on your team and on your company culture.** Think of stress and the heightened emotions that go with it as a magnifying glass that powerfully enhances the impact—good or bad—of your behavior. Use these moments as the golden opportunities they are. Whatever you do in these stressful moments will be remembered and replicated when your team responds to these same or similar circumstances in the future.

4. **Guide your team to discern the impact of what they do and what the company does on each others' lives and your customers.** One of your key responsibilities as a leader is to help shape the meaning your team associates with their work. Are they merely moving bits of data from one pile to another, or

are they helping clients manufacture life-enhancing products by letting them more ably manage a global supply chain? Help your team make the connection between their actions and the good work your company does. Enroll your team in gathering and sharing your client-impact stories. Share these stories at every opportunity. Archive these stories so that the best of them get told and retold inside your company.

5. **Clarify your company's values and make them the filter through which you make all your business's tough decisions.** Encourage your team to use them the same way, and celebrate when they do. From time to time, ask your employees how they used the company's values to make big decisions in the heat of the moment. It's a great barometer of just how deeply your values have been absorbed into the company.

6. **Quickly, clearly, and privately address out-of-bounds behavior.** As discussed in chapter six, if you deal directly with bad behaviors, you're sending a clear message about what does and does not fly in your workplace. And if you consider the importance of this message with respect to your own behavior, it also becomes clear that owning and acknowledging your *own* missteps sets the best example for your team.

7. **Cull low performers.** If you want high performance and personal responsibility to be integral parts of your culture, you've got to cull the low performers *now*. Every company has them: those team members who everyone knows are just getting by. If you give them a pass by not dealing with their poor performance, then the message you're sending to the rest of your team is that subpar behavior is acceptable. Your high performers will resent giving low performers a free pass. Why should they work hard when others are just sliding by? For this reason, it's especially crucial to cull your low performers now and replace them with motivated team members who bring value to the company. Yes, this might cause some short-term pain, but the long-term rewards are worth it.

8. **Start with recruitment.** Emphasize your values and culture in your hiring, selection, and orientation of new team members. Build into your hiring process checks for the workplace

demeanor and values that will align with the culture you want. When you invite a new person to join your team, make sure that you communicate your company values and culture, not just with a ten-minute talk or a handout in your new employee onboard package, but rather by sharing stories that make your values and culture real. Take four to five of your most important cultural elements and have a story to share with your new hire that makes each of these culture items come alive.

For example, if one of the key elements of your culture is that you believe deeply in giving each team member a clear development pathway to grow professionally, you might tell the story of Arjun, an engineer who started with you ten years prior. You can tell how he joined the company after finishing his graduate school program and how the company mapped out a career development pathway that included getting him a series of internal mentors and putting him on handpicked project teams, so he could gain the diversified real-world experiences he needed to make his academic lessons come alive. Today, you might share, Arjun manages one of your most important product development teams. Real stories that illustrate your company culture mean more than any slick slogan you could tell about how "at Acme Inc., we believe in giving team members professional development opportunities." Stories, not slogans, convey culture.

9. **Intentionally make the hard decisions that shock your team into realizing how seriously you believe in your vision and values.** This might mean firing a key client who just doesn't fit with the direction and mission of the business. Or it could be a decision that costs the company quite of bit of money in the short term, but clearly is the right thing to do. Symbols matter when creating culture; sometimes a single action or hard decision can be a powerful symbol.

10. **Apply gentle pressure—relentlessly.** Culture evolves over time. Rarely do you change or move it all in one magic moment. Just like coaching individuals, guide your company culture with the gentle influence of consistent pressure relentlessly applied over time. It's the slow effect of flowing water that, over time, carves out a massive canyon.

Which Economy Does Your Culture Embrace?

As you strive to upgrade and refine your culture, remember to ask this critical question: Does your current culture embrace the Value Economy, or do you push your employees to live in a time and effort world? A simple test is to look at how your company deals with email, texts, and focus time. When you send a team member an email, do you expect an immediate answer? Do you feel like you have to continuously scan your inbox for new messages? Do you and your team regularly handle email or other nonemergency messages at night and on weekends?

How does your company do meetings? Are they overloaded with participants there to "look good," or do you have a minimal number of direct players in any one meeting to get real work done, with a recap sent to keep other interested parties in the know about what you decided or accomplished? If internal politics influences who is in a meeting, then your company is drifting dangerously close to the rocky shores of the Time and Effort Economy.

CONSIDER THE EXAMPLE OF JONATHAN, the senior VP in charge of sales and marketing for North America at one of the world's largest integrated manufacturers. When Jonathan first stepped into his leadership role, he was given an opportunity to build his own team and do things his way. At least, from the outside, that's what it appeared to be. That was about the time that Jonathan brought my company onboard to help him do this important work the best way possible.

But we soon uncovered a clear challenge: Jonathan's company said they focused on value creation, with high standards and challenging performance targets, but their culture gave the opposite message. For example, the way they ran their meetings was rooted in the Time and Effort Economy and wasted thousands of hours of their most expensive talent and attention every year. Before each meeting, they would send out an advance packet for all participants to read. While this was a solid idea to maximize their meeting time, these advance packets regularly were over fifty pages long. When it came time for the actual meeting, the organizer knew that not all participants had read the advance packet, so he or she would take meeting time at the start to summarize the entire advance packet. Their meetings were made worse by having too many participants from too many internal teams present at each meeting. As this bureaucracy evolved, appearances become more important than results. Senior leaders routinely would ask questions they found interesting, even if they had no direct bearing on the subject at hand.

Paul, one of Jonathan's key subordinates whom we also coached, shared an example of how his boss's boss asked him a question at a monthly strategy meeting. Paul gave him an approximate answer.

> "For the purpose of the decision we needed to make, we didn't need the exact number; it wouldn't make any difference. The approximate answer told the story we needed to hear," Paul shared. "But my boss's boss said he wanted an exact answer. I explained that I could get him an exact answer, but it would take ten to fifteen hours of research, data collection, and spreadsheet work, whereas the approximate answer showed what the decision likely should be. He just said he still wanted the precise answer. So, I put in the work, even though it pulled me off of other projects that had a higher yield for the company, and gave him his number. It was a pure waste of time, but he wanted what he wanted, so I did it."

Multiply Paul's experience across hundreds of senior leaders, and this culture robbed the company of its best attention from projects and initiatives, costing this company billions of dollars.

The reality was that there were some changes Jonathan could make for his team, and other changes he couldn't. He focused on the areas he could impact and let go of the ones that were beyond his control. ♦

Maybe you, like Jonathan, are not in a position to change the broader culture of your company. But, as he did, you *can* make your corner of the company operate more effectively and create more value. You *can* do your best to shield your team from the most destructive elements of a Time and Effort culture.

We've discussed the topic of email in the context of reclaiming your best time. Let's briefly shine the spotlight of culture on the email issue. Do you want to improve employee retention and maximize engagement? Tell your employees to stop checking email late at night and on weekends and, instead, to enjoy their families. Chances are, you will have received a new email, text, or alert before you've finished reading this chapter. Your phone will buzz, or your computer will ding, or your watch will vibrate. Probably all three. Will you check your message or keep reading this chapter?

You know as well as I that companies of every size and across every vertical are succumbing to an Always On culture. Employees and leaders alike have become beholden to their notification centers. Even when the office lights go off, leaders and employees still stay on: email, text, apps—whatever their medium of choice. Not only is this culture inefficient, with people spending three to five night-and-weekend hours per week on low-level emails and messages, but it breeds more insidious problems, like higher rates of employee turnover, burnout, and disengagement. Employees' families develop resentment and pass that resentment on to your employees.

No leader wants this for her staff. You want your employees to thrive, to love their work, and to engage with it enthusiastically. And while most business leaders don't intend to create an Always On culture, what they don't realize is that in the absence of intentional effort in the other direction, the tide of today's world will pull you that way. It's the default direction.

I first felt the impact of the Always On world right after a merger one of my earlier companies went through about a decade ago. At the time, I didn't appreciate the impact that disparities in company culture could have on the success of a merger. The woman who became my new business partner was intelligent, talented, and driven. But she also had an air of anxiety about her, and it defined her company's culture. She would send out emails as late as one or even two in the morning, sending follow-up emails early the next business day if she didn't get responses. Of course, her entire staff learned that they needed to be on 24/7. This compounded the problem, as more people responding at off hours further reinforced the culture that in this company, you must be available and responsive day and night.

The merger seemed to make sense for many reasons. We'd already been strategic partners for years, and during this time our combined activities had created millions in profits. We each brought a different service offering to the table, but both our firms served the same core audience: small and medium-sized owner-run companies. Still, post-merger, without realizing it, my original team and I gradually found ourselves joining these late-night threads. Nobody explicitly asked us to. Our company's policies hadn't changed, but our company's culture had.

I remember lying in bed one night, it was about 11 PM, and I felt the overwhelming compulsion to go into my home office and check email (this was before smartphones had become ubiquitous, or I'm sure I just would have leaned over to pull my phone from the bedside table and checked there). I actually got out of bed, walked down the hall to my home office, and started responding to email at 11 PM at night. I thought, *Something is seriously wrong here.* First of all, there wasn't anything in my inbox that couldn't wait until the morning. There almost never was. And in those rare instances, my staff shouldn't have emailed me; they should have called me.

Then another thought struck me: *I'm one of the partners in this firm. If I feel this way, what's the impact on my team?* That wasn't the company I wanted to build for my team members. I learned from that experience that, as business leaders, we need to be careful about the unspoken messages we send our employees. When our two companies merged, my new partner's late-night emails subtly communicated an expectation that all of us should be on email all day, every day. I ultimately bought out my business partner when it became clear that we couldn't align our cultures with both of us owning the company. Sadly, over the next twenty-four months, we also ended up replacing many of the staff she brought to the merger because they just couldn't adjust to the Value Economy culture the rest of the company had embraced.

This is an extreme example, and I realize that most business leaders don't intend for their late-night emails to define the company culture, but it does. For example, one of my business coaching clients, Andrea, manages retail sales for the western third of the United States. She initially shared with me that she only constantly monitors email during off hours for fear of missing something critical—an emergency with her Indian or Chinese suppliers, or perhaps an urgent customer message that, if left unattended, could lose her a major account.

But when I asked how many of her incoming emails met this sort of mission-critical standard, she said it was about one email out of every five thousand. That's .02 percent of all her emails! When I pointed out to her that she was Always On, answering emails on nights and weekends, injuring her relationships with her employees, her vendors, her family, and herself, all for fear of missing out on that one email in five thousand, she realized that she needed to make a change.

YOUR TURN: I encourage you to look at your own business—at your messaging practices and those of your team. Are you and your staff Always On? How is that affecting your business? What is it costing your company in terms of burnout, disengagement, and turnover? If you want you and your employees to have the opportunity to turn off—if you want to reduce turnover and boost engagement—here are three steps to start this change.

Step #1: Talk with your team.

Bring key staff together and ask what prompts people to feel like they need to check and respond to messages on nights and weekends.

I think their answers will surprise you. In many cases, you'll discover that employees believe that you expect them to be on 24/7. Perhaps they worry about letting down the company or their coworkers, about losing a promotion, or even losing their jobs. You may find that, for other employees, the problem is an addiction to email and their other project management tools. They're obsessed with staying up to date and can't bear to leave a message unanswered or an issue unaddressed.

This candid adult conversation is the first step. Ask your team if they think that obsessively answering email or interrupting their day to filter and screen their inbox or feeds increases or decreases the value they bring to the company. Explore if and when being available during off hours actually helps the company and when it hurts the company long term.

Finally, lay out what a more rational set of expectations might look like. For many businesses, messaging can stop at the end of the workday and the work week. If your business requires more responsiveness, perhaps you can establish schedules for who needs to cover which nights and weekends. Remember that even in 24/7 industries, from medicine to security to tech, employees have time off. Companies in these industries use shifts to simultaneously ensure full coverage and healthy lifestyles. Your company should, too.

Of course, emergencies do come up in any field, so you should establish a procedure for handling them. But, even as you establish these safeguards, be sure to clarify that emergencies don't come up daily or weekly or even monthly. They come up one or two or three times a year. They're one in five thousand. And if you *do* have emergencies coming up more often than this, you need to take a deep look at your company's culture.

An effective emergency protocol can be as simple as guaranteeing employees that they will receive a call or text alerting them when they have an urgent message in their inbox. Knowing that there's an emergency procedure in place will assure your team that it's safe to turn off.

There is no one-size-fits-all answer here. My coaching advice is to work out your own shared set of ideal expectations with your team and then experiment to determine your best practices.*

Step #2: Design and conduct a ninety-day experiment.

With your ideal expectations in hand, agree to try out living these new social and business boundaries for ninety days. Remember that this experiment isn't only about your employees; it's about you, too. If you continue to send out messages outside of business hours, your team will follow suit. So, lead by example and change your own behavior.

Thirty days into your experiment, meet again and ask, "What's working well? How is this making us more productive? Happier?" Also ask, "What specific things do we want to adjust going forward that would make things work even better?"

Agree on the tweaks you are going to make and get back to work. Continue to pay attention to what is and isn't working. Keep a running list and be ready to meet again at the sixty-day mark. At the end of ninety days, do your final debrief. Make a collective decision if you should formalize your experiment and make it your new normal. Or, if the process didn't improve value created and team happiness, discuss what you learned and how you might apply those lessons moving forward to reach these goals.

Step #3: Make it okay to talk about availability and accessibility.

If you want to change the culture, you must give people implicit permission to discuss it. Periodically revisit how things are going over the year. Continue the conversation and help break the taboo by holding one-to-one check-ins where you discuss with individual employees the impact of the culture experiment and how it's working

---

* I'll have more to say in chapter nine, "Leverage Better Design," about leveraging buffers, filters, and better design to enhance your team's value creation.

for them. Periodically check in at larger meetings, too. This is a great way to make it clear that it's okay to discuss these things at your company, and that together, you're committed to building a culture where people can do great work and have a vibrant personal life, too.

Ultimately, culture is what integrates and aligns team member behavior to the Fewer, Better focus so that collectively, you crush your company goals and still have a rich personal life, too.

In chapter two, "Reclaim Your Best Time," you learned how to structure your week so that you have regular focus blocks of one to four hours for you to do your A- and B-level work. In chapter three, "Invest in Your Fewer, Better," you learned to create a one-page Action Plan and how to use the Big Rock Report to improve your weekly execution. In chapter four, "Develop Strategic Depth," you learned how to design and build your company or team's UBS, your master system to store, retrieve, and organize your systems. These are all simple yet powerful examples of how you've already been introduced to using better design to make the Freedom Formula work faster. In the next chapter, I'm going to share with you suggestions and best practices to leverage structure, filters, and better design to enhance your team's ability to consistently focus its best attention on your highest-return activities and projects.

CHAPTER 9

Accelerator Five:
Leverage Better Design

The most successful business leaders—and here I'm using "success" in its larger, whole-life sense—know that in the race of business, structure and environment win over willpower. Willpower can help you win a sprint, but building a company and career is a marathon. In fact, it's an *ultra*marathon carried out over multiple years.

This is why Accelerator Five is so critical to your long-term success. When you leverage better design, including your systems, filters, workflow, tools, and time structures, you're able to create more value with fewer hours and less effort. The Time and Effort Economy pushes you to brute-force results: "Work harder; come into the office earlier and stay later; personally do more." The Value Economy knows that often a more elegant design—of your day, your plan, your team, your process—means less can produce more. With less waste and greater concentration of your best attention on the vital few things that matter magnitudes more, you and your team can produce massively more value and still have a life.

First, let's agree on what we mean by "design." In this context, design simply refers to the way an object, process, activity, environment, or tool is structured and built. This could be a product you make, a service you provide, a process your staff follows, an activity like a sales call, the physical workspace of your office, or a tool like a standardized report *(fig. 10)*. Each of these has an element of design—good or bad—that impacts the utility and ease of use, and hence the value created. And each of these is a potential opportunity to leverage better design to increase the value of the output and reduce the cost and time of the input. **This is the essence of Value Economy thinking—looking for ways where you can do more with less (efficiency) and opportunities where less is more (elegance). Great design gives you** *both*.

Processes	Tools
• Your onboarding process for a new employee, vendor, or client • Your sales process • Your production process • Your fulfillment process • Your accounts payable process • Etc.	• Your project management platform • Your CRM • Your UBS • Your standardized forms or reporting • Physical tools your production team uses • Etc.
Activities	**Environments**
• Recurring meetings • Posting on social media • Outbound sales calls • Conducting a new client intake • Ongoing accounting work • Etc.	• Workstations on your shop floor • The layout of your office space • Your office or cubicle • Meeting spaces • Common areas • Etc.

Figure 10   Examples of design in the workplace

Great design incorporates three essential elements. First, great design means something serves its intended purpose exceptionally well. It is highly *functional*. Second, great design is something that is easy to use. Its form serves its function. It is *transparent*. Third, great design is a pleasure to touch, view, feel, and interact with. It's *beautiful*.

Here are a few examples of how several of our coaching clients have used better design to create more value with less effort:

- A surgical practice created a detailed video of preoperative instructions for patients instead of having their surgeons repeat the same conversation multiple times each day. The patient watches the video first, and then the surgeon comes back into the exam room to answer questions. Not only did this save hundreds of hours of their most expensive staff member's time each year, but the practice discovered that patients liked it *better*. The patients felt like they were getting more attention and care, even though objectively they had less live interaction time with their surgeon.

- A web-hosting company was losing 40 percent of its new customers in the first ninety days. They discovered that many of these customers signed up for their web-hosting service but were intimidated by the task of actually migrating their website over. By simply changing the routing of *which* client support team handled new customers so that these new customers got their most experienced support people, and adding in a few proactive outreach phone calls and emails to help new customers do their site migrations, the company reduced their new customer attrition rate by over 60 percent, adding millions of dollars of recurring revenue to the company over the lives of these customers.

- An environmental consulting company generated new business primarily through responding to requests for proposals from governmental agencies. Each proposal cost them fifty or more staff hours to create, and they only captured a fraction of the jobs they submitted proposals for. By templating their proposals, and creating a library of proposal parts to pull from, they were able to speed up this process and generate a better proposal with half the staff hours.

These are all examples of how a little extra thought led to enhanced results. Each of these scenarios required a small investment of their respective companies' best talent and attention to design and create, and each yielded a remarkable return on investment.

Good design often doesn't cost more. In fact, in many cases, good design saves you money. And in almost every case, *great* design increases the value of the output. In this chapter, we're specifically concerned with using great design to better direct and focus your team's best attention on the activities and projects that generate the highest yield for your organization.

Take the Needle Out of the Haystack

In chapter eight, I shared the story of one of our business coaching clients, Andrea, who manages retail sales for the western third of the United States. She found herself checking email after hours and on most weekends, anxious that if she didn't, she might miss that one-in-five-thousand email that she truly needed to handle right away. You've likely heard the expression, "It's like finding a needle in a haystack." In Andrea's case, she was sacrificing her quality of life by constantly monitoring her email inbox, looking for that "needle."

"Andrea," I asked her one day, "why don't we just take the needle out of the haystack and find a way for your team or system to deliver that needle to you directly, bypassing the haystack altogether?"

Imagine you were Andrea and wanted to design a better way to take the needle (a truly important and urgent emergency you need to handle right away) out of the haystack (your email inbox with its one hundred daily messages). How would you do it? If you had an assistant, as Andrea did, you could ask her to screen your email during business hours and to text you or call your cell phone directly if any needle came in. But is there a way you could bypass that need for your assistant to screen for you? What about outside of business hours? Are you unfairly going to ask your assistant to sacrifice her family and personal time to stay on top of your inbox 24/7?

What if you instead talked with your key staff members, suppliers, and vendors and explained to them how best to reach you in those one-in-five-thousand emergencies. Perhaps you give them a hotline number to call or text? Or you give them a separate app that you use only for emergencies? Or maybe there is an "on-call" email that you and your team take turns monitoring so no one person is left to bear the full burden? What you want to do is to design a better mechanism for your team to bypass the haystack and get a critical needle to you directly.

This mechanism doesn't have to be only for after-hours use; you can use it during your workday, too. When you create a way to remove needles from the haystack and deliver them directly, you no longer have the attentional drain of constantly monitoring the haystack of email, apps, and alerts. You can relax and focus your best attention on your highest-value work. You can trust that if needed, during your focus blocks, a needle will find its way to you from a separate channel outside of the normal haystack.

This simple fix allows you to brainstorm with your leadership team for a solution to a pressing problem without your team constantly checking their phones for messages. It allows you to turn your phone off at night when you're with your family or while you're on vacation. I know that when I finally figured this out in my business life, it felt so liberating. Try it! I'm willing to bet that once you experience it for yourself, you'll never go back to the stress, anxiety, and inefficiency of living in your haystack.

Refine Your Processes

SUSAN OWNED A SUCCESSFUL commercial insurance brokerage firm. In her company, her highest-value A-level activity was securing new accounts. But each year she lost four months of selling time to the stressful frenzy known as "annual insurance renewals." The renewal process mattered, but it wasn't Susan's highest-value activity; she just got pulled into it each year because she was the most experienced broker in her small firm. Recognizing that anything that helped free up more sales time would help Susan grow her company, she instituted "Project Renewal," a dedicated company-wide effort to incrementally replace her in all renewal processes. She knew that in order to do this, she would need to refine her company's core renewal systems so that her team, working with these systems, didn't miss anything.

Susan and her staff laid out the renewal process as a flowchart on a big whiteboard. They then detailed the steps that needed to be completed at each stage of the process. They brainstormed ways to simplify this process and determined who besides Susan would be best able to own each step. They then broke down each step, listing what information, tools, relationships, or training the newly assigned non-Susan team member would need to complete their assigned steps successfully. Finally, they put one person—not Susan—in charge of the whole renewal process, so that Susan wouldn't feel pulled back to monitor the work and be the quality control person in the process. If they needed her, they could ask questions or call on her for ideas, but she wasn't the person who would vigilantly monitor the whole process going forward.

The first year they implemented the solution, things went fairly well, a seven out of ten by their reckoning. They learned from their breakdowns and used missed steps to further refine the system. They uncovered steps they could template or even automate, tools they could improve, and domain expertise in which they needed deeper training. In the end, Susan regained hundreds of hours each year, hours she invested to dramatically grow revenue, which was her point of highest contribution for the company. Plus, Project Renewal greatly enhanced the organization's strategic depth. It took expertise to which previously only Susan had access and shared it across a formal system and her team. ♦

YOUR TURN: Pick one recurring activity or process that cumulatively eats up a tremendous amount of your time each month, quarter, or year. Choose something that is *not* one of your highest-value A-level activities. Write it down now . . .

How could you put your own project team together to give this recurring activity over to someone else, or a group, and free up more of your best time for your highest-value work? First, pick your team to be part of this project. Then, collectively lay out the steps to this process as it currently exists. This could be in the form of a flowchart, a Gantt diagram, or a written list of sequential steps. Next, get clear on the purpose and key outcomes of this system. What is it really supposed to do? Why does this matter? Who is the real user or recipient of these outputs? Why do the outputs really matter to that recipient? Have you talked with the recipient about what really matters to them about the outputs?

Keeping in mind the high-level purpose and outcomes of the system, tear apart your current system and brainstorm ways to improve it. How can you make it better? Faster? Cheaper? Higher quality? More impactful? How can you give it greater capacity and scalability?

Which steps are redundant or could be designed out? Which steps could be automated? Combined or simplified? Outsourced? Insourced? Templated?

How could you accelerate the process? Reduce the number of people needed? Make it more robust? More stable? Less prone to error?

Smooth out the ideas you've generated into a new, cohesive whole. Pay attention to the *format* of the system and not just the process. Process ensures the system can work; format ensures that people actually will use the system and get the results you want. For example, would a section of the system work best as an automated email drip campaign? Or as a checklist? Or as mandatory fields in a database? Or as a standardized template? Or . . . ?

Over time, the best systems end up in two levels. Level one is the full system, documented thoroughly. This descriptive form is critical for archiving institutional learnings and giving new users the context and depth to really learn the system. Level two is the abridged version that gives experienced users the simple tools they can use to generate the needed result. For example, an airline pilot uses the level two preflight checklist to quickly and accurately do her review before she takes off. The full, level one version of the preflight system likely has deep documentation that the airline used during training, but an experienced pilot would find the 118-page full version a cumbersome distraction; hence the three-page preflight checklist. In day-to-day use, the checklist is much more powerful for actual system users, but the full version captures key context and institutional knowledge that is valuable for other uses.

New process in hand, assign its steps. Make sure that you choose one person to own the process as a whole.

Finally, implement and track the system. What's working well? What improvements are needed? Who needs what ongoing training? Once this is firmly in place and producing for your company, pick the next recurring process or activity for your team to tackle, perhaps—gulp—even without your involvement!

Standardize Reporting and Structure Information

Standardizing reporting, or any repeating patterns of information, is a way of leveraging structure to make information easier to assimilate and absorb. It reduces the attentional units necessary to understand and use that information. For example, I can get a quick and accurate feel for what's going on in my company, department by department, by reviewing each departmental leader's Big Rock Report. I see what they have prioritized as their Big Rocks, what victories I get to congratulate them on, challenges I may need to support them through, and the other bulleted key updates from their past week. If you've ever enjoyed the speed at which you can get a quick sense of an area of your business by reviewing a powerfully designed dashboard or KPI scoreboard, you've experienced the way standardized information makes things easier.

Standardized information can be the way you set up your customer database, using internal webforms to process and share information across team members. Or it could be a worksheet that your

**Ten Questions to Design an Activity or
Process to Get More Done with Less**

1. How could we radically simplify this process or activity to create more value with less time, attention, or cost?
2. If money were no object, how would we approach designing this?
3. If we had only a fraction of the money or time that we actually have, how would we approach designing this?
4. How could we automate, template, or standardize it?
5. What are the most common and costly mistakes that occur when doing this task or running this process, and how could we redesign this process to completely design out these common and costly errors?
6. How could we spend a little more money, time, or attention on this activity to radically improve its value, quality, impact, durability, or consistency?
7. How could we redesign this process to take less time, attention, or money and get the same or better result?
8. How could we design this activity or process to be easier and more obvious to use?
9. How could we make this activity or process so obvious and simple that a totally new person could successfully use it to get great results with little or no training?
10. If we were starting fresh, with no sunk costs or historic baggage, how would we design this activity or process *today*?

consulting staff uses when they first meet with a client to make sure they ask for and capture the right information you need to successfully fulfill your engagement. It can be the weekly scheduling tool that outputs a schedule for your staff so that they can see their updated schedule in a visually obvious and clear way.

I encourage you to assess blocks of information that you receive regularly but that come ad hoc or idiosyncratically. How could you standardize the way this information gets reported so that it's easier for your staff to deliver, faster for you to interpret, and more powerful for all parties to use for its intended purpose?

Develop Filters That Work

Simply put, a filter is a porous device for removing impurities and solid particles. In a work context, an effective filter can keep out things like noise, low-value activities, interruptions, and addictive time temptations. Great design can help you filter out these distractions so that they don't pollute your best attention. Your filters can delete tasks that shouldn't be done at all, redirect them to other team members, or allow you to accumulate and batch tasks together so that you can handle them more efficiently during nonfocus times.

Great design can also filter up to your attention high-value opportunities and important urgencies that you need to handle now. In other words, a well-designed filter lets you focus on your highest-value projects for concentrated blocks of time, trusting that if any needle shows up in your inflow haystack, your filter will deliver it to you in a way that gets your attention without you draining your attention through ongoing low-level vigilance and continually scanning your haystack. **Filters help you best invest your finite inventory of attentional units in your highest-return activities and projects.**

Your filters could include:

- Setting up automatic processing of common, recurring emails.
- An assistant who does a first pass to process your email, screens phone calls, and plays a gatekeeper filter for part of your business life.
- Giving different access doors to different people. These could include a direct extension on a phone number or an unlisted cell phone number. It also could include using a junk email address that automatically saves messages in a designated folder. When you sign up for a service or get free information online, you preserve your ability to search and access messages

sent to the junk folder address should the need arise, but you reserve your best email for the people and things that likely matter more.

- An alternate phone to use in your nonwork hours to make sure you don't easily get pulled back to work when you really want to be with your family. (For many people, this freedom is worth the added annual cost for a second line and phone.)
- Setting up your phone to go straight to voice mail during focus blocks or after hours.
- Role-specific email addresses that, while you might have to cover them today, make it much easier for you to later redirect to other team members.

    EXAMPLES: events@mycompany.com or invoices@my -company.com.
- Turning on "quiet hours" on your smartphone during focus blocks and after hours, so you aren't distracted by tempting alerts and messages.

Done right, you even can design your *environment* so that it becomes an ongoing filter that supports you in creating more value in less time.

Design Your Environment for Better Focus Time

MAUREEN JOUDREY IS THE VP OF OPERATIONS and technology at the Information Technology Industry Council, a large trade association focused on advocating for public policies, whose members represent the entire spectrum of technology. Collectively, their members have a combined market value in the trillions of dollars. When Maureen first began learning to use the formula, she said, "I love what I do. I get to work with some of the brightest policy thinkers in the world. But the nature of my role means that I get hit multiple times a day with urgent fires that I have to put out. This bogs me down and keeps me from focusing on the higher-order strategic work that I need to do to make my biggest contribution to the organization."

In her first week using the formula, Maureen set aside her Focus Day, conscientiously closed her office door, and turned off her phone and email. She was committed to use the three-hour block she had set aside to focus on drafting an important technology plan for her organization.

"But I forgot about my iWatch!" she shared, laughing.

Maureen kept experimenting until she found the setup that allowed her to maximize her focus time:

"Ultimately, what I found works best for me is to get out of my office for my focus time. There are just too many environmental distractions there—folders on my credenza, reminder slips on my wall. Instead I go to a communal workspace in our office, but I bring only my laptop and the *one folder* I'm working on. I find the white noise of other people working, combined with being out of my office, gives me great energy and creativity." ◆

YOUR TURN: What environment is best for *your* focus blocks? Are you like Maureen, who does best going to a different work area in your building? Or do you work best in your office with the door shut and the ringer off? I find I do my best creative work sitting on the couch in my office with my legal pad and favorite pen. I make sure to put my computer into sleep mode, turn off my cell and office phone ringers, and put an away message on my email so I don't feel tempted to check. There is no right answer, only a right answer for *you*. By designing the environment you do your best work in, at least during your five or more hours a week of focus time, you'll create more value than you previously thought possible—without working fourteen-hour days.

Here are a few more tips to better structure your environment to support creating value:

- Set the stage at the end of today for tomorrow's focus block. Clear your desk or electronic desktop of any distractions and take out only the file you need. Or have your "go folder" packed for you to just grab and go to your focus spot.
- Pick an anchored "focus spot." For me it was my office couch; for Maureen it was the communal work space. Where do you do your best focus work? Is it a local café? A favorite conference room? A home office one morning a week? Or simply your office with a cleared-off desk? Environment becomes a strong cue for mind-set and behavior, so pick a special focus spot and use it only for focused work.
- Set your technology (e.g., phone, computer, watch!) to "do not disturb" mode to support your focus time.
- Communicate with your team about the value of focus time. Help them design their own recurring focus blocks. Discuss how you can support one another in getting five or more hours a week of uninterrupted focus time.
- Have a sign that tells the world when you're available or if you're engaged in a focus block. Put a sign on your door. Set an away message for your email. Or even wear a "focus" hat, headphones, or scarf that signals to people that you're doing deep work and to interrupt you only if they have a truly important, urgent emergency that can't wait a few hours.

Maureen reported,

"That first week I made the effort to structure things so I wouldn't have distractions during my focus time was one of my most productive weeks. I've been doing this now for the past four months, and it's made a real impact. I'm getting more of my highest-value work done. I feel calmer because I *know* that no matter how crazy the week gets, I'll have my five or six hours of focus blocks to get my important, non-urgent project work done. My favorite part of doing this is actually the Big Rock Report. This is really the first time I've ever taken the time to think at the end of each week in a structured, written way what exactly did I accomplish that week on my most valuable projects. I love listing my victories because it reminds me that I am making progress and contributing more value. My boss, Dean, has noticed, too. He loves getting my Big Rock Report at the end of the week because it makes his life easier. He gets to see what I'm focused on and areas to better support me. It's sparked him to invest more one-to-one time in mentoring me to grow, which also feels great."

The Eight Meeting Maximizers

One final application of better design is how you do meetings. You and your team collectively spend hundreds of hours in meetings each year. With a little thought about how you design your meetings, you can maximize your team's time and talent, whether conducting a small-group or departmental-level meeting or running a company-wide gathering of minds. Here are eight best practices to leverage better meeting design to get more with less.

1. **Only meet to create value.** Meetings are for creating value, not playing politics, covering your backside, or simply because "that's how we've always done things." If the meeting doesn't create value, cancel the meeting. You'll reap an instant savings from the freed-up staff time for them to do other, more valuable work. Meetings are a great place to brainstorm ideas, reach a key decision, gain full buy-in from your staff, or coordinate execution. Just make sure the area you're brainstorming on, the decision you're making, or the project you're coordinating creates enough value for your company to yield a healthy return on your meeting investment.

2. **Conduct a "standing meeting audit."** Review every standing meeting that your team participates in. Are these recurring meetings still relevant? Could you reduce the number of people participating and just circulate notes after to the people who no longer have to attend? Could you shorten the meeting from an hour to thirty minutes? How about fifteen minutes? Could you reduce the frequency of these meetings? Perhaps you could combine two or more meetings into one? Slash out as many of the wasted employee hours as you can from these meetings; your company and staff will thank you.

3. **Plan the meeting in advance.** All meetings must have a purpose and an agenda. Someone must own the meeting and have planned out how best to accomplish the intended purpose. Ideally, this means a written agenda that gets in the hands of all participants well in advance of the meeting so they can come prepared themselves. At the very least, the meeting owner has invested the time to make the meeting valuable (or to cancel it). If there is specific information, or other preparation work that participants need to have ready, make that explicit on the agenda. This isn't just about creating a "policy" (which in many organizations simply will be ignored), but rather about making it a cultural must-have in your company that this is how we do meetings: we plan them in advance, we have written agendas, and we come fully prepared.

4. **Engage your team right from the start.** Think of opening your meeting like a blockbuster James Bond film: start with an action sequence. This can mean that you go around the room and ask team members to share a quick victory, insight, or relevant challenge. Or it could mean you ask them a provocative question and get each participant to share their initial thoughts. These openings will root your meeting participants in the meeting.

5. **Start and end your meetings strong.** This means starting the meeting on time and expecting all meeting participants to

come prepared. Make sure you end with clear lines of action and a clear "Meeting is over." Don't let your meeting end by the slow leak of air.

6. **Follow your meeting plan.** It's one thing to have an agenda, but altogether another thing to follow it. Make sure whoever is leading the meeting guides the conversation, giving all participants a voice and pushing past unproductive moments when the meeting is on the verge of going down a dead-end spur. Of course, there are times when that tangent one of your team members brings up is brilliant and sparks a whole new way of seeing the situation and a better course of action. Experienced leaders know when to let spontaneity and creativity have a free rein. There are times when ditching your preconceived agenda is the right move.

7. **Clarify and follow up on action items.** It's one thing to have a productive meeting, but to reap its value, stuff has to get done. At the end of the meeting, go back and explicitly clarify action commitments. Clarify who owns which tasks, when they'll complete them, and how they'll "close the loop" by reporting its completion. This is half the accountability battle. The other half is ongoing follow-up to make sure all assigned tasks got done. As a default, the meeting leader should be responsible for holding all participants accountable on assigned action items. Of course, he or she could delegate this follow-up responsibility, but as a default this works well. Send a meeting recap email that lists data points, decisions, and next steps (Who? What? When? How to close the loop?).

8. **Be the role model for the behaviors you want to see.**

The Seven-Week Summer

RC CHAVEZ, A SUCCESSFUL REAL ESTATE ENTREPRENEUR in northern California, grew up poor. Many days after school and on weekends, RC worked with his immigrant parents picking produce in the hot, dusty fields of central California. As he grew up, he was driven to succeed. In college, where he met his wife, Dalia, his hunger for learning pushed him to devour business books, especially on real estate.

He bought his first investment property while attending Chico State University. After college, he and Dalia got married and worked to scale their fledgling real estate company. And grow they did. In less than ten years, RC was at the helm of a juggernaut: buying, fixing up, and reselling or renting hundreds of houses. With Dalia firmly in control of the office, keeping a close eye on their finances and contracts, the business flourished. They were earning a seven-figure annual profit, but this profit came at a cost: RC was *always* working.

A typical day would have him working in the office from 8 AM to 7 PM, and then there was "the phone," as Dalia called it. The phone: such a powerful tool for getting work done, but for Dalia, it now symbolized how her husband was always working. At night and on weekends, contractors would call with construction questions, vendors would call with pricing or payment challenges, staff would call with operational questions, and prospects would call with potential new opportunities of homes to buy or sell. And RC was there to take each of these calls. He was a prisoner of his own competence because for years he had built his company to leverage his talents. It revolved around him—his decisions, his directions, his negotiations, his personal production.

In some ways, Dalia was just resigned that this was the way life would be. It wasn't so bad, she reasoned to herself. She had a husband whom she loved and who was totally committed to his family. The business gave them the financial security that neither of them had ever dreamed possible. It was just that RC worked, and worked, and worked.

When RC first told Dalia that he wanted to join our coaching program so he could stop working so many hours, Dalia was skeptical. It wasn't that she felt the program wouldn't work; it was just that she doubted her husband's resolve to actually stop working so many hours. But when she thought about it, she realized she had nothing to lose. It wasn't as if RC could work any *more* hours, so she gave her blessing.

Initially, RC and his business weren't ready to tackle the business's reliance on him, so we started by working to push back their single biggest limiting factor—capital. We did our Sweet Spot Analysis and created our one-page Action Plan to attack this challenge. We carved out a Focus Day and made sure he got four hours of focus time each week to work on this key area of the business.

Over the course of four months, RC's efforts worked. He found and cultivated a better source of capital that reduced his direct capital costs by half a million dollars a year, while restoring five hours of RC's time per week. He hadn't realized how time intensive it was for him to be constantly cultivating and developing their private investor base to fund projects deal by deal. But his new capital source gave him several million dollars of working capital, which cut the number of private investors he needed to actively work with.

With this initial success and newly reclaimed time, we next focused on making some leveraged changes to the company's core operations. We engaged RC's team for the first time to "own" a few functional parts of the business, versus just being the hands that RC directed every day. They formally created their UBS and worked to refine many of their core systems. This also gave RC back a little more of his time. He started to leave the office at 5:30 or 6:00 PM each day so he could get home and have dinner with his family most weeknights.

But still there was "the phone." It rang during meals, late at night, and even on weekends. And each time it rang, it pulled RC away from Dalia and his family and into the world of the business. It wasn't until six months after we began working together that RC felt ready to tackle the phone. As RC recalls,

"The year before, Dalia and I decided to take seven weeks off over the summer while our two young kids were out of school. We had a great time. Of course, I had to keep in regular contact with the office during that time, and things didn't go so smoothly when I wasn't there at the office every day. Dalia and I wanted to do it again, but this time I didn't want to work while I was away. I wanted to be able to focus on my family and actually be present with them."

When RC shared the goal to take a true seven-week summer vacation with his family, we had five months to prepare. We debriefed what had happened during his time away the prior summer. His Liked Bests included the fact that he had left the office and that their rehab projects had continued while he was gone. His Next Times included figuring out ways that his team could have clearer lines of authority of who was responsible for what in his absence and better accountability so that the acquisition, rehab, and sales divisions of his company didn't slow down just because he wasn't there every day to check up on people.

We listed what the criteria of success would look like if he were to go away for seven weeks with only two scheduled, formal check-ins during his time away. As we did so, we realized we had to tackle the phone, and do it fast. Over the years, RC's cell phone had become the central number that vendors, customers, and team all called to get quick solutions and answers. We took a step back and designed better ways to unpack that phone and direct categories of calls to other team members. First, RC redirected all contractors and suppliers to call Joe, his construction manager. This took a bit of effort, especially retraining these external team members to call Joe and not RC, but after a month it worked. Next, RC redirected the toll-free number he used in his "I buy houses" TV ads from his cell phone to two of his acquisitions people through their web-based phone system:

"This was harder emotionally to do because we got many of our best deals from those ads, and I was the best negotiator in my company. When that phone rang, it felt like if I didn't answer it then we'd be losing opportunity. But that goal of seven weeks of real vacation pushed me to better train my acquisitions team. I worked on their scripting. We role-played buying scenarios. I coached them on the deals they were working on. It took a little time, but I grew my comfort level with letting them handle these inbound leads."

The last category of calls RC had to deal with were the many tenants from his residential and commercial properties. Believe it or not, over the years RC had given them his cell number, inadvertently training them to call him when there was an issue with a property.

"I know it sounds crazy, but the property management companies I had used in the past had just not done a good job with important, urgent things with the properties. I remember this one time a commercial tenant called my property manager about a burst pipe, and the manager didn't answer his phone right away. It cost me thousands of dollars in damages. Looking back, I realize that my solution was just to give my tenants my phone number. What I really needed to do was to address the breakdown with my property manager."

Which is exactly what RC did this time. He worked with his residential manager to clarify expectations and put clear internal controls in place to make sure procedures were being followed and that emergencies were being responded to quickly. He trained an internal team member to manage the repair issues with his commercial properties and transitioned his tenants to call or text this person for emergencies. He also systematized how in emergency situations his tenants could contact his senior repair vendors directly to at least stop emergency breakages from causing more damage. Ultimately, RC was able to design out 90 percent of the calls he used to get and make sure they went to other people in his company who could handle them well. While it was liberating for him, it meant even more to Dalia:

> "I never thought I'd see the day when he'd be home with us and ignore his phone, but it happened. He's now working so much less, and when he's home, he's really there with us."

As RC dealt with each of these key steps to prepare for his seven-week adventure, I also pointed out that he didn't have a leadership team. He had a person in charge of acquisitions, a person in charge of construction and rehab, and two people in charge of the resale of his properties, but they all reported directly to him. RC was the central hub through which they all connected. Without him there, they didn't really coordinate well with each other.

RC is a savvy businessperson. When I pointed this out to him, he immediately saw the truth of it and worked with his team to better design who was responsible for what, how his key department leaders could and should work directly with each other, and how they would coordinate their efforts going forward without RC as the hub.

In the final two months before he left for his trip, I pulled RC's leadership team onto a conference call and asked them what they still needed from RC to set them up to succeed before he went away. His acquisitions manager, who already had a clear process in place to buy houses at auction, needed a better understanding of how the company would fund nonauction deals when RC wasn't there to do the final authorization for wire transfers. His construction manager needed a better process to work with the sales team to be more strategic about which repairs and upgrades they would or wouldn't do as each new house came into the rehab pipeline, so that they could avoid expensive change orders and maximize profits. Collectively, they created a clear plan to handle each of these items.

Finally, the day arrived. RC and his family left for their seven-week adventure. They started in a small community in Mexico, visiting family. This helped because RC's phone didn't actually work there and getting internet was difficult. It was a tough-love way of forcing him and his team to make this summer trip radically different from the prior year. About two weeks into the trip, RC and Dalia got on a conference call with their team and had their first formal check-in. There were some minor issues that needed to be dealt with, but on the whole the company was humming along. They repeated the check-in two weeks after that. Again, all systems go. In the end, preparing for that seven-week trip was the spark the company needed to make the transition to the Value Economy. RC and his team proved that when you engage your team, focus your best attention on what matters most, and leverage better design, you can create a stronger, deeper, and more successful company. As RC reports,

> "I had worked so hard all those years to get to the point where the business was thriving, but I just didn't see the impact of all those calls on Dalia and my kids. What's amazing to me is how quickly this has all happened. In less than twenty-four months of doing this work, our company is stronger than ever. My team is fully engaged in this process and loves the greater autonomy and impact they can have. I love having more time with my family. I just needed a structured map to guide me through this process. My only regret is that I didn't get started doing it sooner." ♦

Congratulations! You've completed part two of the book and have become familiar with the five Freedom Accelerators. In the final chapter, I'll share with you the three most important first steps to immediately put the formula to work in your business life so that you generate real results—fast.

CHAPTER 10

Getting into Action

As I write this final chapter of the book, it's during my kids' holiday break in December. I needed a little quiet, so Heather generously took the boys to play at a friend's house, and I'm getting some much-needed introvert time. So far today I've gotten seven hugs, had three rich conversations, and broken up two fights, and it isn't even 1:00 PM. In another forty-five minutes, I'll meet my family at our local park to go sledding together. Then tonight, while my wife heads out to her weekly meditation group, my sons and I will do Movie Night.

How has the Freedom Formula worked for me in my life? It has allowed me to radically increase my impact on the world as I've scaled my company. It has given me the ability to enjoy challenging and intensely interesting work that has provided well for my family and team members. When I'm at work I focus on creating value, and when the day is done I choose to be with my family. What I've come to appreciate most is that by focusing my time and my company's best talent and attention on those few things that actually matter most, we've collectively created extraordinary business and professional success and still can enjoy rich personal lives, too.

In this book I've done my best to deliver on a simple promise: to give you a clear, concrete road map to succeed in business without having to sacrifice your family, health, or life to do it. I've coached you to do this by embracing the Value Economy and upgrading how you invest your best time and attention into those Fewer, Better areas that will produce the highest return for your company. At the same time, I've been working with you to build ever greater strategic depth into your organization by engaging and coaching your team, developing your systems, and cultivating your culture. Collectively, this upgraded road map empowers you to create a magnitude more value without working around the clock. Essentially, my goal for this book was to operationalize how to work smarter. Not fluff, not theory, but the nitty-gritty mechanics of what working smarter actually means in the real world of business.

YOUR TURN: Once again, I'm throwing down the gauntlet, this time asking you to take the 10-Day Challenge. If you don't see a dramatic impact on the value you create, both at work *and* home, then the next time we meet you can throw your copy of this book in my face and I'll stand there and take it. But if you're anything at all like the thousands of business leaders I've given this challenge to over the past decade, you'll have one of the richest and most productive two weeks of your business life.

The 10-Day Challenge

For just ten business days—two working weeks—apply just the most basic part of the formula to your own business life. Begin by organizing your calendar so you can start the 10-Day Challenge this coming Monday. Right *now*, restructure these two weeks to block out one Focus Day each week with a two-plus-hour focus block. Then, on at least three of your Push Days each week, block out an hour focus block. All totaled, this means you'll reclaim five hours out of the entire week to fill your time plate with your highest-value work. Of course you can do this; it still leaves you with plenty of time for all those other things you "have to get done."

Commit up front that during these five hours of focus time, you're going to block out the world and focus on completing your two or three Big Rocks for the week—the things that you realistically can do that week that would create the most value for your company. List your Big Rocks in writing somewhere visible, such as on a Post-it Note on your desk. Being clear—in writing—on what your A- and B-level Big Rocks are for each week of this 10-Day Challenge is a requirement. Right before your focus blocks, turn off your email; set an away message if you must. Turn off your ringers, bells, and other alerts, and give your full and best attention to doing great work on your highest-value Big Rocks during these concentrated focus blocks. If you are daring, explain to your team how you're taking this 10-Day Challenge and ask for their support.

Each day, when your business day is done, turn off work and go home. Be with your family, take a walk, read an inspiring book, or call a friend. Then, refreshed and renewed, make your next workday even more valuable.

At the end of week one of the challenge, pause and ask two questions: What is working well about this so far (your Liked Bests)? What specifically do I want to do differently next week to make this work even better (your Next Times)? Make week two of this challenge even better by applying what you learned in week one.

It is my belief, based on actually using the formula myself, and seeing firsthand the astonishing impact it's had on the lives of thousands of other business leaders just like you, that you're going to have an extraordinary two weeks. Let your initial success with the formula pull you forward to applying it at a deeper level.

Start with yourself. Get value *yourself*. See the impact both in the office and how you feel at home. Be a role model for the other members of your team. Then and only then, share the formula with a few of your key team members. In fact, I've created a choreographed ninety-day program for you to share and apply the formula with your core team. It's part of the Freedom Tool Kit, and it's my free gift to you, an investment in your success. You can immediately access this quick-start program at **www.FreedomToolKit.com**. I'll pace you and your team via short weekly emails over the ninety days. You'll each study a chapter of this book, watch a *short* video, and use that week's one-page action guide to apply the lessons of that chapter to your organization and team. Then, the next week, you'll do this again, and again. We don't have to complicate things; the formula and action guides are short, simple, and easy to follow. You just make them a priority by investing a small fraction of your work week to applying what you've learned. This ninety-day program will help you apply the formula inside your organization and reap the many, well-deserved rewards.

A Two-Door Moment

In the introduction to this book, I shared about my personal epiphany in 2001, that I just couldn't continue to put in eighty-hour work weeks with all the pressure I felt on my shoulders. But for a few months I was stuck, not knowing how to make the needed change. I was scared because what I had been doing was seemingly working. The business was immensely profitable and growing. But I was burning out.

In October of that same year, my then–business partner and I were sitting in a hotel meeting space in Estes Park, Colorado. We were meeting at the start of a new quarter, as we had done every quarter for the prior five years, planning out the coming ninety days in the business. But this meeting was different. He turned to me and poured out how the long hours were impacting his family. In our own ways, we both had come to the same conclusion: the status quo of long hours and constant travel was no longer sustainable.

Our company had grown—fast—with annual growth over 30 percent. But we both were clear that we wanted to find a better path forward, one that would allow the business to continue to grow, but especially to grow more independent of us as the top leaders and producers. We both knew we couldn't go on working this hard, traveling two or three weeks each month teaching workshops and giving keynote talks at large conferences. We were at a crossroads. We were making more money than we ever imagined we could, but we both felt stretched to the breaking point.

I believe that from time to time, life presents you with what I've come to call "two-door moments." At these moments you have two very clear choices, and your decision about which door you pick has consequences that roll forward for the rest of your life. Some two-door moments—the choice of a spouse, the decision to accept or turn down a job—are obviously pivotal moments. Other two-door moments fly under the radar, and their import is only clear years afterward, looking back.

For my partner and I, this was a two-door moment. We knew that if we kept putting in the hours, focused on the business, we could grow the company. But we both felt that to really build something enduring and special, and to enjoy the process more, we would have to fundamentally change how we operated the business. We'd have to build a team of other leaders who owned functional areas of the business. We'd have to say no to good opportunities so that we focused all our energies on going after great ones. And we'd have to put a hard stop on our hours and force ourselves to take time away from the company, because when either of us was in the office, we tended to be micro-managers who wanted to jump in and personally take over projects and tasks.

What we didn't know was if this radical shift in how we ran the company would actually work. This was a two-door moment for us. We chose the scary door and made the clear commitment that over the next eighteen months, we would build our core leadership team and put clear boundaries on our personal participation in the company.

Fast-forward four years. The bet we placed worked. The company tripled in size and profitability over that period, even as my partner and I cut our working hours in half. That was when I got the phone call.

Heather was in Boston, visiting her dad in the hospital. Since we live in a smaller community, she took advantage of the great medical infrastructure there to follow up on a strange mammogram result. She had a core needle biopsy to look closely at a specific lump in her left breast. I was at home when I got her phone call. She was in tears and frantic as she told me she had breast cancer.

There I was, a thousand miles away, trying to calm and comfort her. I felt helpless. I couldn't hold her or make her feel better. I immediately booked a flight and joined her in Boston for what ultimately was a long series of medical consultations, pathology reports, and second and third opinions, and ultimately three surgeries. Today, my wife is healthy and the cancer is all gone, but at the time, we both were overwhelmed and scared.

Looking back, I can see that the decision my business partner and I made in 2001 to build an owner-independent company was what allowed me to drop everything for four months and be fully present to support Heather. Over the prior four years, my business partner and I had followed the core of the formula I've shared with you in this book. No, it wasn't nearly as refined or simple as I've laid out here, but the bones were there: shift your mind-set from maintaining control to creating value, say no to the good so that you have the time and attention to say yes to the great, reclaim some of your best time each week to invest this time in your highest-value activities, build an engaged leadership team that does the same thing, and strengthen your strategic depth.

In my life, as in yours, I've had many two-door moments. Let me be clear—this is a two-door moment for you right now. One door you could pick is to put down this book and come up with any number of reasons why, although you liked what you read and found the ideas "interesting," you're just too busy to get started applying them now. Of course, if you pick this door, then you're also choosing to accept the deep cost to your company, family, and personal life.

But right now you have a second door ready for you to walk through instead. If you choose this second door and begin to apply the Freedom Formula to your business life, you're affirming that you no longer are willing to accept a work life encumbered with low-value junk and seventy-hour work weeks. You're no longer willing to let work take over every corner of your life. Instead, you'll start *today* to reclaim a portion of your best time so that you can focus on your Fewer, Better activities that truly create value for your company. You're choosing to apply the formula, imperfectly at first, but better and better over time, to find a way to enjoy extraordinary professional success and to have a rich and fulfilling personal life as well.

You can do this. I've shared with you dozens of stories of business leaders just like you who have applied the formula in their companies. Have a sense of humor and know that you'll make mistakes at first, but when you're on the path, you are on your way. You're doing this for the people in your life whom you love. You're doing this for the people you work with and whom you want to enjoy a rich life, too. And you're doing this for yourself.

Like most people, I have regrets in my life. I regret not challenging the misdiagnosis of the tumor in my hip in 1994 that kept me from playing in the Olympics. I regret several special friendships I let fade over the years. But I've never regretted applying the Freedom Formula to my company and life. The formula has given me time to be with my young family at an age when spending time with "Daddy" is something my kids crave. I know this won't be the case forever. Kids grow up. But in this two-door decision in my life, I have zero regrets—I know I have chosen the right door.

There will be a day when you look back at this very moment and the door you picked and say to yourself, "I'm so glad I picked wisely . . ." or you'll say, "If only I'd had the courage to pick the other door . . ."

Which door do you choose?

The Freedom Tool Kit
Your FREE $1,275 Gift from the Author

Dear Reader,

Congratulations on finishing the book. Clearly you're hungry to grow personally and professionally, and I want to support your efforts. This is a huge part of what fulfills me. I want to help.

I've created a unique online tool kit to help you and your team apply the ideas you've learned in this book so that you enjoy *both* business success *and* a rich personal life.

This Freedom Tool Kit includes dozens of video and PDF tools to help you share what you've learned from this book with your team and start applying the formula right away.

To register and get immediate access to this powerful collection of business success tools, just go to **www.FreedomToolKit.com**. You'll get:

- **Over a dozen short training videos** to make applying the formula to regain control of your life faster and easier.
- **Free PDF downloads** of the business tools I shared in the book (including the *Time Value Matrix*™, the *Leverage Your Personal Assistant* tool, the *1-Page Quarterly Action Plan*, the *Sweet Spot Analysis*™ tool, and all the others).
- **A 90-day action guide** to apply the formula to your business life the most effective way possible.
- **And much more . . .**

Not only will this special tool kit empower you to take smarter action; it will also give you a proven way to enroll your team in the process. And as we spent so much time on together in part two of the book, your team is your secret accelerator for succeeding faster and healthier.

The tool kit gives you five simple Action Guides to help your team apply the formula inside your company. Each downloadable Action Guide has a concise summary of the key points for each step of the formula, a provocative list of discussion questions, and a simple assignment to immediately apply what you learned to enjoy fast results. It's that easy.

We've even added an entire enterprise section of the tool kit for leaders inside larger companies who need to find the best ways to apply the formula on that scale.

Limited-Time Extra Bonus:
A Free, Private 90-Minute Business
Coaching Session

For a limited time, if your business qualifies, you'll get one more bonus from the Freedom Tool Kit: a confidential **90-minute Strategy Session** with one of my senior business coaches.

This deep-dive working session will help you pinpoint the key constraints to growing your company, division, or team and map out the best path forward. Think of this as your way to get our concrete coaching as you apply the concepts and strategies you've just read about to your specific company and personal circumstances.

For over a decade we've worked with thousands of business leaders, executives, and entrepreneurs to help them succeed in business without sacrificing their family, health, or life in the process. This is your chance to explore the possibility of our working together to help you grow your company the right way.

Register Now to Get Immediate Access to This Free Bonus

Simply go to **www.FreedomToolKit.com** and register right now. In less than sixty seconds, you'll be able to create your account and have full access to this powerful collection of business success tools. This special bonus offer is available for a limited time only. You don't want to miss out.

You'll also receive regular updates, articles, and ongoing invitations to web-based trainings that you and your key staff can leverage as you learn to work smarter, not harder.

Again, I want to thank you for reading this book. I wish you a lifetime of professional success and happiness. And I look forward to playing a small part in your life's journey. Enjoy your "graduation gift" of the Freedom Tool Kit!

Your friend,

David Finkel

P.S. Because this free tool kit is a limited-time offer and may be changed or pulled at any time, I strongly encourage you to go to **www.FreedomToolKit.com** and register *now*.

Acknowledgments

The Freedom Formula is about focusing your best time, talent, and attention into those Fewer, Better projects, activities, and areas with the greatest impact. This book never would have come to be without the enormous talent, creativity, energy, and commitment of a diverse group of people.

First, I want to thank the entire BenBella team. You made this book so much better than I ever thought possible and are a pleasure to collaborate with. I need to give special thanks to my editors, Laurel and Leah, who helped me shape, cut, clarify, and polish. You are both stars in my book. Thank you also to the production and marketing teams at BenBella; with every interaction I am struck by just how good you are. Glenn, you did an amazing job putting this team together.

Next, I want to thank the business leaders featured in this book. Thank you for sharing your stories with me, knowing that your experiences will touch a lot of lives. You are a remarkable group of people, and I learned so much working with you.

To my clients at Maui Mastermind—thank you! You inspire me, challenge me, and spark me to grow. You've taught me far more than I've ever been able to share with you. Many of you have grown to be personal friends, and I am grateful to have you in my life. Thank you for helping to change "business as usual" in the world.

I wanted to give a special thank you to the editors at *Inc.com* for the platform you've given me to share these ideas with millions of readers around the world.

To my team at Maui Mastermind—from the bottom of my heart, thank you. Your commitment to our business coaching clients has made a real difference in the world. I want to thank our leadership team—Theresa, Larry, Steve, and Kim—for so ably running the company. To our coaching and advisor team of Patty, Doug, Phil, Jennifer, Carrie, Ralph, Kevin, Jeff, Stephanie, Alan, Kiran, Gene (of blessed memory), Bill, and Steve—thank you for sharing your personal insights and leadership with our clients. Thank you also to the behind-the-scenes team of Marilyn, Oscar, Maggie, Michelle, Cyndi, Elena, Candice, Katie, Diamond, Chris, and Mike. And a special thanks to Tiffany and Emily, who manage my business and personal life with grace, class, and ease—I couldn't do any of this without your competence and support.

I want to give a shout out to my personal mastermind group—thank you for challenging me to grow and savor.

Finally, I want to thank my family. Dad, I treasure our long walks and intimate talks. Mom, thank you for the sacrifices you made raising us. Alex, Laurie, and Stacey—I love you. Grandma Gerry, you are a true gift in my life, and I am so grateful for you. To Grandpa Morrey—I miss you. I wish you could have met your other great grandkids. To Matthew, Adam, and Joshua—I am so proud of each you, and I marvel watching you grow up. And to Heather, my best friend and life partner—thank you, sweetheart, for sharing your life with me. You are my forever.

Notes

1. Corporation for National and Community Service, "Volunteering in America," accessed February 20, 2019, https://www.nationalservice.gov/vcla.
2. Rafael Diez de Medina, "Volunteers Count. Their Work Deserves to Be Counted," UN Volunteers, November 2, 2017, https://www.unv.org/swvr/volunteers-count-their-work-deserves-be-counted.
3. Amy Adkins, "Employee Engagement in U.S. Stagnant in 2015," Gallup, January 13, 2016, https://news.gallup.com/poll/188144/employee-engagement-stagnant-2015.aspx.
4. See "State of the American Workplace" to view the report from Gallup.com, https://news.gallup.com/reports/199961/state-american-workplace-report-2017.aspx.
5. David Brown, et al., "Culture and Engagement: The Naked Organization," Deloitte Insights, February 27, 2015, https://www2.deloitte.com/insights/us/en/focus/human-capital-trends/2015/employee-engagement-culture-human-capital-trends-2015.html.
6. See "State of the American Workplace" to view the report from Gallup.com, https://www.gallup.com/workplace/238085/state-american-workplace-report-2017.aspx.
7. Lori Goler, et al., "The 3 Things Employees Really Want: Career, Community, Cause," *Harvard Business Review*, February 20, 2018, https://hbr.org/2018/02/people-want-3-things-from-work-but-most-companies-are-built-around-only-one.
8. Dr. Singh and I collaborated along with Alan Gassman on *Grow Your Medical Practice and Get Your Life Back* (Bradstreet and Sons, 2018).
9. Steven Kutz, "NFL Took in $13 Billion in Revenue Last Season—See How It Stacks Up Against Other Pro Sports Leagues," *Forbes*, July 2, 2016, https://www.marketwatch.com/story/the-nfl-made-13-billion-last-season-see-how-it-stacks-up-against-other-leagues-2016-07-01.
10. Kurt Badenhausen, "The Average Player Salary and Highest-Paid in NBA, MLB, NHL, NFL and MLS," *Forbes*, December 15, 2016, https://www.forbes.com/sites/kurtbadenhausen/2016/12/15/average-player-salaries-in-major-american-sports-leagues/#51496dcb1050.
11. Kurt Badenhausen, "The NFL's Highest-Paid Players 2018: Aaron Rodgers Leads with $76 Million," *Forbes*, September 20, 2018, https://www.forbes

.com/sites/kurtbadenhausen/2018/09/20/the-nfls-highest-paid-players-2018
-aaron-rodgers-leads-with-76-million/#35f59f5a117b.

12. BBC Sport, "Premier League Average Weekly Wage Passes £50,000, Says New Study," *BBC,* November 27, 2017, https://www.bbc.com/sport/football /42130297.

13. Brandon Wiggins and Cork Gaines, "The 25 Highest-Paid Players in the English Premier League for the 2017–18 Season," *Business Insider,* August 26, 2018, https://www.businessinsider.com/premier-league-highest-paid-players -2018-8#6-sergio-aguero-220000-weekly-150-million-annually-20.

14. Maurice Moton, "The 10 Highest-Paid Coaches in the NFL," *Bleacher Report*, February 5, 2018, https://bleacherreport.com/articles/2755442-the -10-highest-paid-coaches-in-the-nfl#slide10.

15. Michael Potts, "Premier League Manager Wages: Every Top Flight Boss Ranked by Salary in 2017/18," *Express*, January 28, 2018, https://www .express.co.uk/sport/football/910809/Premier-League-manager-wages-salary -2017-2018-sportgalleries.

16. International Coaching Federation, "2016 ICF Global Coaching Study," December 2017, https://coachfederation.org/app/uploads/2017/12/2016ICF GlobalCoachingStudy_ExecutiveSummary-2.pdf.

17. See George A. Miller, "The Magical Number Seven, Plus or Minus Two: Some Limits on Our Capacity for Processing Information," *Psychological Review* 63, no. 2 (1956): 81–97.

About the Author

Photo by Maui Mastermind

Serial entrepreneur **David Finkel** is the CEO of Maui Mastermind®, one of the world's premier business coaching companies, which has worked with over 100,000 business leaders, helping them grow their companies and get their lives back. David's clients enjoy an average annual growth rate five times higher than the average privately held company in the United States, and at the same time, these business leaders have dramatically decreased their working hours. Over the past twenty years, David and the other Maui coaches and advisors have personally started and scaled companies with an aggregate value of $63 billion.

David eats his own cooking, which has allowed him the time to start, scale, and sell multiple successful ventures and be on the boards of several other companies, all while holding his working hours to under forty hours per week and taking ten weeks of vacation each year. The *Wall Street Journal*–bestselling author of eleven books, David's syndicated business articles on *Inc.com*, *FastCompany.com*, and *Forbes.com* have garnered millions of readers. His work has been featured in such prestigious media outlets as the *Wall Street Journal*, *Bloomberg Businessweek*, *Fox Business*, *MSNBC*, and the *International Business Times*.